Incarcerated Resistance

Incarcerated Resistance

How Identity, Gender, and Privilege Shape the Experiences of America's Nonviolent Activists

Anya Stanger

LEXINGTON BOOKS
Lanham • Boulder • New York • London

Published by Lexington Books
An imprint of The Rowman & Littlefield Publishing Group, Inc.
4501 Forbes Boulevard, Suite 200, Lanham, Maryland 20706
www.rowman.com

86-90 Paul Street, London EC2A 4NE, United Kingdom

British Library Cataloguing in Publication Information Available

Library of Congress Cataloging-in-Publication Data

Name: Stanger, Anya, 1979–, author.
Title: Incarcerated resistance : how identity, gender, and privilege shape the experiences
    of America's nonviolent activists / Anya Stanger.
Description: Lanham : Lexington Books, [2022] | Includes bibliographical references and
    index. | Summary: "Grounded in the lives of some of its most committed nonviolent
    activists, Incarcerated Resistance tells a story of anti-war resistance, what it means to
    'go to jail for justice' in the contemporary United States, and shows how identity mat-
    ters in both the activation of prison witness, and as a key shaper of individual experi-
    ence"—Provided by publisher.
Identifiers: LCCN 2021046604 (print) | LCCN 2021046605 (ebook) | ISBN
    9781793605634 (paper) | ISBN 9781793605627 (epub)
Subjects: LCSH: Passive resistance—United States. | Civil disobedience—United States.
    | Peace movements—United States. | Prisoners—Political activity—United States.
Classification: LCC HM1281 .S729 2022 (print) | LCC HM1281 (ebook) | DDC
    303.6/10973—dc23
LC record available at https://lccn.loc.gov/2021046604
LC ebook record available at https://lccn.loc.gov/2021046605

To Professor John Samuel Burdick. Your memory is a blessing.

Contents

Preface

An hour or so into my first interview, I asked Ann Tiffany what had changed as a result of her 1997 line-crossing at Fort Benning. Brightly and without hesitation, she replied, "me!"[1] In that moment, I knew that I wanted to tell this story through the prism of its participants, centering their lives rather than the strategy they chose to employ. This required a theoretical framework that was broader and more intimate than what I had found in social movement or civil resistance scholarship. At the same time, I realized that a transnational feminist framework could shed light on Ann's experience; for its insistence on beginning with the personal while connecting to the global, and for its work on the subjects of identity, privilege, and solidarity. Hence, in under two hours of actual "research," the edifice of the project I had first imagined transformed, and this project took shape.

In the research and writing process, the choice to focus on personal accounts as windows into larger structural patterns did not always feel comfortable. Almost all of the people represented in this research have dedicated their lives to challenging the forces that drive injustice. Over and over, participants told me that their activism was not about them. Yet there I was, writing a book about them. However, because of the unusual and intentional ways in which my participants live, by centering them, this book is also about the issues they care so much about. In the end, I hope that my participants agree that what can be learned through their personal stories significantly reveals the workings of violence in all of our lives, and how necessary it is to resist it.

This book is the result of years of research and work, only some of which is my own. It exists because of the generous (and ongoing) gifts of time, trust, and wisdom provided by its 43 participants. It is their lives that I share here: their intelligence, experiences, moral clarity, humor, courage, and faith that provide all of the ideas that are most interesting and important. To the extent that what I may offer is useful, I remain convinced that it is because I have such "good data." To all of my participants, I thank you for doing your work, and for sharing so much of it with me. For your ongoing assistance, I especially thank Brian Terrell. So many of my own understandings would not be complete without your steady aid. All remaining errors, of course, are my own.

The research for this book began when I was a graduate student at Syracuse University, and was fundamentally shaped by the most extraordinary team of advisors. My deepest thanks to Professor Chandra Talpade Mohanty; not only did you help me formulate and carry out this project, you also forever altered how I see and understand the world. From feminist organizing to parenting, solidarity activism to wearing brighter colors, your influence on my scholarship and life choices is daily present. I carry it all as a life-long gift. Professor Sharon Erickson-Nepstad has been an extraordinarily generous advisor, with unmatched subject expertise and needed perspective. This book has benefitted in uncountable ways from your superb scholarship and work, Sharon, both published and personal. Professors Angela Davis and Gretchen Purser provided careful guidance and methodological support, and I still cannot believe my luck to have had you both on my team.

My writing has also benefitted from the help of brilliant scholar-friends: Dylan Hendricks, Dana Hill, Kellea Miller, Estelle Manticas, Terry Reeder, Dianna Winslow, and Diane Swords—all of you have made this book, and my life, better. For taking such good care of my children while giving me space to write, I thank Deborah Gutierrez and Rosie Campos.

This book is dedicated to the late Professor John Burdick. It was your enthusiasm in life that propelled this project initially, and it was your heart-breaking passing that finally compelled me to write it. It is no exaggeration to say that it would not exist without you. I have written it as an offering toward keeping the legacy of your scholarship and activism an ongoing project, with a lifespan generations beyond your own. John Burdick, présenté!

Finally, for your unwavering trust that writing a book has been a good idea, I thank my family. My parents, Diane and Dale Jacobson, have been steadfast cheerleaders, and have supported me at every step of this bewildering life choice to be a scholar-activist. Since 2007, my mother-in-law Rachel has been ever-helpful, providing a listening ear, childcare in a pinch, and a hands-off sense of trust that surprises me still. My siblings and their spouses: Heather and Luke Hunt, Clare and Patrick Ryan, and Bo Jacobson—have been quietly insistent in their encouragement, as well as dependable sounding boards and reliable first readers. Many an idea has been talked through late into the evening after the children have been tucked in to bed, and I've counted on your insights and critiques throughout these many years. To my own children, Isa and Leo, whose lives have influenced this project in every way, from content to timing: I write this in spite of you, because of you, and for you—and from the bottom of my heart. And last, to my husband Dave. The more I have learned about justice action, peace work, radical politics, and being a good person on the planet, the more I love and appreciate you. You get so much right, without all of these words. Thank you for being my partner in this life, Dave. I love you.

NOTE

1. Ann Tiffany, Interview by author. Syracuse, NY, February 22nd, 2010.

Introduction

The idea for this book was gifted to me when I was a graduate student in 2009—at choir practice, of all places. Every Wednesday, the Syracuse Community Choir sings songs for peace and justice in the tradition of Pete Seeger. One evening after practice, soprano Nancy Gwin announced that she was planning to "cross the line" (illegally trespass) onto the base at Fort Benning during the annual School of the Americas Watch vigil that November. My reaction was immediate, despite my long interest in non-violence. *Who would do that?* Happily, this question has kept me going ever since. Indeed, focusing on the identities of justice action prisoners in the United States has helped me better understand contemporary American imperial power and its resistance, through the lived experience of individual people. The 43 lives highlighted here provide a snapshot of what organized resistance to state violence looks like in this current moment. From nuclear weapons to torture, weaponized drones to prison, the issues that justice action prisoners care about, *as well as* how participation affects their minds, bodies, relationships, and future activism, reveal how the interconnected, complex, and varied processes of militarized global empire are experienced and lived in the U.S. today.

The activists who I call *justice action prisoners* employ a tactic called "prison witness," a nonviolent technique of "going to jail for justice" to put particular issues such as war, nuclear weapons, and U.S. foreign policy on trial.[1] It is a high-risk tactic, one of the most extreme in the nonviolent toolkit. It entails intentionally breaking the law, most often through crimes of trespass onto federal property or the destruction of federal property. Such acts are illegal, and may result in lengthy jail time (ranging from several days to decades).

Though they have knowingly broken the law and generally expect to be incarcerated as a result of their actions, justice action prisoners do not actually court imprisonment.[2] Their goal is to raise awareness and to resist, but not necessarily to go to jail. Indeed, the majority of justice action prisoners seek not-guilty verdicts, and use the space of the courtroom and subsequent media attention as opportunities to share information about their issues of concern. They do this through questioning the logic of weaponized drone use during their trials, for example, or the (il)legality of nuclear weapons. Often, they argue that their acts are "necessary"—a small violation required to stop much larger crimes. As such, their acts align with both international law and the laws of a Christian God. They are considered both righteous *and* legal.

Despite their belief in their own innocence, justice action prisoners rely upon the punishments acquired to further and strengthen their resistance. Their arrests provide them with opportunities for media outreach and public speaking. Their nonviolent actions work as a permanent and public testament against state policies. Their court statements go into the public record, creating a searchable constellation of grievances against various forms of state violence that are impossible to make disappear or distort across time.

The incarceration that results from illegal actions facilitates entrée for justice action prisoners into public forums such as classrooms, courtrooms, and the media. The actions create stories that are tangible and human, they provide a way to talk about issues that otherwise feel overwhelming or incomprehensible. Justice action prisoners gain credibility through their identities as "moral" prisoners, and their nonviolent actions give them validity to speak as political, legitimate, and ethical actors. In the words of participant Brian DeRouen, being an ex-convict is "a sexy position" from which to speak, and one's status as a former prisoner makes other people take one's actions "seriously." Hence, in Brian's experience, being an activist who has served jail time provides him with a "unique position from which to be more helpful" to the causes and people he cares so much about.[3]

WE ARE NOT PRISONERS OF CONSCIENCE
AND WE ARE NOT DISOBEDIENT: NAMING

What we call things is important. My first challenge in terminology came early in my fieldwork, when I identified the people I study as prisoners of conscience, or POCs. Amnesty International coined the term, defined as any person imprisoned because of their identity, beliefs, or status. Because those who are incarcerated for nonviolent resistance in the U.S. have broken laws, Amnesty International does not recognize any POCs in this country.

Many U.S. activists and movements, however—including the School of the Americas Watch—proudly claim the term and its legacies.[4]

Participant Kathy Kelly was the first person to tell me that she does not like being called a prisoner "of conscience." For her, it is "not even honest" to describe herself as such, because "all prisoners" are "prisoners with consciences."[5] In a personal email, participant Karl Meyer further explained:

> I detest the designation "prisoner of conscience." I am not a prisoner of my conscience. My conscience and I get along very well and have a completely voluntary relationship. . . . When we are in prison we have been classified legally as convicts and as criminals, and those are good, honest terms, with no attempts at euphemism. We are prisoners of the federal or local governments, not prisoners of conscience. I also would not favor "prisoners on purpose," because I generally regard myself as innocent of the crimes charged, and believe that I should be acquitted and released. . . . I also do not like to be separated out from other prisoners by designation as a "political prisoner," because all prosecutions and imprisonments are based on political and social values and judgments.[6]

In this same email, Karl suggested the terms *justice action prisoner* and *peace action prisoner* as alternatives to "prisoner of conscience." In 2013, I held a focus group in Syracuse, NY, in part to ask for participants' feedback on Karl's suggestions. The response was enthusiastic. My decision to use the term *justice action prisoner* instead of *prisoner of conscience*, *peace people*, *prisoners on purpose,* or some other phrase is grounded in these exchanges.

"Civil disobedience" (versus "resistance") is another troublesome term. It was participant Sr. Carol Gilbert who first alerted me to how seriously Plowshares activists consider what they do to be acts of resistance rather than disobedience—she made me read Ellen Barfield's pamphlet "Defending Resistance" before signing her interview consent forms.[7] Participant Ed Kinane explained the difference simply. He wrote, "Civil disobedience entails (justifiably) *breaking* the law, whereas our direct actions seek to *enforce* the law—international law."[8]

This is not simply an issue of semantics, for in resisting imperialism and upholding international law (rather than intentionally disobeying particular laws), justice action prisoners see what they are doing as confronting the "system" of violence, rather than a specific instance of it. In their view, in their resistance they are not breaking laws. Rather, they are upholding them—and the system of just protections guaranteed therein. Further, their resistance does not create a disturbance to the democratic system, but rather exercises and protects it. Resistance is understood to be an essential exercise of democratic governance, a necessary and ongoing push that is required to keep the whole system robust. During her interview, former nun and Plowshares founder Liz McAlister explained that her resistance is "not against a particu-lar law, it's a whole culture . . . it is a whole network of things."[9] In this way, many activists see what they are doing as upholding domestic, international, or even "God's law," as they may also be practicing "divine obedience." Such terminology is common among faith-based activists, and oral historian Rosalie Riegle notes that disarmament activists often claim to practice moral obedience, Gospel obedience, divine obedience, and civil resistance, terms that encompass their feelings that "it is their government that disobeys the law, especially international law, not they."[10]

Participant Karl Meyer rejected the term *civil disobedience* for still differ-ent reasons. For him, the term does not accurately describe what he does. He explained, "I don't like to sit in the middle of an expressway and stop traffic over these issues." Instead of obstructive action, Karl participates in what he calls "defensive" actions. "I'm doing defense of civil liberties," he explained, "particularly as they try to take them away." For example, when police des-ignate protest zones—which is common practice for public actions today—in Karl's understanding it is the police who are breaking the law, not the protes-tors. "The whole public area of the USA is a free speech zone," Karl told me. "The first amendment says congress shall make NO law" infringing on the public's right to free speech and assembly, "so my view is that it's the govern-ment . . . who are breaking the law . . . thus disobeying the Constitution and laws." This distinction mandates that the protests for which arrest is likely be understood as *nonviolent resistance actions.* Fundamentally, they are *not* instances of "disobedience."[11]

For clarity, a few other notes on naming are worth mentioning. First, because so many of the people involved in resistance are vowed religious (and specifically Roman Catholic, which I often abbreviate as "Catholic" in my writing), it is helpful to review the terminology of the Catholic Church. A "father" (Fr.) is a priest, and most priests are considered clergy. A sister (Sr.) is an apostolic, or "in the world" vowed woman. A nun is a contempla-tive vowed woman, one who lives a spiritual life withdrawn from the world, cloistered. However, it is at times acceptable to use the term *nun* for sister. Among my participants, the vowed religious women are all sisters. However, I take advantage of the leeway allowed in the terminology and for clarity sometimes refer to them as nuns. Also, several of the participants involved in this research are former priests or sisters but think of themselves as Philip Berrigan described himself: as a "priest who happens to be married." In honor of these self-identifications, I refer to such participants as vowed religious—though upon first introduction, note their "former" status.

OUTLINE OF THE BOOK

The arc of this book is chronological, and follows what happens to justice action prisoners engaged in prison witness from planning of action through release from prison. The focus is on what happens to them, how they experience it, and the meaning they make from it. Telescoping out from the individual stories reveals patterns across participants, and the patterns reveal more general truths about activism, identity, and the unequal structures that shape our lives. The first chapter introduces the project overall: the theoretical and methodological frameworks that give direction to the research, as well as introduces the participants, movements, and issues of activist contention. The second chapter locates the strategy of prison witness historically, and as it fits within nonviolent praxis. In practice, prison witness is a relatively uncommon technique of nonviolence. Though not popular, prison witness is recognized to be vital to the success of social movements over time—historically, going to jail has often been necessary for movements to accomplish their goals. The second chapter also includes discussion of the "theory of the trial" activated by justice action prisoners, as well as activist notions of efficacy. Chapters 3 through 6 detail the research findings, tracing the experiences of justice action prisoners chronologically; from the decision to participate in an action (ch. 3) to the "moment of action" (ch. 4), the experience of prison (ch. 5) through the personal changes and reflections that may occur upon release (ch. 6). The concluding chapter (7) brings together some of the most useful contributions of the work, for both activist and scholarly purposes.

Throughout the process of research and writing, my goal has been to be truthful to what I have learned from my participants, as their stories fit within a larger political and social context. My beloved graduate advisor, the late professor John Burdick, extolled me to be "excruciatingly accurate" in the stories that I tell, and this has served as my standard in determining precisely what and how to write. Most simply, the effort is to more widely share some of what justice action prisoners know and do, so that we may jointly better pursue a world of increased justice, fairness, and liberation for all.

NOTES

1. In scholarly and activist literature, such activists are generally called "prisoners of conscience" (POCs), as they are incarcerated for reasons of conscience—for their values and beliefs. A goodly number of my respondents, however, do not like this label, so I refer to them by the term suggested by participant Karl Meyer, as "justice action prisoners." Karl Meyer, telephone interview by author, March 27th, 2013.

2. This is not straightforward, as further chapters will show. Not all justice action prisoners believe that they have broken the law, and some *do* court imprisonment. Fr. Dan Berrigan insisted that the activists broke *no* law, and the fact that they were prosecuted was itself a crime. (Daniel Berrigan. *The Trial of the Catonsville Nine.* New York City: Fordham University Press, 2004.) All this said, the above statement is more often true than not, and accurately describes prison witness as a strategy.

3. Brian DeRouen, interview by author, Columbus, GA, November 18th, 2011.

4. School of the Americas Watch, "Prisoners of Conscience," accessed May 3, 2013, www.soaw.org/poc. Unlike political prisoners (such as Nelson Mandela and Leonard Peltier), justice action prisoners go to prison by choice: they willingly engage in acts that they know can result in prison time, and they do so in obedience to their conscience.

5. Kathy Kelly, interview by author, Syracuse, NY, February 25th, 2012.

6. Personal email, March 2013.

7. Ellen Barfield. "Defending Resistance." *War Resisters League,* Spring 2011. http://www.warresisters.org/content/defending-resistance.

8. Ed Kinane, "Think Global, Act Local: Grassroots Opposition to Weaponized Drones" (presented at Historians Against War conference on "The New Faces of War," Towson University, April 2013).

9. Elizabeth McAlister, interview by author, Baltimore, MD, March 13th, 2012.

10. Rosalie Riegle, *Crossing the Line: Nonviolent Resisters Speak Out for Peace* (Eugene, OR: Cascade Books, 2012b).

11. Meyer, interview.

Chapter 1

Justice Action Prisoners in the School of the Americas Watch and Plowshares Movements

If you think one person can't be effective, you've never been in bed with a mosquito.—War Resisters League

The activists included in this book share a lot in common besides their obvious commitments to peace and justice. Indeed, almost all war-resisting justice action prisoners in the U.S. today are white, well-educated, financially stable, Christian (mostly Roman Catholic), and over the age of 60. To those familiar with these movements, this is not new information; the mainstream American peace movement has always been largely white and Christian. This demographic has been problematic historically: through careless attention to the politics of race, for example, radical pacifists of the 1940s–1970s reified many of the oppressive patterns they sought to transform.[1] As such, the particular and privileged demographic of the American peace movement is not tangential to work towards peace and justice, but fundamental to it. Centering the identity of those who engage in prison witness thus becomes key to understanding it as a strategy of resistance against an imperial state. This focus helps explain how the strategy works and where it fails, as it sheds light on what, in effect, prison witness actually does.

The privileged identities of nonviolent peace activists is the starting place for this analysis, rather than treated as a troublesome corollary to the history of justice organizing. The focus on social privilege is especially significant in the stories of how justice action prisoners come to activism, what their resistance is "for," and how and why they—given their social locations—are able (or not) to bring attention, pressure, and movement to an issue. High-risk nonviolent resistance is a useful way to see how social inequalities are reified, as privileges (of whiteness, class, citizenship, etc.) affects both the effectiveness and experience of the actions performed. In other words, nonviolent

1

resistance may be viewed as an area in which social privileges may be performed, utilized, contested, and better understood.

In the stories participants told during interviews, the centrality of their public identities (and especially their race, class, and gender) emerged as crucial defining influences over what happened to them, how prison witness works more generally, and how they interpreted the various events of their lives. Interestingly, these identities were often intentionally inhabited as platforms for action that were distinctly political, and many justice action prisoners intentionally *used* their privileged identities—and particularly their whiteness, citizenship, education, and professional status—to make *more* and *differently* visible the various violences they protest. In their resistance actions, many of this book's participants purposely "used" their privilege, intentionally, and "for good."

Though they were often aware of how their identities mattered in their activism, participants rarely noted their gender identity (as male or female) as a significant part of how they thought or what had happened to them. However, in this research, gender proved to be a reliable dividing line in terms of what people experienced. Even when circumstances were quite similar, women and men relayed stories of action and incarceration that were different from one another in strikingly patterned ways. Hence, the central questions addressed in this book are: 1) How do justice action prisoners' conceptions and enactments of identity matter during their journeys through prison witness? and 2) How does gender shape their experience?

Studying prison witness from the starting point of identity illuminates how "who we are" matters in what we can do (our agency) and how we experience what happens to us, as it makes differently visible the social structures within which we live. An emphasis on identity also highlights the dangers of relying upon unequal and/or hegemonic social roles in one's efforts toward profound and systemic change. The challenge, as so perfectly articulated by Audre Lorde, is how to dismantle the master's house while using the master's tools—to work against and rebuild the unjust structures of this society, while participating, living, and struggling within them.

METHODOLOGICAL FRAMEWORK: THE WHO IS THE WHAT

This research is based on qualitative interviews with 20 men and 23 women that took place between 2010 and 2014 in various locations throughout the United States. Thirteen of those interviewed are Plowshares activists and 29 are involved with SOA Watch, (though several have been active in both movements). Two are anti-war activists not connected with either movement, and one (Tim DeChristopher) is an environmental activist. At the time of their interviews, all had been released with time served for actions that took place between 1980 and 2009. Thirty-six participants spent at least six months in jail, while the others served slightly shorter sentences but were included for different reasons. Reflecting the older demographics of the group, four participants have died in the time between their interviews and publication. Jerry Berrigan, Sr. Ardeth Platte, Lois Putzier, Sr. Megan Rice, and Dr. Dan Sage, ¡presente!

The homogeneity within the group confirms the demographic limitations of the movements: only two of the 43 participants identify as people of color, the rest as white. Most are formally well-educated and financially stable. For some participants, this stability comes from actual monetary sufficiency, for others it comes from belonging to faith communities that eschew the material world but that still provide sustenance (such as vowed religious and Catholic Workers). Several participants are materially poor, but through community and faith commitments, are able to endure long stretches of incarceration without prohibitive hardship (such as eviction or loss of professional certifications). Many have heterosexual families and have or are retired from high-status careers. Only eight do not identify as either Catholic or Protestant; however, several of these eight credit a religious upbringing with their development of "conscience." In sum, the justice action prisoners interviewed are firmly a part of a dominant American "mainstream," in all ways other than their politics. All participants wished to be known by their real names (which is itself revealing of how they feel about their participation in resistance actions and this study—they are proud of what they do). There is nothing pseudonymous in this work.[2]

All but one interview happened in person (I interviewed Karl Meyer by phone), and began with the same question: "tell me a little about yourself and your activism." For most participants, this was the only question beyond the occasional probe—though when time allowed, my scripted second question was "what do you wear when you know you will be arrested?" (a neutral way to get at notions of privilege). This open-ended format strengthened the rigor of the research as it cemented its most prevalent themes.[3] There were no "leading questions" about privilege or gender, for example, that could be identified and answered strategically. In addition to interviews, I conducted several follow-up phone calls and emails with a handful of willing participants—several of which included direct questions from me about specific content, as well as preliminary research findings.

The research is also informed by participant observation. In the years between 2011 and 2014, I attended multiple court trials in the Central New York area (for anti-drone actions at Hancock Air Force Base), as well as a variety of multi-day protests and meetings.[4] I also attended planning meetings for several nonviolent actions, as well as public presentations given by justice action prisoners themselves.

The Participants

To be included in this research, a person must have completed a prison or jail sentence of six months or more, as a result of nonviolent action performed in the United States. The focus on nonviolence precludes investigation of significant resistance against the state that includes violence (such as the struggle for Puerto Rican independence), but works to isolate a group of activists motivated by similar beliefs about social change. My insistence on lengthy prison sentences limits the scope of movements examined—to two peace movements, essentially—though some of the most inspiring nonviolent action in this country today is around structural racism, the environment, and political or economic reform. The focus on Plowshares and SOA Watch is necessary, however, for an analysis of the strategy of prison witness itself.

Importantly, nonviolent action is *not* any action that is "not violent" (i.e., harmful to people) but instead describes actions that are guided by nonviolent theory and strategy. The six-month incarceration mark delimits inclusion to those who have endured prison as a result of effort and planning, and as a way to exclude those who are arrested without intending to be; for example, for being on the wrong side of a police line. Insisting upon nonviolent action conducted in the United States and adding *time* to my criteria brought my research group into ready view: those who go to prison for nonviolent resistance in the U.S. and are alive today are almost always peace activists and, most often belong to either the SOA Watch or Plowshares movements (though some belong to neither/no movement). With these criteria established, the "who" of my research became peace activists in the United States who have served lengthy prison sentences as a result of protesting imperialism, militarism, war, and nuclear weapons.

Participation in prison witness almost always happens intentionally. It is most often a result of what activists call "discernment"—a process of planning, thinking, and sometimes praying with like-minded others about what best to *do* to actively resist violence. There are rare exceptions to this; however, a nonviolent action leading to incarceration is almost always carefully planned, with the expected result of personal hardship.[5] This makes justice action prisoners stand apart from other activists: they are a unique group.

This unique group would seem to be very small, though precise numbers are impossible to obtain. There are about 120 Plowshares activists (who may or may not have spent time in prison) living in the U.S. today, while there are 247 people who have served time for SOA Watch violations, though many of these served sentences shorter than six months.[6] There are also resisters who are not affiliated with either/any movement, but who act on behalf of disarmament: opponents of war-taxes, the Missouri Peace Planters, STRATCOM, and so on.[7] Most resisters wish to make a public stand through their actions, but some want their witness to remain private and unpublished even within activist circles. Hence, simply counting justice action prisoners is not feasible. Obtaining accurate numbers from court documents is similarly impossible, as justice action prisoners are imprisoned for things like illegal trespass, not "resistance." Most likely, there are fewer than 1,000 people who meet the criteria to be included in my research, 43 of whom are included here.

Locating Myself in My Research

My identity is accounted for and transparent in this research. At the time of my interviews, I was in my early thirties, a heterosexual married white woman, a graduate student studying social movements and nonviolence. In effect, this made me similar—non-threatening and likeable—to those I study. Further, the year that I conducted interviews was the year that I became a mother. Road-tripping across the country with my spouse and infant daughter, we often stayed overnight or shared meals in the homes of research participants. Hence, while the official interviews were recorded and transcribed and form the basis of this book, much of my broader learning came from chatting with participants at their dinner tables, nursing my daughter after a recorded interview, and taking walks before getting back in the car with a little baby.

Traveling as a new mom during the research process, I was grateful to be part of a feminist tradition that sees the subjectivity of the researcher as fundamental to the process of knowledge production, and provides tools for how to account for this in one's research. My gratitude for these tools deepened when I analyzed my data, and it became clear that "who I am" seemed to prompt much of the content of the research itself. Women shared details of marriages and families while men spoke of issues and policies in part because they were speaking *to me*—known among my participants as "the researcher with the baby."[8] In this case, the "what" truly cannot be disentangled from the "who," and so my analysis has to be clear enough to hold both.

I recognized early on that a different methodology could have made my subjectivity less important to the research overall. However, the rich variety of stories that resulted from the wide-open, in-person, and seemingly informal "tell me about yourself and your activism" question kept my interest. The fact that I heard such different stories from men and women when starting from the same (rather boring) question was itself fascinating data. Indeed, in the end, I believe that it propelled many of this book's most significant findings and themes.

Methodological Outlook: Focus on the Good

I have made a very specific choice to focus on the stories and examples from justice action prisoners demonstrating what I consider to be the most insightful, sophisticated, and progressive things in their activism. This focus is not meant to conceal shortcomings among justice action prisoners, or within the movements. I heard such stories, and recognized the more mundane or even destructive practices they represent. However, I rarely re-tell them, but rather deliberately uplift and highlight what I consider to be the *most useful* models for transformative change that my research can provide.

This methodological choice is unusual, but purposive and critical. It is not used as a screen to obscure facts that do not neatly "fit" the overall narrative, and remains both supported by evidence and scientific. While I do not spend many pages on personal or movement weaknesses, I also do not hide them. Such shortcomings are present, visible on the page. They are just not "the point." (Because really, how interesting is it to know that yet another activist has acted without awareness of their privilege? Water is wet. What is interesting, useful, and important to learn from is when someone has the wherewithal to challenge this—and to do things differently).

The discussion on privilege in Chapter 4 shows how this methodological practice works. In this chapter, I carefully examine the stories of ten justice action prisoners who expressed nuanced understandings around how they use their privilege strategically in their activism. This focus comes at the expense of the 33 other participants who expressed less developed views (or refrained from discussing privilege at all), and it serves a very simple purpose: for those who are interested in how to do progressive activist work that responsibly crosses various lines of power, centering these ten individuals offers practical, insightful ideas that are helpful, and may move us forward. Not delving into the other 33 stories is not an attempt to ignore imperfections or to provide cover for other participants, but instead to concentrate on what is the most widely interesting and useful. The ten individuals of focus are not presented as "typical" of the movement, or even of the smaller group of justice action prisoners included in this research. Rather, their interviews anchor the discussion of privilege because they offer the most informed and informative perspectives. Hence, they have the most to offer to the rest of us.

THEORETICAL FRAMEWORK

This book is guided by transnational feminism, both theoretically and methodologically. It is also informed by intersectionality and post-positivist identity theory. Through grounding analysis in individual identity, and particularly emphasizing the difference that gender makes in shaping justice action prisoners' experiences, the research still makes evident justice action prisoners' fundamental concerns. However, by centering attention on people rather than issues, it further shows how "who we are" matters, both politically and personally, in ways that are essential to account for in collective organizing and justice activism.

Transnational Feminism

Transnational feminist analysis is rooted in individual identities and experiences, and theorists such as Chandra Talpade Mohanty posit that one may better understand the intimate and the global, the personal and the political, by grounding knowledge in the individual body.[9] Beginning from the level of the individual does not mean that we can "know" the world from this single scale, rather that transnational trends and local realities may be made visible through it, as people's daily lives are shaped and constrained by global forces. Transnational feminist work is committed to understanding global patterns and drawing connections in ways that are located and specific, without flattening differences across groups or identities. In this, it is concerned with the oppression of women as a part of a *network* of oppressions—gender is just one axis by which people may be oppressed, and while there is not "sameness" between people (there is no meaningful category "women," for example), there is space for coalition and working together across groups.[10] This happens through struggling *against* structures of oppression, in ways that do not rely upon some static notion of identity ("oppressed woman") to make sense. It is thus inherently "feminist" to expose the effects of such things as transnational capitalism, neocolonialism, and the prison industrial complex, for one is never just studying "women," but that which shapes and constrains one's life and life chances. Transnational feminism is a pro-active, justice-seeking approach that works towards the liberation of the individual and society.

Intersectionality

Importantly, transnational feminism is not simply interested in "women's" bodies and experiences—but in how various forces shape all bodies: an intersectional approach.[11] A commitment to intersectionality mandates that understanding be neither reduced to one aspect of identity ("female") nor made so specific that predictable lines of power are obscured (i.e., that women are systematically oppressed in relation to men). In practice, intersectionality translates into a privileging of experience: seeing each person as inhabiting a unique location shaped by a multitude of forces, including gender, race, religion, sexuality, ability, geographic location, class, caste, and ethnicity. Intersectional research requires attending to the multiple axes of identity and oppression people face simultaneously—to locate this in context, structure, and history (the work must be concrete and situated), and to account for the relations among and between identity categories and power.[12]

Post-Positivist Identity Theory

"Who we are" is both structurally determined (the impact of our race and class, for example) and influenced by personality, knowledge, and experience. Identities, then, are both constructed and real.[13] This post-positivist conception sees identities as "sites" of knowledge and meaning-making, our social location shaping what happens to us, as well as how we understand the world and our place within it. We are particularly shaped by our "visible identities" (race and gender), which are powerful and accurate predictors of how we will experience our lives.[14] As a result, post-positivist identity theorists argue that we are affected by the society in which we live (its categories and spheres of belonging), and that we always also retain some power over who we are. We can transform some aspects of our being, but we are always located in time and place.

Beginning with the individual experiences of justice action prisoners, this research confirms post-positivist notions around how "who we are" affects the ways in which we know and act; what we can do and accomplish, as well as how we learn, interpret, understand, and value our experiences. This is true in terms of both our "public" identities—what we look like, where we were born—and our personal senses of self, our "subjective" identities. The stories told in this book further reveal that our identities influence the structural and political powers that we may wield—shaping not only our experiences, but also what we may "do"—in intention and effect—both politically and personally.

THE MOVEMENTS

Almost all of the participants come from one of two movements, Plowshares and the School of the Americas Watch (SOA Watch). Plowshares is an anti-nuclear disarmament movement based in the Prophetic Tradition in Christianity, a tradition that emphasizes resistance to imperial violence as essential to being a true follower of Christ.[15] Plowshares actions are marked by their methods, which include illegal trespass, the destruction of property, and Catholic symbolism.[16] The first recognized Plowshares action occurred in 1980 in King of Prussia, Pennsylvania, when the "Plowshares 8" broke into a General Electric plant where the nosecones for Mark 12A nuclear warheads were manufactured. They beat the warheads with household hammers and splattered them with their own blood, in symbolic but also direct protest to the death they represented.[17] To date, there have been over 100 Plowshares actions carried out by more than 200 activists in the U.S., Germany, Sweden, Great Britain, Australia, and Holland.[18] More than 50 of these have occurred in the United States, carried out by about 120 activists.[19] The most recent Plowshares actions in the United States include the 2012 "Transform Now" action at the Oak Ridge nuclear facility in Tennessee and the 2018 Kings Bay Plowshares at the Kings Bay Naval Submarine Base in Georgia.

The School of the Americas Watch is a solidarity movement founded in 1990 to close a military training school for Latin American military personnel located at Fort Benning in Columbus, GA. Every November between 1990 and 2015, activists convened at Fort Benning to participate in a conference, vigil, and planned disobedience (illegal trespass) to protest the school. Today, the SOA Watch movement continues its work to close the school and protect human rights in Latin America, but since 2010 has focused more on issues of migrant justice.[20] Since 2016, the annual gathering has occurred at the border of Nogales (Mexico) and Sonora (Arizona). Importantly, with the expanded mission has come a change in tactics, and no one connected to the movement has committed civil disobedience at the school since 2011.

Plowshares

Plowshares is an anti-nuclear disarmament movement that takes its name from a biblical verse in the Book of Isaiah advising Christians to "beat swords into plowshares"—to transform weapons into something useful and productive rather than destructive and violent. About 80% of those involved in the Plowshares movement are inspired by their belief in the "Prophetic Tradition" of Catholicism, a perspective advocating that to truly "live" one's religion, resistance in necessary.[21] Representative of the deep faith that Plowshares calls to action, 19% of the movement's activists are vowed religious (priests or nuns), and 37% belong to faith communities such as the Catholic Worker.[22] The vast majority of Plowshares activists are white, and about one-third are female—though this third "includes several of the most frequent participants" (including Sr. Carol Gilbert, Liz McAlister, Susan Crane, and the late sisters Ardeth Platte and Jackie Hudson).[23]

The Prophetic Tradition interprets the life of Jesus Christ as committed to nonviolent struggle.[24] In this thinking, Jesus died for resisting the imperial state, and he did what he believed to be right without concern for popularity or efficacy. In Plowshares philosophy, resistance is biblically and morally necessary, and it is also the most accurate way to emulate the life, as well as the death, of Jesus Christ. In the tradition of prophetic protest, it is impossible to separate thought and action, word and deed—and so to be faithful, one must *live* one's commitments to God. This understanding mandates resistance.[25] Supported by such beliefs, about 30% of the estimated 120 living Plowshares members have participated in more than one serious nonviolent resistant action, while several are serial repeat offenders who have cumulatively spent more than a decade of their lives incarcerated as foot soldiers for Christ.[26]

The Plowshares movement has its genesis in the Vietnam War, when nine people (among them priest-brothers Daniel and Philip Berrigan) raided a U.S. draft-board office in Catonsville, Maryland, and burned over 300 draft files with homemade napalm.[27] This controversial act led to a long jury trial and prison sentences for all participants. Simultaneously, it consolidated a new form of activism in the American anti-war movement: dramatic nonviolent civil disobedience that included the destruction of property, illegal trespass, and intentional interference with national security.

From its inception, the movement has benefited from powerful leadership, in the team of the late brothers Fr. Daniel Berrigan, (former) Fr. Philip (Phil) Berrigan, and (former) Sr. Elizabeth (Liz) McAlister. Through their founding of the movement, intellectual and spiritual leadership, honored identities as vowed religious, and direction of Jonah House, "the Berrigans" have had a profound influence on the philosophy, practice, and culture of the Plowshares movement. The intellectual and inspirational hub of the movement is Jonah House, an intentional faith community located in Baltimore, Maryland. Founded in 1973 by husband-and-wife Phil Berrigan and Liz McAlister, Jonah House is committed to nonviolence, faith, and resistance.

Those involved with Plowshares are traditionally (but not exclusively) leftist-Catholics who identify nuclear weapons as instruments of death that rely upon and support U.S. empire, destructive capitalism, and military expansion. By their very existence, nuclear weapons "kill every day," according to the 2018 Kings Bay Plowshares statement—even without being used.[28] The ultimate logic of such weapons is "omnicide," the destruction of all forms of life (a word that did not exist before the advent of nuclear weapons). During the 2019 Kings Bay Plowshares trial, attorney Bill Quigley explained that Plowshares actions are intended to save "all of our lives."[29] From this view, there is no quibbling regarding nuclear weapons; they are instruments of mass death that are illegal according to international law and contrary to both scripture and common sense. They have "no right" to exist, in the words of Liz McAlister, and must be resisted.[30]

In Plowshares philosophy, the trouble with such weapons is not limited to their potential use; their very existence is harmful and dangerous. Specifically, nuclear weapons are directly linked to domestic problems—and most pressingly, to poverty. The way Plowshares sees it, the billions of dollars spent annually on national defense is money not spent on healthcare, education, social services, and so on, hence comprising a "theft from the poor," in the words of participant Kathleen Rumpf.[31] Weapons of mass destruction are thus at once a divestment in human needs and an investment in an aggressive consolidation of American military power, inequality, and coercive violence both domestically and around the world. Hence, focusing their resistance efforts on nuclear weapons is a way to make their positions on each of these issues clear. They are interconnected.

To bring attention and hoped-for change to the issues they care about, Plowshares activists engage in actions that are both public and illegal (although participants will often argue that it is refraining from protesting nuclear weapons that is truly criminal). As Catholics, their tactics are "legitimate" in how they are biblically appropriate to those who use them. The elements of a Plowshares action are symbolic and/or actual destruction of property, the spilling of blood, illegal trespass, and the use of household items such as hammers to destroy property that has no right to exist in the first place. Fr. Daniel Berrigan explained that "our tradition is sacramental. It is full of symbols: human blood, ashes, water, oil. . . . You shed your own blood rather than the blood of others; your own body is broken rather than the body of others. This is the heart of the Gospel."[32] These symbols are activated in a Plowshares action, communicating a new vision for a place otherwise committed to violent destruction.

Plowshares actions are riskier and more controversial than other forms of nonviolent peace action. Participants sneak onto restricted military property and "symbolically disarm" nuclear weapons and related machinery. They jackhammer missile silos and swim to nuclear submarines. In highly securitized sites, they bang on military equipment, pour their own blood to represent the ultimate purpose of the weapons, and post incriminating evidence against the war machine. Activists do this because they believe that the threat of war, nuclear weapons, and unchecked militarized imperialism are dangerous, imminent, and urgent problems, and because they are willing to endure incarceration as a consequence of their action. Their choice of tactics is symbolic, principled, and authentic to who they are. Plowshares actions are highly secretive in their preparation (they must be, as U.S. law is unforgiving in matters of conspiracy) and daring in execution. Plowshares actions stand out, as elderly priests and retired professors carrying wire cutters, sneaking into aircraft hangars, and splattering blood make for good press *and* force moral reckonings.

The Plowshares movement occupies a special space in the peace movement. It is the most radical type of nonviolent activism currently practiced. At the same time, it is controversial even within the peace movement—for its destruction of property (are the actions truly "nonviolent"?), religious symbolism (do these messages translate?), techniques employed (they are secretive and destructive), and for the questions Plowshares actions bring up concerning efficacy (is spending time in jail the best use of a committed activist's time?). At the very least, such concerns spur important conversations. The Plowshares movement also provides a model of what a very small group of committed activists can produce. The movement represents a persistent attempt to keep a difficult issue alive—nuclear threat as a daily threat—globally and personally. With only a handful of people involved at a given time, Plowshares has kept such conversations alive in the peace movement, as it has also provided framing around how to think about nuclear weapons. Further, Plowshares actions provide narratives for other peace groups to organize around, as well as issues to prioritize. Finally, Plowshares is a sort of lightning rod for the peace movement more widely—a fringe from which other movements may exist in relation. For all of these reasons, in the United States and elsewhere, its role in the peace movement is important.

The School of the Americas Watch

Participants in this book were also drawn from the campaign to close the School of the Americas (SOA), a military training school for Latin American military personal in Columbus, Georgia. Alumni of the school have been linked to some of the region's most egregious atrocities; the 1981 El Mozote massacre in El Salvador determines the date of the annual SOA Watch vigil, but numerous other (and equally horrific) crimes could reasonably take its place.[33] Founded in 1990 by a Maryknoll priest, Fr. Roy Bourgeois (canonically dismissed in 2012, for his support of ordination for female priests), the School of the Americas Watch is the longest ongoing movement of civil disobedience in the U.S.[34] Though the movement has shifted its energies from closing the school to migrant justice, for those included in this study, the school itself was the primary object of protest and "crossing the line" the primary tactic. The fact that prison witness is no longer the cornerstone technique of the movement does not make its examination irrelevant, but in fact sheds more light on the complexity and challenges of the strategy overall.

The first really large SOA Watch protest gathering occurred in November 1997, when over 2,000 people attended a vigil held outside the gates. In 1999, over 10,000 people attended, 4,408 of whom "crossed the line"—illegally trespassing onto the military base housing the school—in an act described by the movement as an instance of mass "civil disobedience." The pressure from the movement culminated in 2001, when Congress voted to close the School of the Americas. A few weeks later, the school re-opened under a new name: the Western Hemisphere Institute for Security Cooperation (WHINSEC).[35]

The campaign to close the school "resists this new world order doublespeak" and continues to refer to the school as the School of the Americas, nicknamed the "school of the assassins" by the movement.[36] As of 2021, 247 people have altogether spent more than 100 years in prison for resisting the school.[37] From 2001 onwards, they have almost always served the maximum penalty for the offense, which is six months in federal prison.

For everyone arrested at Fort Benning, trials were held in the single court-house of Muscogee County, GA. Until 2000, all School of the Americas cases were presided over by Judge Robert ("Maximum Bob") Elliot; by Judge Mallon Faircloth until 2010; and later by Judge Stephen Hyles. Each judge has preferred the maximum punishment for a charge of illegal trespass, which is a six-month stay in federal prison. Participant Brian DeRouen explained that in his trial statement, he "thanked" Judge Faircloth, because "without him, our movement doesn't work. Nobody pays attention to people on pro-bation. So, I was like, 'thank you for being our Bull Connor. Thank you for being the great injustice that makes this whole thing work.'"[38]

SOA Watch has also engaged lobbying efforts in Washington, DC, and internationally and has satellite offices in Chile and Venezuela. The move-ment has been a critical player in seven Latin American countries' decisions to withdraw their troops from attending SOA/WHINSEC. Explaining his 2012 decision to stop sending military personnel to the school (after meeting with SOA Watch delegates), Nicaraguan president Daniel Ortega explained that "the SOA is an ethical and moral anathema. . . . All of the countries of Latin America have been victims of its graduates. The SOA is a symbol of death, a symbol of terror."[39] Such thinking must be at least partially credited to the efforts of SOA Watch, its message amplified by the efforts of justice action prisoners.

THE ISSUES THAT MOTIVATE
JUSTICE ACTION PRISONERS

On the face of it, nuclear weapons and a school of torture in Georgia are the issues of most pressing concern for the activists included in this book. However, for most justice action prisoners, these two instances of violence are understood to spring from much larger, and even more concerning, sys-temic issues. Thus, the goal of most justice action prisoners is not "simply" to close a school or change some bedrock military policies, but like Dorothy Day, they want to "change the system. We need to overthrow, not the govern-ment . . . but this rotten, putrid, industrial capitalist system which breeds such suffering."[40] What most activists are working against are U.S. imperialism and globalized militarism, and they resist these broader forces as they manifest in places like Fort Benning and Kings Bay.

U.S. Imperialism

Participants share an analysis that names U.S. imperialism—basically economic, political, and social domination maintained through force—as the root enabler to diverse violences around the globe.[41] U.S. imperial power works to coerce nations, individuals, and policies, and is maintained through both threat and militarized power, including the use of militarized violence. In this view, the capitalist domination that is enabled through U.S. hegemony globally entrenches inequalities between individuals and nations, and results in environmental destruction, poverty, and other structural inequalities that are harmful to positive life chances. Ultimately, imperialism enriches dominant nations, corporations, and groups, as it divests power and wealth from those it marginalizes.

To confront the interconnected problems created through U.S. imperial policies and practices, Plowshares analysis leads activists to dismantle and disarm nuclear weapons. Nuclear weapons provide the threat (and the reality) of violence that ensures the (necessarily temporary) smooth running of U.S. global supremacy. SOA Watch analysis of the same problems leads participants to protest the SOA and U.S. foreign policy in Latin America. However, the intent is always broader in scope. The goal of both movements is to transform U.S. empire by destabilizing its supports, thereby improving the quality of regular people's lives all over the world.

The concern with imperialism, writ large, is evidenced by the fact that a goodly number of this book's participants are currently most invested in work against weaponized drones and for migrant justice, rather than involved with either Plowshares or SOA Watch. Such shifts indicate not movement disloyalty but in fact *issue allegiance*: weapons of mass destruction, military training schools, weaponized drones, and children in cages are understood to be *manifestations* of aggressive U.S. imperialism, instances around which people can organize but are not the core of contention itself. Of course, the specific effect of each recognized instance is terrible—and what is protested is at once the violent manifestation as well as the system that supports, legitimizes, and furthers it. Describing how he determines where to focus his resistance efforts, participant Fr. Louis Vitale said, "I just keep bouncing from one thing to another. It's all connected, though. I see them all as connected. It's all about injustice."[42] Imperialism is the logic that connects the injustices of focus, and is the foundational issue of concern for all of the justice action prisoners included here.

Globalized Militarization

Justice action prisoners recognize that American economic, political, and social power is maintained through militarization, including the use of force. At this writing in 2021, the U.S. has been continually at war in the Middle East since 2003. The various wars in this region have resulted in millions of mostly civilian deaths, and (regardless of formal U.S. presence in the region) there is no end to the hostilities in sight. The U.S. has the world's largest military budget, constituting 43% of the world's military expenditures, as well as the second-largest number of military personnel after China.[43] The U.S. Armed Forces also controls large quantities of valuable equipment: ships and submarines, manned and unmanned aircraft, infrastructure, and weaponry. Further, the geographic reach of the U.S. military is global: in 2021, there were approximately 165,000 U.S. military personnel permanently stationed in more than 150 of the world's 192 countries, *excluding* those serving in the active combat zones of Iraq, Syria, and Afghanistan.[44] The U.S. occupies over 1,000 military bases internationally, American outposts on foreign soil.[45] These bases make up 95% of *all* foreign military bases operated by any country worldwide, and it is from these sites that even the most remote corners of the globe can be monitored and controlled.[46] The reach of the U.S. military is vast: well equipped, well-funded, trigger-ready, and omnipresent.

Nuclear Weapons

Plowshares emphasizes nuclear weapons as the linchpin to the smooth running of U.S. dominance worldwide. In 2020, it was estimated that there were about 14,000 nuclear weapons in existence.[47] The overwhelming majority of these belong to either the United States or Russia, and many remain on hair-trigger alert. This number is small compared with the estimated 70,000 that existed in 1986—the height of the Cold War—in large part because of national participation in disarmament treaties such as the 2017 United Nations Treaty on the Prohibition of Nuclear Weapons. However, the numbers are again growing. In 2019, the U.S. withdrew from the Iran Nuclear Deal and the Intermediate-Range Nuclear Forces (INF) Treaty with Russia. Subsequently, the U.S. has established a new Space Force (which is intended to have nuclear capacities). The U.S. has also developed a new smaller nuclear warhead, the W76-2, to be used in what is euphemistically called a "limited" nuclear war.[48] Nuclear weapons are expensive. The Ploughshares Fund (not connected with the Plowshares movement) estimates that in the next decade, the U.S. will spend between $620 billion and $661 billion on nuclear weapons and related programs—a huge sum of money for weapons that, everyone hopes, will never actually be used.[49] Widespread concerns exist about nuclear accidents and nuclear weapons falling into the "wrong" hands—specifically, the "wrong" states or non-state actors with terrorist intentions.

Since the 1960s, nuclear weapons policy in the U.S. has been justified politically as "deterrence." Nuclear deterrence is the idea that, in a world in which nuclear weapons exist, having the biggest stockpile is the best way to prevent nuclear conflicts. Deterrence "works" because the reality of actually using the weapons is too destructive for any party to ever truly consider. As a framing idea, deterrence shows the central role nuclear weapons play in maintaining U.S. power abroad. They exist as a constant threat of superior force—and hence, effectively maintain U.S. hegemony.

The School of the Americas

Since at least the 1850s, the United States has pursued an expansionist and interventionist agenda in Latin America. In pursuit of capitalist markets that are open to U.S. trade and political structures that are amenable to U.S. interests, the United States government has toppled democratically elected leaders and supported dictators throughout Latin America, funded civil wars, and provided weaponry to insurgent groups, crippled local movements and assassinated those who disagree with the U.S. agenda.[50] Such actions were particularly flagrant during the decades between 1970 and 1990, when many of the region's most brutal civil wars (in Argentina, Chile, and most of Central America) were exacerbated by U.S. interference and financial support (officially intended to quell communism, but never to protect regular people).

The School of the Americas has played a supporting role in this history, as a military training school that has taught tens of thousands of Latin American military personal since its founding in 1946, including "some of the most notorious dictators and human rights abusers" in the region.[51] Indeed, the Latin American countries with the worst human rights records have consistently been the ones with the highest number of students attending the SOA. A 1993 Congressional analysis confirmed that "dictators, death squad operatives, and assassins" had been trained at the school.[52] Largely because of the pressure exerted by SOA Watch, the content of the training offered at the SOA came under scrutiny, and in 1996 the school gained national attention when the Pentagon released seven training manuals—the core curriculum of the SOA. The manuals provided instructions for various forms of torture, explicitly supported executions, advised on strategies such as arresting the relatives of those being questioned by authorities, and suggested the targeting of union organizers and others who advocated against the government as legitimate methods to quell dissent. These manuals confirmed what activists had long believed, as they showed the direct support of the U.S. government (and its citizens' tax dollars) in supporting horrific abuses of human rights, political interference, and death across Latin America.[53] In 2021, the school remains open.

A GLOBAL STORY, ROOTED IN IDENTITY

The strategy of prison witness makes logical this book's focus on the individual in relation to the political. Unlike more popular nonviolent tactics, such as marches and sit-ins, prison witness is inherently and already personalized. As will be made clear in the next chapter, prison witness "works" by creating a moment of cognitive dissonance around what is "just." As "good people" going to jail, prison witness is meant to jar the public into more critical thinking about the issues of activist concern. As a method of action, then, prison witness is uniquely well suited to tell this blended story of the personal impacting the political and vice versa, despite my participants' oft-voiced complaint that their witness is "not about me, it's about the issues."[54] In fact, their actions are the result of both elements: it is their identities that provide the platform and much of the power for their protest, and it is through their bodies that their public and political messages are conveyed. So no matter how they might wish otherwise, their witness is already and always also about *them,* the contexts in which they live and work, as well as the issues that they care so much about.

This focus on identity is not tangential or inconsequential to justice action, but is in fact deeply relevant to much contemporary activism. Peace and justice activists are increasingly concerned with issues such as solidarity, allyship, and privilege. Of particular relevance in these conversations are some of the ways in which justice action prisoners think about and "use" their privileged identities (especially their citizenship, whiteness, and status within a community) intentionally—as a way to elevate and further their activism's impact. Most often, this action is thoughtful; it is always challenging. Acting "in solidarity" with others is not straightforward, especially when acting "for" those who occupy positions of less power than oneself, and for whom one feels responsible. For example, SOA Watch activists protest the school because they feel responsible as the citizen taxpayers who fund it, but also because those most affected by what the school does are unable to safely lodge their own resistance. As participant Randy Serraglio explained to Judge Faircloth during his 2004 trial in Columbus, GA, he was there because he *could* be. He added, "If I were a campesino, I would be dead in a ditch somewhere."[55] Hence, it was his identity (as a U.S. citizen) that motivated Randy to resist, and it was his privilege (as a white man) that made his protest possible.

Quite basically, beginning with the individual body of justice action prisoners is an effective way to tell many stories at once. It provides a mechanism to understand the issues of activist concern and the logic of prison witness. The embodied story of justice action prisoners also shows how "who we are" matters, as it illuminates structures of violence, reveals gendered impacts on identity and experience, and highlights novel practices for activist engagements into the future.

NOTES

1. Marian Mollin, *Radical Pacifism in Modern America: Egalitarianism and Protest* (University of Pennsylvania Press, 2013).
2. See Mitch Duneier's appendix for a discussion of this method. *Sidewalk.* New York: Macmillan Press, 1999.
3. Marjorie DeVault, *Liberating Method: Feminism and Social Research* (Philadelphia: Temple University Press, 1999).
4. Events included the 2011 SOA Watch vigil, 2012 April Days of Action, the fall 2010 Atlantic Life Committee retreat in Camden NJ, and a 2012 Peace Walk in support of Susan Crane beginning her sentence for the Disarm Now Plowshares.
5. For example, Peter DeMott's 1980 Plowshares action at General Dynamics Electric Boat shipyard in Groton, CT. Without prior planning, Peter drove a shipyard van into a Trident submarine because he noticed that the keys were in the ignition.. Similarly, participant Tim DeChristopher's 2008 environmental action of "buying" public lands at auction to keep them safe from energy development was not planned beforehand, but Tim went to the auction hoping to disrupt the proceedings somehow. He knew about prison witness as a strategy, and he was willing to use it. Hence, both men were "looking for a way to get arrested," in Tim's words, though their acts themselves were spontaneous (Tim DeChristopher, interview by author, Nevada City, CA, January 2014).
6. Sharon Erickson Nepstad, *Religion and War Resistance in the Plowshares Movement* (Cambridge University Press, 2008). This number remains approximately accurate, with a few new participants added since 2008, and a few who have since passed away. *School of the Americas Watch*, www.soaw.org.
7. *The Nuclear Resister*, www.nukeresister.org.
8. Feminist methods account for these impacts, and see owning one's subjectivity as a way to create "better" knowledge—knowledge that is more accurate precisely because it does not claim objectivity when there is none to be had. The reality that my research is shaped by who I am does not muddy its "truth," so long as I remain reflexive and accountable to my role on the process. Marjorie DeVault, *Liberating Method,* 1999; Alison Jaggar, *Just Methods: An Interdisciplinary Feminist Reader* (Routledge, 2015); Trinh T. Minh-Ha, *Woman, Native, Other: Writing Postcoloniality and Feminism* (Bloomington: Indiana Press, 1989); Shulamit Reinharz and Lynn Davidman, *Feminist Methods in Social Research* (Oxford University Press, 1992).

9. Chandra Talpade Mohanty, *Feminism without Borders: Decolonizing Theory, Practicing Solidarity* (Raleigh: Duke University Press, 2003). Hyndman and Mountz explain, "The working woman's body holds intimate knowledge of the global powers of transnational corporations. While she may not have crossed international borders to work, she finds herself simultaneously displaced by poverty and held in place by global capitalism. Learning this one woman's story can tell us something about the realities of capitalism, poverty, and corporate practices through how they *affect* the working woman." Alison Mountz and Jennifer Hyndman, "Feminist Approaches to the Global Intimate" (2006): 446–463. See also M. Jacqui Alexander, *Pedagogies of Crossing: Meditations on Feminism, Sexual Politics, Memory, and the Sacred* (Duke University Press, 2005); M. Jacqui Alexander and Chandra Mohanty, eds., *Feminist Genealogies, Colonial Legacies, Democratic Futures* (New York: Routledge, 1997); Inderpal Grewal and Caren Kaplan, eds, *Scattered Hegemonies: Postmodernity and Transnational Feminist Practices* (Minneapolis: University of Minnesota Press, 1997).

10. Mohanty, *Feminism without Borders,* 2003, 55. Kaplan and Grewal (1997) similarly argue that in linking struggles across lines of difference, transnational feminism must be interested and attentive to local struggles, border crossings, cultural flows, material realities, and relations of power. The idea is not simply to "connect" oppressions, but to construct a theory of gender oppression that operates via "scattered hegemonies" around the world (pp. 17–18).

11. Kimberly Crenshaw, "Mapping the Margins: Intersectionality, Identity Politics, and Violence Against Women of Color," *Stanford Law Review,* 43, no. 6, 1991, 1241–1299. See also Avtar Brah and Ann Phoenix, "Ain't I a Woman? Revisiting Intersectionality," *Journal of International Women's Studies,* 5(3), 2004, 75–86; Sumi Cho, Kimberly Crenshaw, and Leslie McCall, "Toward a Field of Intersectionality Studies: Theory, Applications, and Praxis" in "Intersectionality: Theorizing Power, Empowering Theory," *Signs,* 38(4), 2013; Kathy Davis, "Intersectionality as Buzzword: A Sociology of Science Perspectives on What Makes a Feminist Theory Successful," *Feminist Theory* 9, 2008, 67–85; Leslie McCall, "The Complexity of Intersectionality," *Signs: Journal of Women   in Culture and Society,* 30(3), 2005, 1771–1800; Nira Yuval-Davis, "Intersectionality and Feminist Politics," *European Journal of Women's Studies,* 13, 2006, 193.

12. Hae Yeon Choo and Myra Ferree, "Practicing Intersectionality in Sociological Research: A Critical Analysis of Inclusions, Interactions, and Institutions in the Study of Inequalities," *Sociological Theory,* 28, 2010, 129–149; Ann Phoenix and Pamela Pattynama, "Intersectionality," *European Journal of Women's Studies,* 13(3), 2006, 187–192.

13. Linda Martin Alcoff, "New Epistemologies: Post Positivist Accounts of Identity" in *The Sage Handbook of Identities,* ed. Margaret Wetherell and Chandra Mohanty (London: Sage Publications, 2010), 144–163. See also Alcoff, Linda Martin, Michael Hames-Garcia, and Satya Mohanty, eds. *Identity Politics Reconsidered.* (New York: Palgrave Macmillan, 2006); Michael Hames-Garcia, *Identity Complex: Making the Case for Multiplicity* (Minneapolis: University of Minnesota Press, 2011); Satya Mohanty, "The Epistemic Status of Cultural Identity: On *Beloved* and the

Postcolonial Condition," *Cultural Critique* 24, 1993, 41–80; Paula Moya, "What's Identity Got to Do with It? Mobilizing Identities in the Multicultural Classroom" in *Identity Politics Reconsidered*; Paula Moya and Michael Hames-Garcia, eds., *Reclaiming Identity: Realist Theory and the Predicament of Postmodernism*, (Berkeley: University of California Press, 2000).

14. Linda Alcoff, *Visible Identities: Race, Gender, and the Self* (Oxford University Press, 2006).

15. Ronald Sider, *Nonviolent Action: What Christian Ethics Demands but Most Christians Have Never Really Tried* (Brazos Press, 2015); John Howard Yoder, *Nevertheless: The Varieties and Shortcomings of Religious Pacifism* (Herald Press, 1992).

16. Sharon Nepstad, *Religion and War Resistance*, 2008.

17. Arthur Laffin and Anne Montgomery, eds. *Swords into Plowshares: Nonviolent Direct Action for Disarmament, Peace and Social Justice* (Perennial Library, 1987), 31.

18. The Nuclear Resister, "A History of the Plowshares Movement—a talk by Art Laffin, October 22, 2019," https://www.nukeresister.org/2019/11/02/a-history-of-the-plowshares-movement-a-talk-by-art-laffin-october-22-2019/.

19 Kristen Tobey. *Plowshares: Protest, Performance, and Religious Identity in the Nuclear Age.* (University Park: Pennsylvania State Press, 2016), 36.

20. Chandra Russo, *Solidarity in Practice: Moral Protest and the US Security State* (Cambridge University Press, 2018); Lesley Gill, *The School of the Americas: Military Training and Political Violence in the Americas* (Duke University Press, 2004); Sharon Nepstad, *Catholic Social Activism* (NYU Press, 2019).

21. Sharon Nepstad, *Catholic Social Activism*, 2019. See also Sharon Nepstad, "Persistent Resistance: Commitment and Community in the Plowshares Movement," *Social Problems* 51, no. 1, 2004b, 43–60.

22. Kristen Tobey, *Performing Marginality: Identity and Efficacy in the Plowshares Nuclear Disarmament Movement* (University of Chicago, 2010), 45. The Catholic Worker (CW) is a network of "houses of hospitality" founded in 1933 by Dorothy Day and Peter Maurin in New York City. In her interview, participant Kathleen Rumpf explained that the CW is about "performing . . . the corporeal acts of mercy . . . it is also to confront the system, it is about systemic change, too." (Kathleen Rumpf, interview by author, Syracuse, NY, April 28th, 2010).

23. Tobey, *Plowshares,* 2016, 36.

24. Nepstad, *Religion and War Resistance*, 2008.

25. Yoder, *Nevertheless*, 1992, 57.

26. Tobey, *Plowshares,* 2016, 36.

27. There were two draft board raids previous to the Catonsville 9 (one in Baltimore with Fr. Phil Berrigan and Tom Lewis, and one by Barry Bondhus in Minnesota); however, this was the action that galvanized the movement.

28. Kings Bay Plowshares 7, https://kingsbayplowshares7.org/; see also Brian Terrell, "A Judge's 'Doubtful Proposition' on Nuclear Weapons," *Consortium News*, 11/18/2019, https://consortiumnews.com/2019/11/18/a-judges-doubtful-proposition-on-nuclear-weapons/.

29. "Kings Bay Plowshares 7 Guilty Verdict 10–24–2019," *YouTube*, https://www.youtube.com/watch?v=MONkguTdryA&feature=youtu.be.

30. Elizabeth McAlister, personal interview, Baltimore, MD, March 13th, 2012.

31. Rumpf, Interview.

32. Quoted in Walter Wink, ed., *Peace is the Way: Writings on Nonviolence from the Fellowship of Reconciliation* (Maryknoll, NY: Orbis Books, 2000), 94.

33. Gill, *The School of the Americas*, 2004.

34. Sara Koopman, "Imperialism Within: Can the Master's Tools Bring Down Empire?" *ACME: An International E-Journal for Critical Geographies* 7, no. 2 (2008a): 283–307.

35. Sharon Nepstad, *Catholic Social Activism*, 2019.

36. Sarah Koopman, "Cutting through Topologies: Crossing Lines at the School of the Americas," *Antipode*, vol. 40, no. 5, 2008b, 830; see also Selina Gallo Cruz, "Negotiating the Lines of Contention: Counterframing and Boundary Work in the School of the Americas Debate 1." In *Sociological Forum*, vol. 27, no. 1, pp. 21–45, 2012.

37. *School of the Americas Watch*, www.soaw.org.

38. DeRouen, interview.

39. Marcel Evans, "Nicaragua: Ortega announces withdrawal from US Army School of the Americas," *Costa Rica Star*, 9/12/2012, http://news.co.cr/nicaragua-ortega-announces-withdrawal-from-us-army-school-of-the-americas/14348/.

40. Sharon Nepstad, *Catholic Social Activism*, 2019, 164.

41. Arthur Laffin and Anne Montgomery, *Swords into Plowshares*, 1987; *Jonah House*, www.jonahhouse.org; Ed Kinane, "Think Global," 2013; Rosalie Riegle, *Doing Time for Peace: Resistance, Family, and Community* (Nashville: Vanderbilt University Press, 2012a); Rosalie Riegle, *Crossing the Line: Nonviolent Resisters Speak Out for Peace* (Eugene, OR: Cascade Books, 2012b); *School of the Americas Watch*, www.soaw.org; Brian Terrell, "Pro Se Defense in the Catholic Worker Tradition," *Voices for Creative Nonviolence*, 2011, http://vcnv.org/categories/writings-by-brian-terrell; "Legal Arguments," *Transform Now Plowshares*, http://transformnowplowshares.wordpress.com/legal-arguments.

42. Fr. Louis Vitale, interview by author, Oakland, CA, December 22nd, 2011.

43. $934 billion for 2020–2021. Kimberly Amadeo, "US Military Budget, Its Components, Challenges, and Growth," *The Balance*, updated 09/03/2020, https://www.thebalance.com/u-s-military-budget-components-challenges-growth-3306320#:~:text=Estimated%20U.S.%20military%20spending%20is,Defense%20alone2%EF%BB%BF%EF%BB%BF; Murtaza Hussain, "It's Time for America to Reckon with the Staggering Death Toll of the Post-9/11 Wars, *The Intercept*, 11/19/2018, 8 p.m., https://theintercept.com/2018/11/19/civilian-casualties-us-war-on-terror/.

44. "Number of Military and DoD Appropriated Fund (APF) Civilian Personnel Permanently Assigned By Duty Location and Service/Component (as of March 31, 2021)," June 2021.

45. Hugh Gusterson, "Empire of Bases," *The Bulletin of Atomic Scientists*, 03/10/2009, http://thebulletin.org/empire-bases.

46. Gusterson, "Empire of Bases," 2009.

47. *Bulletin of Atomic Scientists* columnist Kingston Reif explains that even if a U.S. president decided to use nuclear weapons, he or she would need "only a handful, not the thousands the United States currently possesses." https://www.bbc.com/news/newsbeat-51091899.

48. William Arkin and Hans M. Kristensen, "US Deploys New Low-Yield Nuclear Submarine Warhead." Federation of American Scientists, January 29, 2020, https://fas.org/blogs/security/2020/01/w76-2deployed/.

49. Joel Rubin, "What Nuclear Weapons Cost Us—It's the Right Time for a Debate," Ploughshares, http://www.ploughshares.org/what-nuclear-weapons-cost-us; see also Elaine Scarry. *Thermonuclear Monarchy: Choosing Between Democracy and Doom.* (New York City: W.W. Norton & Company, 2014); Kristensen, Hans, and Robert Norris. "Global nuclear weapons inventories, 1945–2013." *Bulletin of the Atomic Scientists* 69, no. 5 (2013): 75–81.

50. See Gill, *The School of the Americas*, 2004, for a more thorough review of this history.

51. Sharon Nepstad, "School of the Americas Watch," *Peace Review* 12, no. 1 (2000): 67–72, 67.

52. Koopman, "Cutting through Topologies," 2008b, 828.

53. Ibid., 829. See also "Category: SOA Graduates in the News," *School of the Americas Watch,* https://soaw.org/category/resources/soagradsnews/.

54. Tiffany, interview.

55. Randy Serraglio, interview by author, Tucson, AZ, May 13th, 2012.

Chapter 2

Nonviolent Resistance
in an Imperial State

Prison Witness

There were five of us who gathered, and we took time in prayer and reflection over a period of several months, and we decided to say no to the warheads. . . . In the middle of the base there's this separate facility, it's called the Strategic Weapons Facility Pacific . . . SWFPAC. So we went onto the base at night, and we cut through a fence. We had hammers with us, to symbolically disarm, and we also had blood with us, our own blood, to mark the weapons if we could get to them.

We had heard that we wouldn't be able to get on the base, because there was so much security. There were perimeter guards and ferocious guard dogs and cameras . . . so we were pretty surprised when we got on the base, and when we kept walking towards the middle. . . . Later, at shift time, all the cars were passing us, and nobody stopped. We just acted like we were going to our shift, I guess. Kept walking. And we got to the area where the bunkers were, where the nuclear weapons were being held. There's woods all around this area that's enclosed with a double fence, and then between the woods and the second fence there's this big bulldozed area—just dirt, so they can see people approaching. So . . . we gathered, said a prayer, and we walked across the dirt. Nothing happened, no alarms. Went through the first fence, nothing happened. We cut (the fence), with bolt cutters. . . . We got up to the second high security fence and it was a double fence. . . . So we cut through that and we were on the grass and held our banner up, and there were armed guards at that point . . . maybe 20 feet away.

(At this point) it was dawn. It took us a long time to travel, because Bix couldn't walk very fast because of his heart problems. . . . So the marines came up and separated us, put us down on the ground, put hoods on, hand-cuffed us, and held us there about 4 hours. . . . We hung the one banner on the side of the high security fence before we came in, and then we held the other banner when we came in and were confronted by the guards. It said: "Disarm now, Plowshares. Trident immoral and illegal." We knelt down and held the banner. Put our hammers and bolt cutters down. . . . They released us later that

same day. 10 months later, they brought charges.—Susan Crane, September 5, 2010, interview with the author, describing the 2009 "Disarm Now" Plowshares Action in Bangor, Washington

Civil disobedience leading to lengthy imprisonment ("prison witness") is a specific strategy in the nonviolent toolkit. High-risk and intentional, prison witness entails breaking the law in principled resistance.[1] It is a way to signal disagreement, to make one's own position clear, and to bring attention and change to an issue. There is a long legacy of disobedience in Western thought: Judeo-Christian stories are full of acts of rebellion and defiance against the state, and ancient Greek philosophy explicitly supports the idea that a just person must disobey an unjust law.[2] In the modern era, prison witness was most clearly promoted as a strategy of resistance by Henry David Thoreau in his seminal *Civil Disobedience,* an essay prompted by his spending the night in jail for refusing to pay poll taxes supporting the Mexican-American war. In the essay, Thoreau argues that one is justified in breaking the law if the "machine of government" requires one to be an "agent of injustice to another." Living in a state that permitted both slavery and war, Thoreau believed that those working for their abolition must live their lives as a "counter-friction to stop the machine." Famously, he explained that "under a government which imprisons any unjustly, the true place for a just man is also a prison." [3] Armed with this reasoning, going to jail for principled reasons, even in direct disobedience to the state and its laws, is recognized a way for a person to make their position against systemic injustice clear and to "do" something against it. Disobedience highlights injustice as it removes material and moral resources from an authority. Simultaneously, it gums up the systems supporting unjust laws and policies.

As a tactic of nonviolence, prison witness was first widely used during the Salt March of 1930, when Gandhi advocated for those struggling for independence to fill the jails—overextending the administrative system and bringing the opposition to a position more prepared to bargain. "Filling the jails" was also a key strategy during the American movement for women's suffrage, as well as the American movement for Civil Rights.[4] Indeed, a principled refusal to obey an authority—leading to known or expected punishment—is a cornerstone of nonviolent action in the United States.

Civil disobedience is fundamentally different from other forms of dissent expression, such as voting, participating in a march or rally, letter-writing, or boycott. Instead, it is an "illegal" intervention that exists outside of the political or legal system, a technique in which one "goes to jail for justice." This may happen in one of two ways: an activist may break an unjust law to protest the law itself (e.g. Jim Crow), or they may break a "neutral" law (e.g. private property) to bring attention to an area of concern. Prison witness can be integrated within a large-scale movement, as it has been with SOA Watch; it can be an individual action not affiliated with any movement (e.g. tax refusal); and it can be a clandestine activity involving secrecy and nonviolent sabotage, as with Plowshares actions.

To be incarcerated for a lengthy period of time as a result of nonviolent action does not happen accidentally or necessarily easily. It is relatively simple to get sent to jail for a night or two for nonviolent resistance—or longer for violent resistance—but being handed a sentence of weeks or more for nonviolent acts generally requires intentional efforts and planning. Illegal trespass (of highly securitized or politicized federal property) and destruction of government property are the two most common forms of "disobedience" carried out by peace and justice activists. Such acts carry a wide range of consequences in the contemporary United States, where sentences for justice action prisoners have varied from several days to as long as 18 years.

Prison witness may be conducted as an act of civil disobedience, and it may be performed as an act of nonviolent "resistance," a distinction that matters. In his 1970 article on the subject, philosopher Berel Lang argued that for an act to qualify as civil disobedience, three criteria must be met: 1) the act must violate the law, 2) the act must be performed intentionally—and in part to change the law or policy, and 3) the actor must take responsibility for the act. In nonviolent resistance, none of these criteria is essential. Indeed, those motivated by nonviolent resistance may see what they are doing as *upholding* rather than violating the law—and their aims may be more revolutionary than reform-oriented.[5] For example, civil disobedience may entail sitting at a lunch counter to protest segregation laws. Nonviolent resistance would be banging on a nuclear weapon to *enforce* the international laws that make such weapons illegal, in an all-out effort to save the planet and its inhabitants from nuclear annihilation. It is performed as act of law enforcement, rather than criminality. Such resistance is understood to be *legal,* by actual law *or* by necessity. Justice action prisoners almost always view what they do as nonviolent resistance rather than civil disobedience, and prison witness is their *moral, chosen,* and often *legal* strategy of action.

At first glance, prison witness may seem extreme, unorthodox, or unusual. However, it is actually an essential tool for protesting an unjust system from within that system itself. In the United States, prison witness works as a check on democratic institutions and the rights of the people, as enshrined in the Constitution. Justice action prisoners are quick to remind folks that the U.S. Constitution grants "the people" significant power. American democracy guarantees citizens the right to resist; to speak and protest; to challenge, change, and even overthrow the government and its laws. As a result, resisting that which harms or fails to fairly represent people is quintessentially *democratic* behavior, and absolutely American. It is, in fact, a democratic duty for "the people" to stand up for what they want and need. One way to interpret the actions of justice action prisoners is not as disrupters, but rather as essential safeguards of democratic governance; citizens who are using the tools provided them by the U.S. political and legal system (free speech, dissent, the courts, trial by jury), to protect the institution of representative government itself, government *by* and *for* the people.

This chapter begins with a review of prison witness as a historical tool for legal, social and political change in the United States, one that has been activated across time, context, and issues. Further elucidating prison witness includes an overview of nonviolent methods, mechanisms, and power. Nonviolent power is expanded to include a notion of "privilege power," to more accurately account for the role of status and identity in the use of prison witness. The chapter also examines prison witness as it has been imagined and practiced by justice action prisoners from the SOA Watch and Plowshares movements more specifically—including the role of the court trial. Last is a discussion of what prison witness accomplishes, and the slippery notion of "efficacy."

PRISON WITNESS AND NONVIOLENCE IN U.S. HISTORY

Though nonviolence is often thought of as beginning with Gandhi in India, it is actually much older, and a characteristically American, method of dissent. Historian Stephen Kohn explains that in the U.S., "civil disobedience and resistance to unjust laws are an integral part of the American democratic tradition."[6] Nonviolent resistance has been used against the British to win independence; to fight slavery; to win rights for women, laborers, and minorities; and in various (and ongoing) struggles for peace and justice. The potential for civil disobedience "lies deep in American attitudes and thought," according to historian David Weber, and has been present throughout American life "out of all proportion to its number."[7] Though many people remain unaware of the history of nonviolence in America, it has fundamentally shaped this country's policies, laws, ideals, and people.[8]

Notions of nonviolent resistance are woven into the formation of the country itself. The Quakers were early white settlers from Europe who refused, on religious principle, to take lands from or fight against the Native Americans. They also refused to own slaves, pay taxes for or be conscripted into the monarch's wars.[9] Their positions were individual and religious rather than directly political; however, the Quaker's views had an outsize effect on their nascent country. Through their pacifist commitments, they enshrined resistance to political policies and laws for reasons of personal liberty or conscience as *valid* and *legally protected* forms of citizen engagement. In our rights to the freedom of religion, the separation of church and state, and other personal liberties, American citizens owe much to these early religious pacifists.

The American Revolution is most often taught as a story of violence working, but the war was pre-dated by decades of nonviolent resistance to colonization. One can see resistance to British rule in the development of institutions articulating colonial interests (and against British controls), through open resistance to specific acts (the Stamp Act, Townshend Acts, and the Coercive Acts), through mass noncooperation with British authority, and through the creation of "parallel institutions"—most importantly, political organizations that could take the place of British rule.[10] Through the use of such tactics, colonists experienced noncooperation as a form of power, and their ongoing resistance made the longstanding success of British rule untenable—even before the official "start" of the Revolutionary War.

In the movement to abolish slavery, American abolitionists were even more active and organized than the early settlers. They based their resistance against state powers not on religious conviction, but on direct action around the rallying cry "No compromise with evil." The American abolitionist leader William Lloyd Garrison is often identified as the first person to outline the political doctrine of nonviolent resistance to oppression; he extolled that slavery was so immoral that *every* person should interfere "with its daily operation" and work to overthrow it.[11] The abolitionist view required *absolute non-participation* with the unjust state: one must categorically refuse to be a part of a system that enables and profits from the abuse of human beings. Garrison urged people to violate military laws, to break "unjust" laws, and to willingly suffer the consequences. Such action was considered a moral imperative overriding all other issues, and all people had a duty to participate. This articulation of mass (and yet personal) direct action inspired thinkers like Thoreau and Tolstoy—and later Martin Luther King and Gandhi.

Daily nonviolent resistance to slavery also came from the enslaved themselves. These acts included intentionally breaking tools, feigning illness, or working slowly to cut into slave owners' profits.[12] The Underground Railroad must also be understood as a "disobedient" network, a secretive system to transport enslaved people northward in direct defiance of the Fugitive Slave Act. Little of what the enslaved people or the abolitionists did was "legal" at the time—but all of it was moral, necessary, and justified from a nonviolent perspective.

The campaign for the 19th amendment relied heavily upon nonviolent direct action and imprisonment. In their long struggle, American suffragists petitioned, picketed, paraded, were arrested, and went to jail to win the right to vote. The women often refused to work and went on hunger strikes. They used the tactic of the "jail-in": when the police arrested protesting women, more women were recruited to fill their places. Those arrested would refuse to pay fines—taxing the administrative capabilities and jail facilities—and forcing authorities into difficult positions regarding what to *do* with all of these troublesome incarcerated women.[13] When they were in jail, the women fasted, and were painfully force-fed through their noses by prison authorities. A turning point in the suffrage movement came on November 14th, 1917, at Occoquan Workhouse, a women's prison in Virginia. On this night, 32 women were badly beaten, chained to their beds, and otherwise brutalized for their participation in a peaceful action in front of the White House. This "Night of Terror" galvanized widespread condemnation of the women's treatment.[14] Ultimately, the women's willingness to endure incarceration proved essential to securing the passage of the 19th Amendment.

The First World War provided an opportunity for the early religious underpinnings of American resistance to meet the abolitionist calls for direct action, in the form of draft resistance. Draft resisters at the time did not seek to *avoid* the draft, but for the first time actively "courted prosecution" for their refusals, intentionally interfering with the draft system's ability to function.[15] Draft resisters during the First World War framed their resistance as a civic and moral duty in a democratic state, wherein conscription itself (and not just the war) must be protested. Crucially, this form of action was enabled by the idea that the legitimate power of the people is a relevant force—and that resistance against both the *instance* and *system* of injustice are necessary if one is to confront either.

The First World War period also saw socialist-anarchist activists Eugene V. Debs, Emma Goldman, and Alexander Berkman incarcerated (for crimes such as "sedition") that drew links between U.S. participation in the war and imperialism, exposing connections between the class system and the profit-making of the war machine. At his trial, Debs framed his act as "for" the common worker, "because" of the effects of the capitalist system of wage labor, and "against" the institutions of a greedy state.[16] Such thinking popularized philosophical and ethical support for resistance actions, as appropriate behavior for moral citizens in an unjust state.

After the First World War, U.S. activists continued engaging in nonviolent direct action, through various struggles protesting racial segregation, as well as to secure better rights for workers (the bold tactics of the Labor movement have often resulted in incarceration, but also won us the weekend). During the Second World War, conscientious objectors (COs) were sent to prison across the United States. Many men entered prison for religious reasons, however during their incarcerations they were exposed to the more political aspects of war resistance. As a result, many left prison politically radicalized, several of whom went on to become leaders in the movement for Civil Rights.[17] In 1955,

Dorothy Day and the New York Catholic Workers led a highly publicized protest of the air raid drills ordered in New York City, and were sent to jail in punishment.[18] In 1958, the ship *Golden Rule* defied an injunction by sailing five miles into a restricted Pacific nuclear testing zone before being stopped by the U.S. navy.[19] Bolstering the practice of such disobedient actions, religious thinkers and activists such as A.J. Muste, Thomas Merton, and Dorothy Day framed resistance to violence as fundamental Christian practice, constructing the moral infrastructure that became so essential to the philosophies of later peace movements.[20]

The American movement for Civil Rights is the most well-known nonviolent movement in U.S. history, led by the Reverend Dr. Martin Luther King Jr. In his *Letter from Birmingham Jail,* King explained how nonviolent direct action works, and why "breaking the law" is so essential to its success. He wrote:

> Nonviolent direct action seeks to create such a crisis and establish such creative tension that a community that has consistently refused to negotiate is forced to confront the issue. . . . We have not made a single gain in civil rights without determined legal and nonviolent pressure. History is the long and tragic story of the fact that privileged groups seldom give up their privileges voluntarily. . . . We know through painful experience that freedom is never voluntarily given by the oppressor; it must be demanded by the oppressed.
>
> You express a great deal of anxiety over our willingness to break laws. This is certainly a legitimate concern. . . . One may well ask, "How can you advocate breaking some laws and obeying others?" The answer is found in the fact that there are two types of laws: there are just laws, and there are unjust laws. I would agree with St. Augustine that "an unjust law is no law at all."
>
> Now, what is the difference between the two? How does one determine when a law is just or unjust? A just law is a man-made code that squares with the moral law, or the law of God. An unjust law is a code that is out of harmony with the moral law. . . . Any law that uplifts human personality is just. Any law that degrades human personality is unjust. All segregation statutes are unjust because segregation distorts the soul and damages the personality. It gives the segregator a false sense of superiority and the segregated a false sense of inferiority. . . . So segregation is not only politically, economically, and sociologically unsound, but it is morally wrong and sinful.[21]

These words injected oxygen into the Civil Rights movement, giving energy and shape to the techniques employed by the thousands who marched (often without permits), sat down at lunch counters (in defiance of segregation laws), participated in boycotts, and registered people to vote in communities where this "right" was far from secure. For their violations, participants were often harshly punished: their families, homes, and businesses threatened and destroyed; their bodies beaten, arrested, and thrown in jail; their busses and cars set on fire.[22] Eventually, the movement secured the passage of the Civil Rights Act of 1964. At the same time, it solidified nonviolent direct action as the most powerful force available to ordinary people who were organized: strong enough to win—even over the objections of white supremacists, the legal and cultural system of the American south, and the state itself.

The Vietnam War provided another significant development in American nonviolent practice, once again through resistance to conscription.[23] Draft violation is an individual form of resistance and, historically, is almost always enacted because of the resister's religious beliefs. By 1973, however, conscientious objection had become a *collective* and *political* act.[24] In that year, more than 73% (of the tens of thousands) of inductions resulted in a legal exemption from military service—most of which were granted to people who were not religious. This massive, public, and moral engagement in disobedience effectively felled the entire system of conscription, and in 1975 the draft registration requirement for young men was terminated for a five-year period. This is an important instance of nonviolence "working" in concrete terms—and testament to the power of numbers in escalating nonviolent resistance and efficacy.[25]

Since the war in Vietnam, nonviolent resistance has continued in a variety of movements across the United States. There have been movements around global capitalism, international trade, and corporate policies (protests against the WTO and NAFTA, Occupy Wall Street, Citizens United), environmental destruction and climate change (Earth Day, the Keystone Pipeline, Sunrise Movement), war (War Resisters League, Women's International League for Peace and Freedom, Code Pink), weapons and weapons systems (the Nuclear Freeze movement, Plowshares, the Nevada Desert Experience), labor (the United Farm Workers, Fight for 15, pay equity), racism and discrimination (the disability, gay, transgender, and women's rights movements, #MeToo, immigrant justice, the movement for Black Lives), and more. Indeed, looking across this nation's history with an eye for nonviolent civil resistance, it begins to seem omnipresent; regular people are constantly organizing against the authorities that constrain their lives and life chances, and towards the creation of a more just and fair way of living.

Highlighting the history of nonviolent action in American history shows it to be responsible for an outsize number of accomplishments, policies, and protections that most of us consider to be "good": the achievement of basic human and civil rights, protective labor laws, environmental regulations, universal public education, civil rights legislation (across gender, race, ability, and sexuality), voting rights, and many others. Each accomplishment (unfinished and vulnerable as it may be) must be seen as at least partly the result of nonviolent struggles enacted by ordinary people against the state or relevant authority. More often than not, these struggles have included acts of breaking the law and incarceration. In fact, in no case mentioned here has an authority granted a provision demanded without the coercion of regular people organizing to protect themselves and one another. Nonviolent action, then—centrally including time in prison—is part of a vital, quintessentially American tradition of resistance that works against vested power and "for" ordinary people. The work is never complete and "wins" are ever vulnerable (as evidenced by the assault on voting rights following the 2020 presidential election—a struggle justice advocates have been fighting for centuries that is still so far from secure). Rather, gains must be vigilantly guarded and continually bettered. The resistance required to achieve and protect these "good things" may feel radical or uncomfortable, but nonviolent action must be understood as an essential framework and method of action for ensuring, enforcing, and increasing justice and democracy that is home-grown, and effectively works to better people's daily lives.

PRISON WITNESS AND NONVIOLENT ACTION: THE THEORY BEHIND IT ALL

Prison witness, or "court witness" as it is sometimes called, is exemplary of the philosophy and practice of nonviolent resistance more broadly. Most basically, nonviolence is a form of action that is powered by non-cooperation— withdrawing one's complicity (i.e., power) from an authority (regime, policy, law, corporation, boss), and forcing that authority to respond in ways that expose the structural and direct violence already present in the system. Breaking (or upholding) laws, going to court, and enduring lengthy prison sentences in protest are emblematic of what it means to not cooperate, actively expose, and resist an unjust law or authority. This section articulates prison witness as a strategy within nonviolent praxis, briefly describes nonviolent philosophy and practice, confronts common misconceptions about nonviolence and direct action, and reviews nonviolent methods.

Prison Witness

Prison witness is the nonviolent method of going to jail for justice—of doing something that does not harm others but results in one's own arrest, which is then followed by a court trial and incarceration. As Sr. Anne Montgomery writes in her essay, "Spiritual Power Behind Bars," most people can understand civil disobedience, but they do not understand going to jail. Even among activists, Sr. Montgomery explains, prison is often considered a "waste of time," something that prevents people from keeping up their activist work, or deters them from committing bolder action.[26] However, for justice action prisoners, prison witness is considered to be an act of resistance in and of itself, as it also provides a variety of opportunities for further resistance. Here, the discernment process (the spiritual, communal, pedagogical process of determining to act), the moment of action, the criminal trial, the experience of prison, the spiritual training, and the media attention enabled by each step provide opportunities for protest and for potential change—personally and politically. Prison witness, then, is best understood as a process rather than a moment; a process of saying "no" to state violence, as it simultaneously offers authorities opportunities to do better; to change or uphold laws and policies, whereby the state can more accurately reflect its democratic, legal, and justice-oriented ideals.

In the peace community, the word "witness" is meaningful, and the term "prison witness" intentional. The idea of witness is to see and to testify; in a way that may be interpreted as religious (to see and testify to God's will) and also legal (to see and testify to a crime). Both parts are activated in prison witness: one bears witness to crimes of state violence, usually in conjunction with an appeal to a higher authority such as God, morality, or justice.

The idea of witness comes from the Quakers, for whom witnessing means demonstrating one's belief in biblical scriptures. In this, what is important is one's allegiance to conscience and God, but not one's obedience to a state or other authority. Witness is thus an individual commitment and enactment, and entails prioritizing one's own "inner laws" (morality, faith) over what is easy, popular, or legal. The word "witness" derives from the Old English word "witan"—meaning "to know," so witness inherently touches on qualities of wisdom or skill. The idea of witness has taken on multiple forms over the years in the peace community, including "eyewitness, an expression of conscience, a communication with 'the heart' of others, antinomianism (the belief that moral and legal systems are of no use, faith alone determines salvation), (and) witness as (oppositional) presence."[27] This last form—that activated by Greenpeace, SOA Watch, and Peace Brigades International, is a form of "being there"— in areas of injustice—to witness and protest the violence of that place. Witness as "oppositional presence" is a form of "radical witness" involving "the entire body," according to Gibbon. To engage in prison witness, then, is to *embody* one's principles, to literally put one's body where one's beliefs are.[28] From this frame, prison witness is serious and total; there is nothing more that one can give.

In her study of solidarity activists in the U.S., Chandra Russo identifies witness as a *practice* that confronts state violence; a means of seeing, knowing, and coming to act—for and against things that are hard to see, know, and do anything about.[29] She cites Witness Against Torture (WAT), a nonviolent movement working to close the prison at Guantanamo Bay, for how they have activated witness as *practice*. By occupying important public spaces in their orange jumpsuits and hoods, WAT forces people to see what the state has tried to obscure. Through symbolic action, WAT forces a vision of torture. To witness, then, is not a passive act. Rather, it is an active form of engagement that demands a response. It may be uncomfortable, and it may be interpreted as weird, ugly, or distasteful, but it cannot be unseen.

Prison witness is a nonviolent form of protest in that it does not hurt any-one, although there is disagreement about whether the destruction of property and/or self-inflicted harm (of being in a "shoot to kill" zone, for example, where one may be killed but also force another to kill) "count" as truly non-violent. This book does not delve into these arguments and simply accepts such actions as nonviolent when so articulated by their actors; however, fur-ther reading is footnoted for those interested in these debates.[30]

Nonviolence

Around the world, nonviolent civil resistance is one of the most effective, prevalent, and misunderstood forces of social and political change. There is a strong ethical tradition supporting civil disobedience that can be traced at least as far back as Antigone, of ancient Greece.[31] However, it was not until the last century when, ridding India of British colonialism, Gandhi systematized nonviolence as a method of struggle, clearly distinguishable from (though often concurrent with) moralistic beliefs about pacifism, the principled opposition to war.[32]

Nonviolence is *not* pacifism—it is not an avoidance of conflict, haphaz-ard, or accidental, nor is it the only option for those lacking violent means. Rather, it is *a form of conflict itself*: a method of generating and engaging in conflict, a way to escalate tensions and make "suffering" visible so that it may be challenged and transformed. Commonly assumed to be a form of con-flict resolution, nonviolence is in fact a way to *engage in* conflict. One does well to remember that "those who use nonviolent action . . . did not come to make peace. They came to fight."[33] The fight is not violent but it is *against* violence.[34] This "two-sided" phenomenon takes place outside of standard institutions, and is carried through by "regular" people.[35] Indeed, the state or corporation can never be the initiator of nonviolent action, while nonvio-lence works well to challenge elite interests such as militarism and economic exploitation. Most often, the target of nonviolent action is the state.[36]

As an offensive, intentional form of action, nonviolent campaigns are effective. In their analysis of over 300 nonviolent versus violent revolution-ary movements across the 20th century, Maria Stephan and Erica Chenoweth found that nonviolent campaigns are more likely to accomplish their goals (and do so with less loss of life) than are violent campaigns (53% effective vs. 26%). They are also more likely to lead to democratic societies in the long term.[37]

Unlike violence, nonviolence relies upon mass participation; indeed, the extent to which regular people feel they can participate is the greatest indicator of movement success. According to Chenoweth's research, on average, nonviolent campaigns have about 11 times more participants than violent campaigns, participants who are diverse across age, class, ability, and other indicators.[38] Anyone can be an important part of nonviolent resistance, for in a nonviolent movement, everyone holds power. This is one of the reasons why nonviolent campaigns may be so successful; they are additive. Of course, participation in nonviolent action does not guarantee one's safety or the efficacy of one's struggle—and the resulting reactions can be brutal. Still, both one's safety and the success of one's campaign in the short and long term are *more* likely via nonviolent rather than violent action.

Nonviolent Methods

Nonviolence is marked by its methods, which are specific, creative, and multiple; but nonviolence is *not* anything that is not violent. Nonviolent methods can be coercive and risky (such as with prison witness), but they are never physically violent towards oneself or others. In his campaigns and writings, Gandhi clarified the repertoire of tactics that could be used to challenge oppression: tactics of protest (petitions, marches, and walk-outs), tactics of noncooperation (boycotts, strikes, and civil disobedience), and tactics of disruption (blockades and seizures of property).[39] In 1973, Harvard political scientist Gene Sharp extrapolated this to include 198 methods of nonviolence, divided into areas of protest and persuasion, non-cooperation, and nonviolent intervention.[40] The intensity of these methods is linear (i.e., disruption is more serious than noncooperation), and build towards escalation.

Sharon Nepstad articulates nine forms of nonviolent action used in civil resistance struggles. These include forms of "everyday resistance"—the subtle, often hidden ways in which individuals may confront injustice (working slowly, evasion, feigning ignorance), people power revolutions (overthrowing a regime through collective action), third-party nonviolent intervention (accompaniment, work that supports rather than directs those struggling in situations of intense conflict), and what she terms "symbolic moral witness." Plowshares acts fit into this last category, actions that are meant to "strip away" heroic readings of the past, as they reveal the systemic oppression inherent in a system.[41] Simultaneously, symbolic moral witness may point to alternative ways of living. For instance, in spilling blood at sites of violence, Plowshares activists resist the "sanitation" of war, using an

appropriate Catholic symbol that is at once alarming to behold and authentic
to who they are.

The most familiar methods of nonviolence include boycotts, sit-ins,
marches, and civil disobedience—acts of breaking the law. Methods can
demonstrate the illegitimacy of existing systems, and they can demonstrate
what "better" justice looks like.[42] Familiar nonviolent methods include work
slow-downs, walk-outs, teach-ins, die-ins, taunting and haunting of officials,
overwhelming of administrative systems (thousands of phone calls!), giving
of mock awards and holding of mock elections, strategic withholdings (of
work, sex, obedience), vigils, humorous skits and pranks, mourning, fasting,
the creation of alternative structures and systems, and more.

Nonviolent methods are inclusive—just about anything (that does not harm
anyone) can work. What is important is to choose the right method for the
particular moment, issue, actors, and set of opportunities—and to pursue it
with discipline. There have been transformative actions relying on everything
from singing to knitting, eating particular foods to jackhammering on missile
silos, swimming the open sea to wearing particular colors. Under conditions
of extreme oppression, resistance might not look like resistance. Following
the 2021 coup in Myanmar, for example, people are protesting military rule
by intentionally running out of gas on the motorways, or by dropping (and
picking up) individual grains of rice whilst crossing the street—impeding
the flow of traffic, but not doing anything "wrong." The intention is simply
to signal unease with "normal" life, and a lack of acceptance with the new
status quo. The smallest act—Nelson Mandela walking slowly when entering
the prison at Robben Island rather than hurrying as the guards demanded, can
become an act of resistance when performed intentionally and in response to
particular conditions.[43] This flexibility makes nonviolent action accessible for
every kind of participant and in seemingly every condition, wherein people
are limited only by their own creativity and ability to strategize within specific constraints. This does not mean that nonviolent methods will always
work or achieve their goals, but they are a method of action that are available
to everyone—in any circumstance and in any number—and they can work
in ways that are subtle or actively coercive. They can signal disapproval or
apply unbearable pressure, to an instance of harm or a system of violence, as
well as directly challenge an unjust regime or status quo.

Nonviolent methods escalate, from the smallest interventions (dropping
rice) to quite extreme acts (nonviolent sabotage, fasting, prison witness). The
first stage of a nonviolent campaign is to raise awareness of an issue in the
public sphere and to encourage change. In the second stage, one increases the
pressure through legal forms of non-cooperation. Civil resistance—unlawful
acts of resistance, is the last stage of escalation. Of course, escalation may
also be achieved at any stage by adding more people, or more of certain

kinds of people. In the case of prison witness, large numbers of participants are rarely available, and justice action prisoners' seriousness of intent is conveyed by the seriousness of their actions rather than by their numbers. Who they are matters as well, as people with high status in their own communities raise the levels of tension more readily than those who are less well-known.

Principled and Pragmatic Nonviolence

There are two branches of nonviolence, principled (or Gandhian) and pragmatic (or strategic).[44] While those from both traditions may use similar tactics, they have differing motives and goals. Pragmatists are looking for any tactic that will enable them to achieve their objectives, and they are willing to accept a win-lose outcome as long as they are on the winning side. Those in the principled tradition see nonviolence as a way of life. They refuse to humiliate their opponent, and are motivated to achieve a "transformation" of the opponent. Indeed, they see their opponent as a partner to achieving a win-win outcome. The difference rarely matters in terms of methods employed, but shapes motivations for engagement: as either a "way of life" or as a strategic attempt to *win*. Very generally, Plowshares participants follow a more principled path, while SOA Watch participants are more likely to be pragmatic (although exceptions to both are so numerous that even this attempt to classify seems irrelevant). The Indian struggle for independence may be considered a principled campaign, the Velvet and Colored Revolutions pragmatic, and the American Civil Rights Movement a combination of both. Things are a bit messier upon closer inspection, as most movements are made up of a variety of participants inspired by a variety of beliefs.

Principled nonviolence is most often chosen as a result of moral, religious, or philosophical conviction. Gandhi called this *satyagraha*, which may be understood as "clinging to the truth." The principled approach is not "with a view of trying to prevail at any cost" but with seeing "the truth prevail—trying to see that the best solution emerge."[45] The solution sought is win-win, and the principled approach seeks to achieve a change of heart in one's opponent, as well as in oneself. The Czech poet, activist, and former President Vaclev Havel explained this dynamic, stating that everyone who lives under tyranny but does not resist is living a lie, the lie that life is normal. Necessarily, then, everyone who resists the violent state lives "within the truth." Further, everyone who tells the truth denies a system based on lies. Therefore, Havel argued, telling the truth threatens a corrupt system "in its entirety."[46] In Gandhian principles, living nonviolently is a practice of living the truth—exposing the truth, and making it possible for that which is true to be more widely known. This philosophy aligns with the Plowshares perspective, in which the intent is to be a "witness to the truth." The act of

Christian witness, in this case, is understood to be in and of itself resistant and sufficient, even without appeals to changes in policy or the generation of public attention.

Pragmatic nonviolence is more common than principled nonviolence, globally and in practice. Whereas principled nonviolence is a way of life, pragmatic nonviolence is pursued because it is believed to be the most effective form of resistance available. Planning for a pragmatic nonviolent intervention is similar to planning for a military one; for example, in identifying one's opponent's "pillars of support" (the police, military, media, civil servants, business community, NGOs, youth, and/or churches) and asking questions such as "how can we win defections?" from those in powerful positions. The attempt is to pull power away from the state, and towards the activists' cause. Pragmatists plan actions with the intention of garnering media attention, or they use the media to strengthen their goals. In other words, pragmatists enact nonviolence as good *strategy*, rather than morality, though both camps know that the quality of one's tactical choices affects the outcomes of struggle (maintaining the moral high ground, for example, while the authority loses legitimacy through its reliance on force and threat power).

NONVIOLENT POWER: HOW NONVIOLENCE WORKS

The essential dynamic of nonviolence is non-cooperation. Political power is not a monolithic power-over in this formulation, but a relationship that relies on the consent and cooperation of the governed, for power does not come from above but from "below." Erica Chenoweth defines political power as "the ability to elicit others' voluntary obedience"—a definition that highlights people's complicity with prevailing dynamics of power.[47] In his life and work, Gandhi showed that a regime's power depends on people's cooperation, and that people have a choice in where their power goes.[48] Hence, by removing cooperation with an (unjust) ruler, ordinary people can wear down the ruler's power, at the same time as they reclaim their own power. Through non-cooperation, nonviolent power simultaneously divests an authority of its power, as it empowers those who participate in it.

This notion of power is relational, diffuse, and heterogenous rather than domineering and total, and resistance is effective because even the most robust political systems are fragile in that they are not *generators* of power. Rather, they rely upon the exchange-power of those governed.[49] Through their resistance, people may "break up" power relations, for by refusing to comply with a form of power "over," they rob the authority of its power. This notion of power, known as "people power" in civil resistance theory, gives people a tool to uphold, insist upon, and strengthen democratic institutions—and to reject state violence. The idea that one may shake the foundations of political power through a withdrawal of individual consent may sound utopian, but as we've seen so often across history, it also works.

The second element of nonviolent power is that it can be personally empowering for its participants. In this, nonviolence works as a power "to" rather than a power "over." Nonviolent power diffuses monolithic power as it imbues everyday "people" with "power." [50] Indeed, not only empowerment, but a sense of personal freedom may result from engagement with nonviolent activism. Hence, nonviolent action is an individualized, embodied form of resistance that works precisely by its refusal to be disciplined, as it is also a generative form of creative power that empowers people, movements, and ideas. None of this is automatic or guaranteed, of course, but history shows that freedom, democracy, and justice are ongoing projects that require struggle, struggle that is enacted by people who are themselves empowered; empowered with the imagination and personal courage to believe that change is possible.

A nonviolent understanding of power shows state power (monolithic, authoritarian, political) to be ever vulnerable—for if people have both consciousness and organization, the worst tyrants may be overcome through ordinary citizens refusing, en masse, to cooperate. When they are organized, regular people are stronger than any other force. One of the first tasks of a nonviolent campaign, then, is to awaken people to their own personal power. As Desmond Tutu explained, "When people decide they want to be free— once they have made up their minds to that—there is nothing that can stop them." [51] Of course, this does not mean that nonviolence always works or that people will not be harmed along the way. Only that it can, and more effectively than other forms of resistance.

The Power of the People

Reviewing historical struggles, it is evident that participation in nonviolent action is an effective method for people with less political power than their opponents to create social change. In the popular imagination, the most common images of nonviolent resistance are of poor, relatively powerless people (often, people of color) struggling against more powerful people (often Western and/or white). It is easy for most of us to recall images of young African American girls being fire-hosed by Bull Connor's cronies, or of Indian men bloodied by Englishmen on horseback. These images come from what are called "dilemma actions," actions that force authorities to choose between two bad options: enforcing an unpopular law, or appearing weak through not enforcing it. [52] Gene Sharp called this "political jiu-jitsu"—noting that brutalities against a clearly nonviolent opponent "disturb(s) many people . . . thus, wider public opinion may turn against the opponent."[53]

The images that such actions produce—of voluntary suffering, risked in pursuit of change—shake our foundations because they illuminate the inherent violence already present in the systems on which they rely (segregation, colonization, apartheid, and so on).[54] In theory, what is "right" is so clear in these situations that what is "legal" may become obsolete. This is how principled nonviolence works: through making suffering visible by personalizing it, a shift in what is "legal" can better match what is right. The specific actors, in these cases of mass unrest, do not matter. Theoretically, we (the public) do not need to know the names of the young girls being fire-hosed, or even what they look like. We just need to know that they, and their suffering, exist. In this sense, nonviolence truly is a form of power for the powerless—or more accurately, for the anonymous. It does not matter who you are, what you have access to, or what you look like. In situations of grave injustice and with mass participation, anybody's body works.

This has been described in civil resistance literature as "people power."[55] In people power movements, the authority of grandmothers, professionals, and students alike combine to meet and override that of oppressive leaders and policies. As such, nonviolent power is by its very nature a way to de-centralize power away from a violent model of militarized masculinity and toward a model with room for everyone. "People power" is inclusive, additive, and generative. In people power movements, *everybody's* body counts.

Understanding nonviolence as people power and power for the powerless is exhilarating as well as true, but it is not a complete understanding of how nonviolent power works. Nonviolence is effective; it does transform relationships, it can be personally empowering, and it can leave a new system with a better chance at democracy than violence ever can. However, understanding nonviolence only in these ways—as something that anybody with sufficient commitment and organization can do equally well—is an imperfect understanding in contemporary America, and particularly as it regards high-risk, personalized strategies such as prison witness. To the extent that we do not understand nonviolent power better, we constrain our understanding of what makes change happen, what effects our actions may have (on movement goals as well as on participants' lives), what our powers rely upon, as well as what can be.

Specifically, for movements without mass participation, the public story often concentrates on the individual, rather than the issues or the movement. This focus on individuals makes the identities of participants extremely important—a reality that often irks justice action prisoners ("it's not about me!") but which must be accounted for in its consequences. In other words, prison witness is not a form of "people power," but a form of *person* power, and this research further clarifies that *who* the person is critically matters. Indeed, it is most often *privilege power*—the force of one's mainstream status—that is the major form of power animated by the act of prison witness.[56] While the significance of privilege power is likely important in any nonviolent movement, fully accounting for it in the strategy of prison witness is essential.

Most often, prison witness draws on the privileges of race, class, nationality, professional and moral status (as a professor or a nun, for example) as forms of power that can be used to reach movement goals. The participants I spoke with often described a savvy understanding of themselves as people of privilege, purposefully using their citizenship, white skin, social class, age, and other high-status belongings strategically, as intentional platforms to protest U.S. imperialism, militarism, and war. In this, they used their social positions as an intentional tool: "privilege power" was employed as a conscious tactic and source of political and moral power. In general, the choice of justice action prisoners has been to "use" their privilege for good. This is complex terrain, however, and further chapters more fully examine the issues that enacting privilege power brings to the fore.

Privilege Power and the Body

Another noteworthy aspect of prison witness is that it is an embodied form of resistance: one literally puts one's body where one's beliefs are, in a bodily act that makes injustice visible. And bodies, as participant Ken Crowley explained, are serious. The state and media can ignore, lie about, and manipulate other forms of civic involvement, but they "can't ignore bodies."[57] Bodies occupying public space force visibility and unmistakably show numbers and support. What activists sometimes call "somatic politics" is a method of action that concentrates the violence of the system onto the space of the body, making it personal, visible, and potentially transformable. As such, somatic politics is a form of power: through everyday people engaging in resistance, power is generated, shifted, transformed, and confronted. The body and power are thus already always connected: the body is the instrument of nonviolent power, the medium that makes violence visible, and the force that persuades change. For the strategy of prison witness, in which the body publicly performs illegal actions and invites hardship in order to be a witness against gross acts of state violence, the centrality of the body is essential.

Somatic politics is deepened by activists' use of the body symbolically, and popular nonviolent direct actions include "die ins" (symbolically dying together), fasting, pouring blood, and dressing as those one represents. In addition to singing and marching, performing with puppets, and shouting through bullhorns, bodies do things in public spaces that are symbolically appropriate to the specific actor: activists concerned about war dig graves, aunties knit, priests pray, mothers cry. This authentic and strategic use of self can enable and strengthen political action, as explored in Chapter 4.

THE LEGAL DEFENSE: ON TRIAL FOR "GOVERNMENTAL INSANITY"[58]

The trial is an important part of justice action prisoners' activism. After engaging in resistance, justice action prisoners most often (though not always) await arrest, pursue trial, and endure incarceration as punishment for their actions.[59]

Significantly, the efficacy of the trial is not measured by "winning," i.e., securing acquittal, but by widening the circle of those who are aware of and concerned about the issues, as well as by demonstrating consistency between medium and message. For both principled and pragmatic nonviolent activists, the goal of the trial is to put the specific issues and the broader system "on trial," according to participant Kathleen Rumpf.[60] Time in prison is the ticket cost for participation in this undertaking, and justice action prisoners are, quite simply, the people who are willing to pay this price; to put their "action" where their "belief is."[61] The following section describes how this part of the action works: the trial as a tool, the most common defenses used, and how the nonviolent resister's trial fits within a democratic system more widely.

The Trial as Tool

The trial is an opportunity to build awareness and share movement goals, as well as to provide compelling cases about significant matters for the courts to review. The idea is to give the juridical branch the opportunity to uphold and improve the law, both domestic and international, and to create new and better legal precedent. The goal is decidedly *not* to be set free with a "not guilty" verdict. This motivation fundamentally differentiates justice action prisoners from others caught up in the legal system. Thinking through these questions with me, participant Brian Terrell explained that it is "liberating" to go to court with the expectation of going to jail, for it gives one the "freedom to speak one's conscience without regard to consequences."[62] In alignment with this, quite often justice action prisoners defend themselves, though they may be advised by a team of experts and lawyers. This practice better allows the court to hear directly from the defendants, without the restrictions of professional codes or duties.

When the trial is not organized around securing a defendant's release, it can take on a distinctly pedagogical role. Historically and whenever they can, justice action prisoners have used the space of the courtroom as a site to instruct, magnify, and share information. The results can be transformational for those attending. Films and plays have been written directly from the transcripts of select court proceedings—they can be riveting drama.[63] Expert witnesses such as the late Howard Zinn and the late former Attorney General Ramsey Clark have testified on behalf of the activists, locating their actions in resistance legacies and legal precedent to which the U.S. is obliged. At their trials, SOA Watch activists often read the words of those most affected by the school; and the careful thoughts of people who have acted in alignment with their conscience can resound with their simple truthfulness and beauty.

In these ways, the courtroom becomes a public venue afforded justice action prisoners by their nonviolent action, from which they may persuade followers (toward the rightness of the cause, realities of state violence, or the supremacy of God's law) and coerce opponents—forcing authorities into uncomfortable defensive positions from which they must either enforce bad laws or rule on matters they would prefer remain untouched. As Federal Magistrate G. Mallon Faircloth explained in his 2001 sentencing statement of 26 people who crossed the line that year at the SOA, "I'm a pawn in all of this. If I find you not guilty, that makes Fort Benning and the government look like a laughing stock, but if I find you guilty and sentence you to the maximum, I make martyrs of you."[64] This is called a "dilemma" action, in which an authority is forced to either enforce an unjust law or side with activists. It is compelling drama, and "makes for good T.V."

Through their actions and subsequent trials, justice action prisoners show the law itself to be an instrument that can repress, rather than promote, justice. Through their identities as "moral" felons of conscience in court, justice action prisoners facilitate consciousness raising in the broader population. The trial generates local, regional, and sometimes national and international media attention, increases awareness of relevant issues, inspires other activists, and develops organization within peace and justice movements. In all of these ways—and even if found guilty every single time—the trial "works" towards the activists' cause.

The Defense

Indicted for crimes of trespass, sabotage, conspiracy, and so on, justice action prisoners usually consider themselves resisters of state violence rather than violators of particular laws. Hence, they most often craft their defenses not to escape the charges, but to give courts the opportunity to stop such violations in the first place. In their trials, they want to highlight the First Amendment (trespass charges often disappear in the face of citizens' rights to free speech, religion, and assembly), the Restoration of Religious Freedom Act (for many activists, resisting violence is considered part of their religious profession—and is thus both their duty to commit and protected by the Constitution), international law (which prohibits nuclear weapons and the use of torture), and the rights of the jury and democratic citizenry. They also often want to describe their motivations to act, which includes discussion of the issues as well as notions of conscience, God, and scripture. Almost always, defendants are denied such speech on the grounds that this is a trial about X, but in the rare cases when activists are allowed to defend themselves on their own terms, they almost always walk free.

In their defense, justice action prisoners rely primarily upon three tools. The first is the law itself. Appealing to the First Amendment is a formidable defense that may protect justice action prisoners' actions as "legal." In recent research on the arrests associated with the Black Lives Matter organization and political protests of 2020, prosecutors around the country claimed that "cases involving free speech or free assembly rarely succeed in court," while District Attorney Mike Schmidt of Portland, Oregon stated that up to 80% of the arrests in that city (for protest associated with police brutality against people of color) "would not survive constitutional challenges."[65] Though the specific criminal cases cited differ here, the fact that citizens are protected to protest, and even to raise trouble against the government, is legally solid.

More specifically, justice action prisoners rely on international law. This defense expresses a hope that the courts will recognize the legitimacy and supremacy of international law, and especially the Nuremberg principles and the Geneva Convention (but also various treaties to which the U.S. is a signatory), and under which nuclear weapons, proliferation, and torture are prohibited. If a court were to recognize international law, activists would be found to be *upholding* the law rather than breaking it, and they would walk free as the rightness of their action was affirmed. Such an acquittal would be celebrated among activists around the world.

Secondly, justice action prisoners call on the "necessity" defense. Resisters use the trial to show that their actions are moral, justifiable, and necessary—their intent is to *protect* life, never to harm it.[66] Necessity argues that there is a pressing need for their action, an action one must engage in to stop a greater, demonstrable, and urgent threat. The rationale is that sometimes it is better to break a law than to risk the consequences of obeying it. Or even, as the late former attorney general Ramsey Clark testified during the 2010 trial of the Creech 14, there are instances in which a technical violation of the law is the only legal course of action permissible—while obeying the law would be truly criminal. Clark cited "the classic example of someone driving down a street, seeing a house on fire, noticing a child in the third-floor window, hearing the screams, breaking through the front door, violating the no trespass law, and entering the house to save the child."[67] Necessity provides space for something that is obviously right to also be "legal." Of the 1968 Catonsville 9 action (burning draft cards with homemade napalm), Fr. Dan Berrigan relied on necessity when he argued that it is better to burn paper than it is to burn children.[68] In this view, the activists *had* to act against the draft, it was *necessary*. In the face of massive state violence, such trivial illegal acts are required—justifiable, excusable, and legal.

Jury nullification is a more ambitious and nuanced third technique that may be used in the trials of justice action prisoners. One of the primary protections for political resisters within the American political system is the right to a trial by jury. To understand this defense, one must know that in the United States, juries are empowered to ignore the law, if they so desire—and to acquit a person *even if* the person broke that law. This is called the power of jury "nullification."[69] Beginning in the 19th century, it became common for judges to not inform jurors of their powers of nullification. Today, most juries are instructed to decide cases based only on the facts presented, and are never told about their powers of nullification. As a result, even when juries are sympathetic to a particular defense or defendant, if they do not know what they are capable of, they are limited in what they can do. When possible, justice action prisoners attempt to inform juries about their powers of nullification. Doing so is a way to provide a legitimate pathway for regular citizens to re-craft and re-interpret laws in ways that reflect what citizens themselves consider to be fair and just. However, most often defendants are restricted from informing the juries about nullification, making this defense ineffective or mute. [70]

As measured by acquittal, none of these three defensive tools have proven particularly successful for justice action prisoners. "Not guilty" verdicts are extremely rare.[71] It must be remembered, however, that justice action prisoners' commitment to these defenses is not about obtaining their best chance for acquittal. Rather, they are committed to keeping the trials focused on the topics of their concern, as well as to protect court trials as a democratic mechanism available to citizens to transform the legal and political system, a focus that is best maintained through these three legal frameworks.

Also worth noting is that activists are often deeply guided by their religious faith. For these activists, faith works as a higher code than law, and renders the judgements of human courts fairly irrelevant as meaningful signifiers of justice. For these more religious activists, the relevant concern is not around committing civil disobedience, but being sure to commit "divine obedience"—even when the act may not be legal. In any case, what is important is not walking free, but providing opportunities for courts to render different judgments, decisions that more closely resemble the world justice action prisoners work to bring into being.

The "Injustice System"

Most justice action prisoners believe that the modern U.S. criminal justice system enforces injustice, rather than furthers justice. Describing the trial as the "second action" in what is for him a tri-partite act of resistance (discernment and illegal act, trial, and prison), participant Fr. Steve Kelly described the courtroom as "one of the most dangerous rooms in the Pentagon."[72] In general, the participants included in this research do not expect what is legal, just, or holy to prevail in what they see as an enforcing arm of imperial power. They are not willing to demean themselves by playing by its rules (i.e., they would rather go to jail than plead guilty to a crime of sabotage, for example, when they view what they have done as an inspired, necessary, and/or godly act of *enforcing justice*). For many justice action prisoners, the "injustice system," as Kathleen Rumpf calls it, is an instrument of the state, the same state that makes the nuclear bombs.[73] Thus, their resistance must also include resistance to the criminal justice system itself, and this begins with the trial.

To support their contention that the legal process is structured towards injustice, this book's participants shared many examples. The most common was the widespread use of the *in limine* motion during Plowshares trials, what Fr. Steve Kelly described as a "gag-order" limiting what people can say in the courtroom. On trial for trespass or sabotage, defendants and their attorneys are forbidden from uttering such words as "nuclear weapons," "Nuremburg," "war," "God," and even "international law."[74] Such constraints challenge what justice action prisoners can accomplish in court and may work to gut their defenses, as the subject of the trial shifts from their intent—from disarmament and stopping torture to "cutting fence and trespass."[75] Hence, the frequent use of this rule "has precluded the accused from putting on a defense," a defense that Brian Terrell argues is not won by "truth telling" but by "saying super words at the time of argument."[76] In other words, the way to win a court trial is not by exposing what is most just, true, or even what is legal, but by hiring the right people to say the right things in the right kind of way—an opportunity reserved for the well-to-do and well connected in this country. Partly in opposition to the unequal access of quality legal representation available in the United States, many justice action prisoners choose to go *pro se*—to defend themselves.[77] Justice action prisoners sometimes refuse to participate altogether in the trial on the terms defined by the court, though they themselves bear the cost of such refusals. There are also examples of what could be interpreted as direct court harassment: for example, the re-scheduling of Tim DeChristopher's trial (nine times!), a clear—though ultimately unsuccessful—attempt to wear out the movement organizing that his "Bidder 70" environmental action inspired.

Religious studies scholar Kristen Tobey interprets the Plowshares "theory of the trial" as deliberately crafted to maintain participants' marginal identity status as befits their interpretation of the Gospel, and argues that to maintain this identity requires a "guilty" verdict. Needing to serve time in jail to be true to their faith commitments thus explains Plowshares' commitments to the necessity defense and international law, they are chosen precisely because these defenses almost never result in acquittal. For Tobey, conducting the "boundary work" constituting an activist's identity as a Plowshares partici-pant (an identity crafted between the "corrupt" world and other sympathetic peace activists who have not served jail sentences) provides a unique sense of self for the activists, a sense of self that is verified through incarceration.[78]

This study—rooted in personal interviews with activists from two move-ments, but not in trial transcripts or movement rhetorics—offers a different perspective. Indeed, I have no evidence to support the idea that activists deliberately rely on a defense they know will not work for the purposes of identity. On the contrary, this research finds that acquittal is the preference of disarmament activists, but only on their terms.[79] Defendants are simply not willing to waste the opportunity to "put the system" on trial through the use of a less compelling or relevant (to them) defense. After all, the reason justice action prisoners participate in resistance actions is to challenge bad laws or illegal practices, as well as to offer judges and juries interesting cases that can provide pathways for new precedent or the enforcement of existing laws and treaties. With confidence, I can say that justice action prisoners do not *want* to go to jail (especially in today's overcrowded and unhealthy prisons); they are simply *willing* to do so. This willingness, paired with their emphasis on right means and ethical commitments, mandates that the justice action prisoner proceed in very specific ways during the trial. This includes keeping the focus on the issues, wherein acquittal is never as important as highlighting particu-lar policies or protecting the integrity of the trial. Likewise, while being true to oneself is certainly important, it is not the end goal. The goal is to expose the injustice and to remedy it through law. Incarceration is the expected, but not the desired, cost of doing so.

PRISON WITNESS AND THE QUESTION OF EFFICACY

Prison witness is enacted with great seriousness, and is meant to be effective. However, when it comes to questions of social change, how to determine efficacy is never straightforward. (Is a war really over when one side pro-claims victory? Does the 1964 passage of the Civil Rights Act mean that the movement worked?) Social movement scholars recognize that "success" is inherently hard to measure—including for acts of nonviolent resistance.[80] For participants in this study, definitions of what it means for prison witness to "work" range from to changing law and policy ("effective") to being true to oneself and/or one's faith ("faithful")—although it is in the messy middle that most justice action prisoners meet.

As a strategy, prison witness works in a variety of ways, including through raising awareness of an issue (via education, consciousness raising, media attention, and personal or group empowerment), by changing laws or policy, and through the act of nonviolent witness itself. Plowshares co-founder Fr. Dan Berrigan explained that in the Prophetic tradition, one acts "not to be popular or to be seen as having an impact, but to speak the deepest truths that we know."[81] Speaking one's "deepest truths" about an area of entrenched and systemic injustice will almost certainly not result in dramatic social change during one's lifetime, but from a Prophetic (or principled nonviolent) frame-work, it must be pursued. From this perspective, it is the only way toward real transformation. For these justice action prisoners, Sr. Carol Gilbert explained, the important thing is to *start*, and to keep at it because resistance is the right thing to do—but not to worry too much about tangible "results."[82]

For many represented in this work, focusing only on achievable goals is mostly a distraction from the larger concerns. This does not mean that they do not want their resistance to be effective in concrete terms, but simply that winning an election or changing a particular policy is never the end goal: the change that is sought is deeper and more systemic than discreet and measur-able. The problems justice action prisoners are concerned about—nuclear weapons, climate change, war—are complex but also *urgent.* It is thus essen-tial to confront them as such, but not to reduce them to "winnable" or small goals. Staying focused on the complexity of systemic problems is important to keep central, even if it means choosing battles that seem impossible to win.[83] What matters, in this view, is not measurable success based on a series of achievable campaigns (contra Saul Alinsky and most "best practices" wisdom in social movements), but doing the right thing, even in the face of insurmountable odds. For principled justice action prisoners, one must con-tinue moving earnestly in the right direction, even (and especially?) when the destination is too far away to see. As Fr. Dan Berrigan explained, each of us must think, "I am going to turn swords into plowshares and spears into prun-ing hooks. I may never see the transformation myself. It makes no difference. I shall do it. I shall do it."[84]

That said, even those most driven by faith (or the principled perspective) usually also want to see changes "here on Earth"—and ideally, in their own lifetimes.[85] As Cesar Chavez (who is remembered for his principled nonvio-lent commitments) explained, "we're not nonviolent because we want to save our souls, we're nonviolent because we want to get some social justice for the workers. . . . You've got to *win* with nonviolence."[86] And prison witness is a strategy that can work, in the prescient terms articulated by Berrigan and the Prophetic Tradition—but also more concretely.

Nonviolent resistance can topple regimes, secure civil rights, and change discriminatory laws, and it can also raise consciousness and generate power, which are important aspects of "efficacy." Consciousness raising transforms public opinion, and what regular people believe and choose to act upon changes tangible conditions. As nonviolence scholar Jack DuVall insists, revolution is first forged in consciousness.[87] Prison witness is particularly good at generating attention towards particular issues, as participant Ed Kinane explained. "If you are willing to be arrested, to go to court, go to trial, and then suffer those consequences—to go to prison—that has terrific leverage in terms of drawing attention to an issue." For Ed, the initial source of SOA Watch founder Roy Bourgeois's power was his "willingness to go to prison."[88] In a 2001 interview with the *Nuclear Resister,* Bourgeois agreed that prison witness is a critical way to "energize" the movement, rightly guessing that the conviction of 26 SOA violators that year was "going to backfire. . . . What it's going to do is bring more people down here in November to cross that line."[89] This is a classic illustration of how nonviolence works: when one shines a light on an injustice that is already there, one provokes a reaction from the relevant authorities. Quite often, it is this outsized *reaction* that galvanizes public attention, attention that can be focused towards the issue of activist concern. In nonviolence, it is this relational and reactive process that often forces change.

Historically, there are many examples of prison witness working to raise awareness and with it, to generate power. For example, Anne and Carl Braden were a white couple who used nonviolent resistance to challenge racist housing policy in the United States. In 1954, they bought a house in a "whites only" neighborhood outside of Louisville, KY, for a black couple. Ann later explained that Carl's one-year sentence (for sedition) resulting from this act "popularized them." It gave them a platform to "fight back," and they "used it" to protest racial discrimination more widely.[90] The creation of this platform is crucial, as disarmament activist Lisa Hughes explained to historian Rosalie Riegle. "I used to have to really work hard to find places to talk about my times in El Salvador" but "once I was going to prison, all kinds of groups wanted me. And the media pays more attention to you if you've gone to jail; in fact, that is one of the main reasons for doing it."[91]

Justice action prisoners are often asked by journalists (and others) if they are "wasting their time" by going to prison—couldn't their energies be put to better use by continuing to work on the outside? Participant Brian Terrell turns the question back to them: "would you be calling me if I were not going to prison?" And the journalists always respond the same way, he says. "No. That would not be a story at all."[92] In this way, for regular people wishing to challenge systems, prison witness creates a tangible, interesting, public *story* where there was none before; individualized to a particular actor but inclusive of the issues that drive them. Prison witness is thus a form of message amplification, a way to create leverage and interest in the direction of activist concern.

Prison witness can also infuse participants themselves with moral, religious, or political power—strengthening their messages as legitimately *belonging* in a conversation. By engaging in an issue so seriously, non-elite people can gain credibility as subject experts and authorities, and to do so as invested, principled stakeholders. As a result, an experience of living in prison can transform a concerned private citizen into a public figure.[93] As Brian Terrell explained, "I cannot afford face time with a senator. I cannot call a press conference and have the world media come. All that I have is my body to put on the line. . ... Direct action may be the only effective tool people who are not rich have left."[94] Quite simply, then, prison witness provides a mechanism for ordinary, individual people to speak and be heard—on a stage that may be far larger and more powerful than otherwise possible.

In terms of "changing policy," everyone represented in this research seemed to believe that their action was more of a "drop in the bucket" than a final straw—but each person decided to act anyway. This does not imply that they acted without hope of actually *doing* something to create change, but rather demonstrates an honest assessment of their situation (which for those who ascribe to the Prophetic Tradition, mandates biblical obedience regardless of earthly consequences). Prison witness is not likely to change U.S. nuclear policy, for example—but what *can* regular individuals do in this effort? After careful thinking and analysis, participants in this book are among those who have decided that prison witness offers their best—most effective, as well as ethical and appropriate—chance at making a difference. Through their actions, they can raise awareness, change some people's minds, challenge legal precedent, force intellectual reckoning, and render scrutable unexamined beliefs in a broader public. This is not nothing, and it is worthwhile.

NOTES

1. Not all justice action prisoners see what they are doing as "breaking the law." However, as a strategy of nonviolence, this is how prison witness is conceived.

2. For example, the story of baby Moses is a story of disobedience, and Plato's *Apology* promotes resistance to the state. For more examples, see Howard Clark,

ed. *People Power: Unarmed Resistance and Global Solidarity*. London: Pluto Press, 2009.

3. Henry David Thoreau, "Civil Disobedience," in Howard Zinn (ed). *The Power of Nonviolence: Writings by Advocates of Peace*. (Boston: Beacon Press, 2002), 15–36. For further philosophical discussion of civil disobedience, see Candice Delmas. *A Duty to Resist: When Disobedience Should be Uncivil*. Oxford University Press, 2018. See also Howard Zinn, *The Zinn Reader: Writings on Disobedience and Democracy.* New York: Seven Stories, 1997.

4. Benjamin Hedin, *In Search of the Movement: The Struggle for Civil Rights Then and Now* (San Francisco, CA: City Lights Books, 2015).

5. Berel Lang, "Civil Disobedience and Nonviolence: A Distinction with a Difference," *Ethics*, vol. 80, no. 2, January 1970, 156–157.

6. Stephen Martin Kohn, *Jailed for Peace* (New York: Praeger Publishers, 1987), 138.

7. Quoted in Kohn, 123.

8. Staughton and Alice Lynd (eds), *Nonviolence in America: A documentary History* (New York: Orbis Books, 1995); see also Maciej J. Bartkowski (ed). *Recovering Nonviolent History: Civil Resistance in Liberation Struggles*. Boulder: Lynne Rienner, 2013; James Lovell, *Crimes of Dissent: Civil Disobedience, Criminal Justice, and the Politics of Conscience* (New York: NYU Press, 2009).

9. Peter Brock, *Pacifism in the United States* (Princeton: Princeton University Press, 2015).

10. For example, the Stamp Act was a tax on all legal documents and printed materials enacted in March 1765. While the British Parliament expected annual revenues of £60,000, resistance in the colonies (refusal to purchase the stamps) was so great that upon implementation, all legal and financial movement in the colonies became stagnant. Courts were closed, newspapers shuttered, and seaports dormant. In 1766, the British earned only £3,292 from the Stamp Act—less than half their costs of printing. See Walter Coser, "The United States: Reconsidering the Struggle for Independence, 1765–1775," in *Recovering Nonviolent History: Civil Resistance in Liberation Struggles,* ed. Maciej Bartkowski (Boulder: Lynne Rienner, 2013), 299–317, 302.

11. Kohn, 16. See also Brock 2015.

12. For example, see Larry E. Rivers, *Rebels and Runaways: Slave Resistance in Nineteenth-Century Florida* (Chicago, University of Illinois Press, 2012).

13. Katherine Adams and Michael L. Keene, *Alice Paul and the American Suffrage Campaign.* (Chicago, University of Illinois Press, 2010); George Lakey, "'Suffragette' Raises Question of Property Destruction's Effectiveness." *Waging Nonviolence,* 2015, https://wagingnonviolence.org/2015/11/suffragette-raises-question-property-destruction-effectiveness/; Wendy Parkins, "Protesting like a Girl: Embodiment, Dissent and Feminist Agency." *Feminist Theory* 1, no. 1 (2000): 59–78.

14. Nov. 15, 1917: Suffragists Beaten and Tortured in the "Night of Terror." https://www.zinnedproject.org/news/tdih/suffragists-beaten-and-tortured/.

15. Kohn, 26.

16. Eugene V. Debs, Trial Statement, 1918, https://www.marxists.org/archive/debs/works/1918/court.htm. See also Ernest Freeberg, *Democracy's Prisoner: Eugene V. Debs, the Great War, and the Right to Dissent* (Boston: Harvard University Press, 2008).

17. Gretchen Lempe-Santangelo, "The Radical Conscientious Objectors of World War II," *Radical History Review* 45 (1989), 5–29; Lawrence Wittner, *Rebels Against War: The American Peace Movement, 1933–1983* (Philadelphia: Temple University Press, 1984).

18. "June 15, 1955: Protest of Nuclear Attack Drills," *Zinn Education Project*, https://www.zinnedproject.org/news/tdih/nuclear-attack-drill-protest, accessed January 2021.

19. Albert Bigelow, The Voyage of the Golden Rule: An Experiment with Truth (Garden City NY: Doubleday, 1959).

20. Dorothy Day, *All the Way to Heaven: The Selected Letters of Dorothy Day* (New York: Image, 2012); Thomas Merton. *A Thomas Merton Reader* (New York: Image, 1974); A. J. Muste, "The Pacifist Way of Life," *Fellowship* 7, no. 12 (1941): 198.

21. Martin Luther King Jr., "Letter from Birmingham jail," *Liberating Faith: Religious Voices for Justice, Peace, & Ecological Wisdom* (Lanham, MD: Rowman & Littlefield, 177–187).

22. Douglas McAdam, *Freedom Summer* (New York: Oxford University Press, 1988). See also Howard Zinn, *A People's History of the United States: 1492–Present* (New York City: Routledge, 2015).

23. For fascinating relevant histories, see James Tracy, *Direct Action: Radical Pacifism from the Union Eight to the Chicago Seven* (Chicago, IL: University of Chicago Press, 1996) and Jeremy Varon, *Bringing the War Home: The Weather Underground, the Red Army Faction, and Revolutionary Violence in the Sixties and Seventies* (Berkeley: University of California Press, 2004).

24. There were 6,116 convicted COs during World War Two—4,441 of whom were pacifist Jehovah's Witnesses. During WWI, only 0.14% of young men received an exemption from military service, and the Second World War increased this only to 0.15%—when only two-tenths of one percent of the eligible age group requested an exemption (Kohn, 46).

25. Registration for the draft was reinstated in 1980; however, millions of young men refused to register. This made enforcement challenging and may have derailed plans for an actual draft (in the early 1980s, war with the Soviets was possible). Efficacy, clearly, is never easily measured.

26. Quoted in Laffin and Montgomery, *Swords into Plowshares*, 72–75.

27. Gibbon, 205, quoted in Ronald Sider, *Nonviolent Action: What Christian Ethics Demands But Most Christians Have Never Really Tried* (Ada, MI: Brazos Press, 2015).

28. Gibbon, 202, quoted in Sider 2015.

29. Russo, *Solidarity in Practice*, 2018, 21.

30. "The Parameters of Nonviolent Action: What Makes an Action Nonviolent" essays in *War Resisters*, accessed January 2021, https://www.warresisters.org/nva/nva-july-august-2001/parameters-nonviolent-action-what-makes-action-nonviolent.

31. Antigone disobeyed King Creon's demand that her brother not be properly buried. She buried him anyway, rightly knowing that doing so would lead to her own death.

32. Gandhi articulated nonviolence as a philosophy and practice that is "greater" than that of violence, and outlined it as an effective practice against oppression. It is a method of courage, and "where there is only a choice between cowardice and violence, I would advise violence." Quoted in Arne Naess. *Gandhi and Group Conflict: An Exploration of Satyagraha. Theoretical Background* (Oslo: Universitetsforlaget, 1974): 110. This fundamentally differentiates nonviolence from "passive resistance" or absolute pacifism, which never condones the use of force as a matter of *principle*.

33. Peter Ackerman and Jack DuVall, "People Power Primed: Civilian Resistance and Democratization," *Harvard International Review* (Summer 2005): 147–148.

34. Stellan Vinthagen, *A Theory of Nonviolent Action: How Civil Resistance Works* (London: Zed Books, 2015).

35. Hardy Merriman, "Theory and Dynamics of Nonviolent Action," in *Civilian Jihad*, pp. 17–29 (New York: Palgrave Macmillan, 2009).

36. Kurt Schock, "Nonviolent Action and Its Misconceptions: Insights for Social Scientists," in *PSOnline*, 2003, 705–712. One of the hallmarks of the state is that it is the only authority that can use violence "legitimately." Hence, the state always has the upper hand in terms of the legitimacy of violence. On the other hand, when the state initiates violence against peaceful protestors, the protestors earn sympathy.

37. Erica Chenoweth and Maria Stephan, *Why Civil Resistance Works: The Strategic Logic of Nonviolent Conflict* (New York: Columbia University Press, 2011). See also Maria Stephan and Erica Chenoweth, "Why Civil Resistance Works: The Strategic Logic of Nonviolent Conflict," *International Security* 33, no. 1 (2008): 7–44. In another study of efficacy from 2005, *Freedom House* investigated the 67 countries that made the transition from some form of dictatorship to some form of democracy between 1970 and 2004. The study found that nonviolent resistance proved the most effective method of change, as well as instituted the most stable new democracies (Karatnycky & Ackerman 2005).

38. Erica Chenoweth, *Civil Resistance: What Everyone Needs to Know* (London: Oxford University Press, 2021). See also Andrew Marantz, "How to Stop a Power Grab," *The New Yorker*, 11/16/2020, https://www.newyorker.com/magazine/2020/11/23/how-to-stop-a-power-grab, and Erica Chenoweth and Maria Stephan, "How the World is Proving Martin Luther King Right about Nonviolence," *Washington Post*, 2016.

39. Jack DuVall, "Civil Resistance and the Language of Power," International Center for Nonviolent Conflict, https://www.nonviolent-conflict.org/resource/civil-resistance-and-the-language-of-power/2010.

40. Sharp, *The Politics of Nonviolent Action*, 1973.

41. Sharon Erickson Nepstad, *Nonviolent Struggle: Theories, Strategies, and Dynamics* (Oxford: Oxford University Press, 2015).

42. Vinthagen, 2013.

43. When Nelson Mandela was first entering the prison at Robben Island, the guards shouted at him to move quickly, using the word one would use to gather cattle.

Mandela responded by slowing down. From this moment, it was reported, his dignity as a human being was established in that place. He was a man, not an animal, and he would behave as such.

44. For a fuller discussion of principled versus pragmatic nonviolence, see Cynthia Boaz's 2012 article "Must we change our hearts before throwing off our chains?" including the illuminating comments from several scholars in the field—posted on the website *Waging Nonviolence*, http://wagingnonviolence.org/feature/must-we-change-our-hearts-before-throwing-off-our-chains/ (accessed January 2020).

45. Robert Holmes, *On War and Morality* (Princeton: Princeton University Press, 1989), 291.

46. Quoted in DuVall 2010.

47. Chenoweth, *Civil Resistance*, 2021. See also Veronique Dudouet, "Nonviolent Resistance and Conflict Transformation in Power Asymmetries," *Berghof Research Center for Constructive Conflict Management*, 01/08/2008, www.berghof-handbook.net.

48. Vinthagen 2013, 166. If people, in sufficient numbers, withhold their coopera-tion to a system for long enough, the system will "no longer have power. This is the basic political assumption of nonviolent action" (Sharp, *The Politics of Nonviolent Action*, 1973, 64).

49. Kenneth Boulding, *Three Faces of Power* (Fair Oaks, CA: Sage Publications, 1989).

50. Arne Naess, *Gandhi and Group Conflict: An Exploration of Satyagraha. Theoretical Background* (Oslo: Universitetsforlaget, 1974). Martin Luther King Jr. explained that "psychological freedom, a firm sense of self-esteem, is the most pow-erful weapon against the long night of physical slavery."

51. Quoted in Jack DuVall, "Dream Things True: Nonviolent Movements as Applied Consciousness," *Cosmos and History: The Journal of Natural and Social Philosophy* 10, no. 1 (2014): 106–117, 109.

52. Sorensen, Majken Jul, and Brian Martin, "The Dilemma Action: Analysis of an Activist Technique," *Peace & Change* 39, no. 1 (2014): 73–100.

53. Sharp 1973, 658.

54. Dudouet, "Nonviolent Resistance," 2008; Michael Nagler, *Is There No Other Way? The Search for a Nonviolent Future* (Berkeley: Berkeley Hills Press, 2001); Schock 2003.

55. Peter Ackerman and Jack Duvall, "People Power Primed: Civilian Resistance and Democratization," *Harvard International Review*, Summer 2005; Doug Bond, "Nonviolent Direct Action and the Diffusion of Power" in *Justice without Violence* (Boulder: Lynne Rienner, 1994), 59–79; Stephen Zunes, "Weapons of Mass Democracy: Nonviolent Resistance is the Most Powerful Tactic Against Oppressive Regimes," *Yes Magazine*, 2009, http://www.yesmagazine.org/issues/learn-as-you-go/weapons-of-mass-democracy; Stephen Zunes, Lester Kurtz, and Sara Asher, eds., *Nonviolent Social Movements: A Geographical Perspective* (London: Blackwell Publishing, 1999).

56. Stellan Vinthagen gets at this in his understanding that symbolic actions gain meaning based on attributed identity of actors (2013, 112), but this book is more explicit in its arguments.

57. Ken Crowley, interview by author, Chicago, IL, March 7th, 2012.

58. Rumpf, interview.

59. There are interesting examples of resisters defying each of these conditions. For example, after the 1968 Catonsville action, Daniel Berrigan went on the lam—becoming one of the FBI's "most wanted" while continuing to give surprise appearances at various events across the country. By avoiding jail, he generated more attention to his cause, but he did not follow the traditional path of nonviolent resistance. More commonly, defendants will choose to "plead out" or pay a fine rather than pursue trial or endure incarceration, usually because the net benefit of doing so is deemed not worthwhile in the particular case. (For example, Brian Terrell recently paid a $50 fine in Washington, D.C., rather than go to jail for a climate change action, knowing that his fellow defendant—Jane Fonda—would provide enough attention to the issue on her own.)

60. Rumpf, interview.

61. Crowley, interview.

62. Personal email (2020). In the same email, Brian explained that not focusing on acquittal lessens the influence of the grand edifice of "justice"—the beautiful courtroom and formal robes, specialized vocabularies, and bewildering ceremonies. Such intimidation only works, he wrote, if one can be swayed by the threat-power of potential punishment.

63. Dan Berrigan's *The Trial of the Catonsville 9* is the best known, the script only slightly modified from court transcripts.

64. Quoted in Ed Kinane et al., "Two Dozen," 2001.

65. Neil MacFarquhar, "Why Charges against Protesters Are Being Dismissed by the Thousands," *New York Times*, 11/09/2020, https://www.nytimes.com/2020/11/19/us/protests-lawsuits-arrests.html.

66. Shirelle Phelps and Jeffrey Lehman, "Necessity." *West's Encyclopedia of American Law* 7, no. 2 (Detroit: Gale, 2005).

67. Recounted in John Dear, "A Peace Movement Victory in Court," *The National Catholic Reporter*, Sept. 21, 2010, https://www.ncronline.org/blogs/road-peace/peace-movement-victory-court.

68. Fr. Daniel Berrigan, "Catonsville 9 Statement," *Essential Writings* (Maryknoll, NY: Orbis, 2009).

69. A jury has a non-reviewable, non-revokable power to convict or acquit a defendant, hence a state's laws are only as strong as a group of 12 lay people's compliance to these laws. Jury "lawlessness" is an important corrective, a democratic promise against minority rule against the majority, and means that those with the greatest power are still accountable to the will of the people.

70. The 1973 Camden 28 trial allowed the nullification defense (the only large trial I know of that did so), and all 28 defendants were acquitted.

71. Arthur Laffin, "History" (2019). In more than 200 Plowshares trials, Laffin only finds seven instances in which one of these defenses have proven successful— only one of which was in the U.S.

72. Fr. Stephen Kelly, interview by author, Oakland, CA, July 2012.

73. Rumpf, interview.

74. Fr. Kelly, interview.

75. Crane, interview.

76. Brian Terrell, personal email (2020).

77. Terrell explains, "The best trial scenes happen when defendants go to trial with a community of support. Lawyers can be a great help as advisors or representing some defendants, effectively making them 'co-counsel' with those who go *pro se*. The best movement lawyers do not presume to make decisions for their 'clients' but act as collaborators, acting in a sense as tour guides and interpreters to travelers to a strange, exotic and confusing landscape. One advantage to this approach is that judges often will order the parameters of testimony so narrow . . . as to make the proceedings meaningless. While an attorney risks losing her livelihood by speaking the truth in such circumstances, a *pro se* defendant can speak up risking only a reprimand or at worse a day or two in lock up for contempt" ("Pro Se Defense" 2011).

78. Tobey, 2016.

79. On the contrary, they *do* want to win. This is why they put so much energy into things like jury studies. "My dad learned from Angela Davis," Clare Grady explained, and "jury studies" are an "important part" of engaging in trial. (Clare Grady, interview by author, Ithaca, NY. on August 13th, 2010). Similarly, finding the right expert witnesses is emphasized. Procuring experts such as Howard Zinn and Ramsey Clark is a clear attempt to bring legitimacy and legal/historical force to the trials—in order to create precedent, challenge bad laws—and also, importantly, to win cases.

80. Nepstad 2015.

81. Fr. Daniel Berrigan, *Essential.*

82. Sr. Carol Gilbert, interview by author, Baltimore, MD, April 13th, 2012.

83. As Fr. Dan Berrigan explained, "Do not allow yourself to be sidetracked into mini-battles that the system allows you to win" (*Essential*, 2009). In a personal email, participant Brian Terrell wrote, "The trouble is that at this point in the planet's history, we can win every single winnable struggle and still all die in a climate collapse or a nuclear war. The times demand that we take on struggles that have no apparent end but failure. We need to stake our lives on losing causes, or else" (11/17/2020).

84. Joshua McElwee, "Berrigan's Message to Peacemakers: Persevere," *National Catholic Reporter*, 12/08/2010, https://www.ncronline.org/news/people/berrigans-message-peacemakers-persevere.

85. Fr. Luis Barrios, interview by author, Washington, DC, April 14th, 2012.

86. Quoted in Walter Wink, *Peace Is the Way*, 2002, 228).

87. Jack Duvall, "Civil Resistance and the Language of Power" (2014, 107). See also John Burdick, *Blessed Anastácia: Women, Race and Popular Christianity in Brazil* (London: Routledge, 2013); Antonio Gramsci, *Selections from the Prison Notebooks*, edited and translated by Quintin Hoare and Geoffrey Nowell Smith (International Publishers, 1971); Dana Hill, *Opening Our Eyes: How Activist*

Women in Ecuador Learn Critical Political and Self-Aware Consciousness. Syracuse University, 2014; Jane Mansbridge, "Complicating Oppositional Consciousness," in *Oppositional Consciousness: The Subjective Roots of Protest*, ed. Jane Mansbridge and Aldon Morris (Chicago: University of Chicago Press, 2001), 238–264.

88. Ed Kinane, interview by author, Syracuse, NY, March 3rd, 2010.

89. Ed Kinane et al., "Two Dozen Get Prison Time for Crossing S.O.A. Line," *Nuclear Resister*, 07/01/2001, http://www.nukeresister.org/static/nr124/nr1242dozen.html.

90. Anne Braden, quoted in Catherine Fosl, *Subversive Southerner: Anne Braden and the Struggle for Racial Justice in the Cold War South* (Lexington: University Press of Kentucky, 2006).

91. Riegle, *Crossing the Line*, 2012a, 213.

92. Personal email from Ed Kinane, 11/2020.

93. One of the most dramatic examples of this is the 1927 case of Sacco and Vanzetti. In his last letter to Judge Webster Thayer before his execution, Bartolomeo Vanzetti wrote, "If it had not been for these things, I might have lived out my life talking at street corners to scorning men. I might have died, unmarked, unknown, a failure. Now we are not a failure. This is our career and our triumph. Never in our full life could we hope to do such work for tolerance, for justice, for man's understanding of man as now we do by accident. Our words—our lives—our pain—nothing! The taking of our lives—lives of a good shoemaker and a poor fish peddler—all! That last moment belongs to us—that agony is our triumph." https://www.workersliberty.org/story/2010/06/22/last-speech-bartolomeo-vanzetti.

94. Personal email from Brian Terrell, 2020.

Chapter 3

Like a Chiropractic Adjustment

Aligning Actions and Beliefs through Identity-Work

If we create a planet that goes down this path towards privilege and self-ishness and warfare . . . our planet will become uninhabitable. You won't be able to live on it, no matter how high-tech or safe you are in your little imperial cocoon. Your fate is intertwined with the fate of that person in Colombia. I mean, it really is.—Serraglio (interview)

When I asked my participants to tell me about themselves and their activism, most included stories about how they "discerned" their resistance—"deciding what to do and when," in participant Ed Kinane's words.[1] For Plowshares, discernment is usually about how best to emulate the life of Jesus Christ: what one must do to be a good or true Christian living in a violent and imperialist state. For others, the pressing questions are around efficacy, the appropriateness of resistant action, or one's own abilities to carry it through. Almost always, "discernment" takes time—time spent reflecting, learning, praying, and planning. A typical Plowshares action, for instance, involves a small group of people meeting in secret to think through a potential joint act—a process that may take several years. For everyone who mentioned it, discernment entailed thoughtful consideration of particular policies, as well as one's belief system, life circumstances, and sense of self. Discernment is thus the "inner work" of resistance; it is where the work begins, and it can be experienced as personally challenging. Discernment occurs before the illegal actions that we may hear about in the news, but some justice action prisoners consider it to be the most important part of their resistance overall.[2]

This chapter is about the process of discernment, and specifically, what justice action prisoners *know* and *do* to bring their identities into alignment with their beliefs. Most basically, it is the meeting of knowledge and self-concept that generate the particular "doings" of identity—as well as comprise the work that discernment mandates. Hence, the chapter begins with a review of what justice action prisoners "know" that motivates them toward resistant action. The second part examines two areas in which the work of identity happens: learning and the "nonviolent lifestyle," or living in a way most suited to enable participation in resistance. The third part analyzes solidarity as a troublesome but essential activation of identity-work, performed "on behalf of" others. Notions of solidarity bring to the surface activists' understandings of power, privilege, and responsibility—complicating ideas of wanting to "do good" with the reality that doing so as privileged allies may actually strengthen existing hierarchical and colonial relations that privilege whiteness, U.S. citizenship, and so on as more powerful and worthy. Justice action prisoners' ideas about solidarity are thus analyzed in conversation with ideas about "advantaged group allies" in social movements, as well as transnational feminist scholarship—specifically around issues of representation, or what it means (and how best) to speak "for" others.

In each "site" of identity-work—learning, the nonviolent lifestyle, and solidarity—justice action prisoners "do things" to bring their actions into line with *what* they know and *who* they most want to be. In general, the people represented in this research defined themselves personally as active, consistent, and capable. They rarely defined themselves as raced, gendered, religious, or American. Instead, they thought of themselves as "responsible" and "privileged." This chapter's focus on individual identity is not to say that justice activism is "all about me," but instead to show that personal work is a fundamental part of political work. Indeed, in the case of high-risk activism, reckoning with one's subjectivity and place in the world are essential parts of the process.

DISCERNMENT: IDENTITY-WORK AND
THE PROCESS OF ALIGNMENT

Resistance begins in what I call "identity-work." In social movement analysis, *identity work* (no hyphen) is "the range of activities individuals engage in to create, present, and sustain personal identities that are congruent with and supportive of the self-concept."[3] Identity-work (with hyphen) is clarified here, more specifically, as the labor of bringing one's actions and behaviors into alignment with one's values and beliefs. Justice action prisoners want their actions to be in congruence with their ideals, as is appropriate within a nonviolent philosophy that sees means as determining of ends. As if in chorus, my respondents told me that as a Christian, a thinking person, a person of conscience, and so on, "once I knew, I had to act." Thus, identity-work is fundamentally about self-concept, grounded in a political understanding of one's location, privilege, or responsibility—and as they relate to specific forms of knowledge. In other words, deeply knowing "who I am" involves two sets of knowledge—one personal (what are my values? What kind of person am I?) and the other structural/political (what is my public place in this world? What responsibilities do my identities entail?). Being responsive toward one's aligned identity involves attention to both levels: it means behaving as one's truest and most authentic self *and* being responsible for what one knows, in an environment that is understood to be systemically rigged to favor some people over others, a hierarchical system most often achieved through varying but constant levels of oppression and violence.

Those represented in this book ultimately deemed prison witness necessary to "be" who they most truly are. The road to incarceration is long, however, and often riddled with challenges, epiphanies, and long thinking: it is itself a process of labor. This reality puts to rest the idea that high-risk actions are spontaneous or "natural" (a common misperception about nonviolent actions generally). Instead, resistant acts are the result of intentional work and clear thinking; work that begins at the level of "who I am."

PART 1: WHAT JUSTICE ACTION PRISONERS KNOW

Justice action prisoners are generally involved in political activism because they care about and understand certain issues. One of the things that makes them unusual as a group is what this caring and knowledge motivate. For justice action prisoners, the realities of political injustice and violence are not just an accumulation of discouraging facts, but a clarion call to action—to *do* something. There are four essential "foundations" that come into play in the process of discernment; intellectual, spiritual, social, and movement associated.

Intellectual Foundations I: "Counter-Hegemonic Knowledge"

"Counter-hegemonic knowledge" refers to justice action prisoners' ways of thinking about the world. Theirs is an analysis that highlights violence across the globe, sees instances and systems of violence as connected, and under-stands them to be caused by human actions that are changeable. In this view, individual human beings have power—we are part of our social context and historical moment, but we are not helpless bots unable to produce change. Most often, counter-hegemonic knowledge is rooted in some way of thinking based in morality, such as a Christian foundation or nonviolent credo, and it is supported by the rhetorics and ideals of the movements themselves. However, being a "good person" (or a person of faith) is the starting place for aligning one's sense of self with what they do.

Counter-hegemonic knowledge is resistant knowledge: it does not accept ways of living that rely upon violence as reasonable or forgivable, but sees them as systemic and intentional—and wrong. This way of thinking rationalizes and enables opposition to militarism, imperialism, and nuclear weapons, as it makes engaging in serious resistance both necessary and logical. Counter-hegemonic knowledge is like a pair of glasses, and once they are on, a lot of what you see looks like imperial violence requiring resistance. It is this *way of thinking* (more than a particular body of knowledge) that most often motivates action.

That said, counter-hegemonic knowledge is propelled by certain content. Most relevantly, justice action prisoners know about U.S. domestic and foreign policy, national and international law, U.S. military and weapons systems, and the philosophy and strategies of nonviolent action. As evidenced by their prolific writing, they are typically subject experts in the issues relevant to their resistance.[4] The SOA Watch and Plowshares movements are also dedicated to consciousness-raising and education, and justice action prisoners are generally well versed in the areas they are protesting.

Nuclear weapons are the specific area of concern for the Plowshares movement, both in terms of policies and weapons systems, but also as "the centerpiece of the whole strategy of domination," according to Fr. Steve Kelly. Clare Grady described nuclear weapons as the "gun to the head" of U.S. imperialism: a greedy, long-fingered process that has no regard for human life in its pursuit of power (and accumulation of capital). Hence, as long as the U.S. continues to build and maintain nuclear weapons and use them as a threat, Liz McAlister explained, "American superiority is maintained." Sr. Ardeth Platte told me that she acts against nuclear militarism because it "has an effect on every issue of violence that exists . . . whether it be climate change or whether it be poverty . . . it has drastic effect." Fr. Steve put it bluntly: "it is a sin to build a nuclear weapon" as even in its construction, it is a "theft from the poor."[5] Hence, in their own understandings, Plowshares activists are literally doing the same work when serving in a soup kitchen or banging on a nuclear weapon. Each is an appropriate response to the same *system* of violence—a capitalist system of wealth accumulation for the few that relies on violence as it impoverishes both those who pay for it in the U.S. (by funding weapons rather than schools, for example) and are impacted by it elsewhere (by violent force, political influence, resource extraction, and so on).

This perception of interconnections explains how participant Kathleen Rumpf could do her 1983 Griffiss Plowshares action "on behalf of the homeless." A member of the New York City Catholic Worker throughout the 1980s, Kathleen watched "the face of the homeless change" from "men from the road" and veterans who "couldn't quite come all the way home" to addicts and families, while President Reagan's Star Wars program thrived.[6] For her, the bloody and bodily costs of imperial governance were not theoretical: the violence of nuclear weapons was present in her daily life. Heartbroken from what she was seeing on the streets of New York, Kathleen hammered on a B-52 to bring attention to those most affected by the bomber's existence: Americans who are poor and homeless while fleets of airplanes rest on military tarmacs, ever-ready lest others far away dream too clearly of insurrection toward their own freedom.

Present also in counter-hegemonic knowledge is an understanding of how systemic, structural, and nonviolent change occurs. Social movement analysis presents three ways of achieving systemic change: political, legal, and direct. Citizens may participate at any level—letter writing, for example, is a way to put pressure on one's representatives to support political change, while financially supporting the ACLU may bolster legal change. Direct action implies protest, and putting one's body on the line to make one's position known. Sr. Ardeth Platte explained that "there are very few . . . causes that have been won without people going to jail." Liz Deligio agreed, arguing that "civil disobedience is not exotic or extreme, but a fundamental tool in the kit."[7] Justice action prisoners understand prison witness to be essential for progressive change, and it is a tool they understand and are willing to use. They are also often quite knowledgeable of the legal system itself: their rights as a citizen, treaties to which the U.S. is a signatory, the pattern of the criminal trial, and so on.

A counter-hegemonic knowledge legitimates direct action and jail, so that imprisonment is considered a reasonable part of the activist experience rather than a consequence that should be avoided. "It was something missing," Nancy Gwin told me, "that I'd been wanting to do."[8] For committed nonviolent activists, not going to jail may be likened to a mountaineer not climbing an important peak. If you want to be a "46er," you've got to climb all 46 peaks. And a lengthy stay in prison is the Mount Everest of radical nonviolent activism: if you can possibly do it, you don't want to miss it. (This way of knowing is less attentive to *who* may participate in prison witness without serious consequence, and do so with the greatest political efficacy. But these are issues for forthcoming chapters.)

Intellectual Foundations II: The Radical Gospel of Justice Action Prisoners

Also undergirding and shaping justice action prisoners' thought is religion—the faith that guides and directs action, both personal and political. Though it is impossible to accurately capture the beliefs of a varied group of people, it is clear that strong commonalities exist among the faithful represented in this research (the majority). Most importantly, faith-based justice action prisoners share a commitment to living their faith through what they do.[9] Participant Jack Gilroy was one of several who quoted Saint Francis of Assisi during his interview, saying "preach the gospel, and if you have to, use words."[10] Words without action hold little value for the faithful represented here. What is important is what you *do* with your faith—in this life, here on Earth.

Most often, justice action prisoners are supported by either the Prophetic Tradition in Christianity (from the Hebrew Bible, and usually adhered to by Plowshares) or Liberation Theology (a theology of liberation from systemic injustices, more common among SOA Watch activists). Many of my participants cited the Bible as their primary rationale—as well as their guidebook—for action.[11] Most often, participants insisted that Jesus was a trouble-maker, his life *as well as* his death evidence that resisting an imperial status quo is the heart of what it means to be a Christian.[12] Followers of both the Prophetic Tradition and Liberation Theology link the social and political context (injustice, unfairness, poverty, suffering) with their understanding of the Gospel—for them, the worldly and divine are connected. Their faith tells them that imperialism and other forms of violence are not "natural," or God's punishments for sin, but rather systemic and unjust. To be Christ-like under such conditions, they should organize and resist.

Activists inspired by the Prophetic Tradition are Roman Catholics who are fiercely committed to the word of God. They are not constrained by the institutional Church, and they are willing to lose mainstream acceptability to walk their most faithful path (including excommunication and disrobing, which are not uncommon for Plowshares clergy). The Gospel is the only guide that matters to them, its teachings trumping what is legal, popular, or Vatican-condoned at all times.

Beginning in the 1960s, priest-brothers Daniel and Philip Berrigan breathed life into the Prophetic Tradition through their political actions, mentorship, writing, and speaking.[13] This is a tradition that sees Christianity as a "call to justice, mercy, and peace," and is critical of religion not activated into practice.[14] What is essential for the Berrigans is *practicing* one's faith, evident in works that uplift the marginalized and poor, for example, rather than such things as church attendance or tithing. For Plowshares, the aim is to literally imitate Christ—"imitatio Christi" by following his example as closely as possible.[15] In his autobiography, Philip Berrigan wrote that Christ was "never a reformer. . . . He preached that we should dismantle, not attempt to patch, the state."[16] I was reminded during interviews that Christ not only resisted imperialism during his lifetime, he *died* for his resistance to Roman Imperialism. It was "that important" to him, according to Jerry Berrigan. In our interview, Jerry explained that he was proud of his brothers Dan and Phil because they were willing to go "all the way" for Christ, to live as well as to die for him.[17] They never compromised with the violent state.

Following his brothers' lead, Jerry feels he is "on pretty safe ground" in knowing what it means to emulate Christ: it means resisting injustice through nonviolent direct action. During our interview, (former) Fr. Bill Frankel-Streit remembered that it was life-changing for him to hear his friend Phil Berrigan explain that "resistance is the cross." In other words, resistance is the very core of what it means to be a Christian. Fr. Bill explained more fully, "Presidents and pharaohs, they're the anti-Christ. They're what has to be resisted. The whole Bible is about resisting the principalities and powers, those who make war on God's children, the poor."[18] Here, the Bible is "the radical tract" for systemic social and political change—"the handbook for nonviolence and anarchism."[19] For those who ascribe to the Prophetic Tradition, overcoming the imperial state is the goal, and nonviolence the only means. As a result, to live out their faith, bold, risky, and lifelong resistance is necessary.

Toward this goal, Fr. Bill explained that nonviolence is "tough love."[20] It is drawing a line ("thou shalt not kill" being primary) and *doing something* when that line is crossed. Fr. Bill told me that his faith entails a "responsibility to the world" that is compounded for him as a vowed religious man (who happens to be married, but despite excommunication still considers himself to be a priest). Sr. Ardeth Platte, a Dominican Sister and recidivist Plowshares activist who lived at Jonah House in Baltimore (and was the real-life prisoner represented in Piper Kerman's *Orange is the New Black*), was clear about what it means to be a sister committed to following the teachings of Christ. She explained:

> The documents of the Church spell it out. No more war. Abolish nuclear weapons . . . economic justice. Counter racism, make sure you are opposed to the death penalty. . . . And you know if we Sisters don't participate in the change, then I wonder who will? We really entered religious life in order to live the Gospel to the hilt. Luckily somewhere along the line a conversion took place in us, and we said we will give our life to this . . . do good and avoid evil. And when the government in our name defies the principles of our faith, then it seems to me essential to take the stand regarding it.[21]

Sr. Ardeth's commitment to activist work came from her vow to "live the Gospel to the hilt." As a nun, she told me, doing so is "essential." Quite simply, for all who ascribe to the Prophetic Tradition, living one's faith through resistant action is central to what it means to be a Christian, and resistance provides evidence that one's faith and actions are in congruence.

Liberation Theology also directs resistance actions, particularly for those imprisoned for SOA violations. Roy Bourgeois (the founder of SOA Watch) wrote that it was the people in the slums of La Paz, Bolivia (where he first ministered), who "taught me about their 'theology of liberation' and a God who empowers and gives hope to the poor. This theology teaches about a loving God who does not want anyone to suffer from poverty, oppression, violence, or discrimination."[22] In our interview, Fr. Luis Barrios explained that his (liberation) theology works for a just society "here on Earth." He explained:

> I know enough about what is going on, on this planet. And it's a lot of injustice. And I got to the conclusion that if there is a heaven . . . no one is going there without going through Earth. So I think we need to fix what is going on. I don't need to go there (to heaven) to feel the so-called justice of God, where there is equal distribution of resources and there are no abusive people . . . where you can be whatever it is that you want to be—as a woman, as a black person, as a gay, lesbian, as a Muslim. . . . That we create something here, that we guarantee that you can stand, with respect, in this society. That's why I put more attention into building the so-called Kingdom of God on Earth.[23]

Part of how he does this is to make "God" the center, rather than Jesus Christ. "And I call justice 'God.'" In centering *justice* rather than Jesus, Fr. Luis Barrios's theology is inclusive; it makes space for Christians, but also for people of other and no faiths. Liberation Theology instructs people to work for justice "here on Earth"—to not accept inequalities as inevitable or as God's will, but as human-imposed problems that can be transformed.

Of course, even among the Roman Catholics I interviewed, there are diverse understandings of what it means to live in alignment with one's faith. What is constant, however, is a commitment to living the Gospel, through action, toward the betterment of people's lives *here on Earth*. For Plowshares participants, honoring the Gospel and the life of Jesus Christ while living in a war-state requires resistance. For those who align with Liberation Theology, it means illuminating injustice and violence as systemic and preventable rather than divine, which entails empowering people to demand change. For other participants, church teachings serve primarily to support, justify, and rationalize their choices. "It was very easy to get support from the Bible" agnostic Ann Tiffany explained, support that brings righteousness, legitimacy, and coherence to her actions, as it connects her to those she works alongside and for.[24]

Intellectual Foundations III: Know Thyself

Another important piece of justice action prisoners' knowledge is how they know themselves, both structurally (such as their race, gender, and class) and subjectively (as individuals—their personalities, preferences, and quirks). When they defined themselves structurally, participants rarely used words like white, religious, or American. Instead, they defined themselves in context: as "privileged" and "responsible"—responsible as U.S. citizens and privileged by their race, education, class, and experience. Such language was particularly present for participants in SOA Watch, a movement that is committed to deepening understandings around power and privilege. What seemed most important for me to understand, according to these participants, was what these privileged identities meant for this group of activists and how they mandate particular forms of action.

Participation in prison witness is frequently linked with a concept of privilege. Participant Meagan Doty usefully summarized the understanding. She said:

> I have this privilege and I didn't earn it . . . and I need to use that, not to my benefit, but for the benefit of all those who didn't have that great chance. . . . I have power, and not everybody has that power . . . I am part of the 1% who has a college education. . . . I can't just take that for granted. I need to use my 1% power to speak for the people that will never have the opportunity.[25]

The sentiment Meagan describes was widely felt by others, and acting "in response" to privilege plays a crucial part in both justice action prisoners' conceptions of themselves and in directing what they do. Most instrumentally, their privilege comes from their status as U.S. citizens. This citizenship gives them ability to act (without higher risks than temporary incarceration), but it is also what makes it *mandatory* for them to do so. It is *their* government, acting on their behalf and with their consent unless they demonstrate otherwise, whose policies result in hardship and death for others across the globe. As Liz Deligio explained, she crossed the line at Fort Benning because "I had the privilege to protest without being disappeared, kidnapped, tortured and killed. I have a responsibility because of what my country is doing, and the freedom to do it because I don't face the same obstacles and risks that other people might."[26] Fr. Bill Frankel-Streit agreed when he told me that "these are actions for U.S. citizens to take, because as citizens of empire, this is what's required of me."[27] Hence, while they may not identify as "American," justice action prisoners feel compelled and uniquely responsible to act *because* they are citizens of the United States.

Whether for reasons of faith, knowledge, privilege, citizenship, or some combination, justice action prisoners also expressed a sense of *responsibility* for the suffering that takes place globally, in their name. With tears in her eyes, participant Susan Crane said, "What if I had lived in Germany during World War Two? When I see the pictures of people in Hiroshima and

Nagasaki, when I see the woman whose body is burned and she's trying to nurse her child, what do you do with that picture?" For Susan, the answer is clear: Resist. Resist those who are responsible for the violence, the policies that enforce it, the thinking that enables it, the institutions that support it—resist totally, not worrying about results. This certainty is supported by the documents of the Church and a counter-hegemonic knowledge rooted in resistance, but it is activated by a sense of personal responsibility. Susan continued:

> When I sit with those images and with that knowledge . . . and I sit with my faith tradition that says we're supposed to love our enemies, what am I called to do? . . . I don't want to live this normal life in this empire that's killing people. . . . I look at the pictures of babies whose mothers were exposed to depleted uranium, and I think "is it right to do good or to do evil, to save life or to destroy it? What's right?" . . . So I begin to disarm the weapons. By international law they should be disarmed. It's our duty and our responsibility to begin to disarm them, by my faith we need to . . . and someone needs to start.[28]

Being a person willing to "start" is a through-line among justice action prisoners, and key to what makes them distinctive as a group. Indeed, more often than not, participants told me that despite the many challenges of prison witness, "not acting" would be more difficult than doing something—even with the consequence of prison attached. What makes it so very difficult to "not act" is that it would be out of compliance with their conceptions of who they are.

In more personal terms, justice action prisoners identified themselves as *busy*. Fr. Luis Barrios laughed as he told me, "Fighting for justice, there is no way you can say, I've already accomplished my goal." There is "no vacation, no retirement" in this job.[29] As nonviolent resisters, justice action prisoners don't want to "talk," they want to *do*. Collectively, they write, teach, cook, volunteer, attend events and meetings (so many meetings). They travel to learn, to protest, and to support other actions; they care for people in their communities; and they agitate against individuals and institutions who they believe are using their power in unjust ways. In ways large and small, justice action prisoners are busy people.

Interestingly, justice action prisoners rarely describe themselves as "religious," though only eight of the 43 participants are not or are no longer religious. Several live in faith communities such as the Catholic Worker, and 12 are or have been ministers, priests, or nuns. Rather than religious, participants described themselves as committed to *living faithfully*, and this identity was conveyed through what they did. As Nancy Gwin explained, "that is my challenge to myself and the people I interact with. Get out of your pews! Get up off of our prayer rugs! . . . It's time to do something!"[30]

The impact of living faithfully is huge for justice action prisoners—and not just those who ascribe to the Prophetic Tradition. Participant Clare Grady said, "In the mass, we sum it up: to love and to serve. You know, social trans-formation here."[31] Loving and serving are traditional Catholic tenets, but in the hands of justice action prisoners they are also tools for social resistance and change. John Heid encapsulated this when he told me about working on the U.S.-Mexico border, where leaving water in the desert for traveling migrants is illegal. "On the border," he said, "works of mercy are works of resistance."[32] In effect, and as Philip Berrigan described, the work of living faithfully is inherently resistant: faith and resistance one and the same.

Justice action prisoners also hope to be "consistent"—to live what they believe. Most basically, this is the (principled nonviolent, but also Christian) idea of means determining ends. Through embodying right action, one directs and smooths the path towards the creation of a better world. Living "consistently" was also expressed as being uncompromising—never bend-ing on one's values or principles to fit in or make others feel comfortable. Consistency was also interpreted as interior work, an effort to present the same levels of dignity in private as in public. Plowshares philosophy endorses a rigorous adherence to nonviolence in one's personal and political life: to be consistent (and consistently good) with one's sentencing judges and with one's closest family, with the media and in one's private thoughts.

For Clare Grady, the challenge of living consistently is present in how to respond personally to what is being done in her name politically—but it also feels right, and good. Describing how it felt to do a Plowshares action, she said:

> The word "alignment" comes to mind, like any relationship . . . the more you act in that humble way, it literally manifests in your body. . . . And when I ham-mered on that . . . B-52 that was carrying this first strike nuclear weapon for this empire that I live in, I was making that so clear. I describe it as like a chi-ropractic adjustment, *psss-ch!* Like I disarmed the beast, the head of the beast.[33]

This image of the "relief of adjustment" resonates with the ways other justice action prisoners expressed how it felt to participate in resistant action. It feels good to feel closer to where they were supposed to be, doing the work that they were "put here to do." This feeling was anchored in acting consistently.

In addition to being active, faithful, and consistent, many participants sim-ply seem to be born trouble-makers, people who have a life history of bucking authority. "You tell me a rule," Rae Kramer told me, "and my instinct is to break it."[34] Randy Serraglio described himself as a "hot-head" who "cannot stand" arbitrary rules. He recalled a high school teacher telling him that he "always thought" Randy would get arrested—"but not for something good!"[35] As a young woman, Julienne Oldfield was a Labour party councilwoman in England who asked questions (in a room full of older men) about the municipal budget that no one had previously dared voice—confronting generations of silence about municipal priorities.[36] For some, prison witness seems to align with a personality as a rabble-rouser, a natural part of a life-long pattern.

Intellectual Foundations IV: The Role of the Movements

The Plowshares and School of the Americas Watch movements also shape how activists think of themselves, understand issues, and act. Evidence of the two movements' influence informs this section on identity-work overall, but a few parts are worth highlighting and examining in more depth. First is how the two movements articulate a notion of "activist" that inculcates a sense of goodness, ability, religiosity, and a special commitment—the movements revere those who go to prison. Second is the way the movements collect and frame information, around the issues of concern as well as strategies for action. Last are the ways in which the movements provide the moral and/or religious foundations from which nonviolent activism, including arrestable acts of resistance, become considered both essential and ethical. Each movement works as a resource for those involved, with its framing of the issues, principles, commitments, and communities shaping how activists think of their actions and themselves. Both movements define activists as good, devout, and also ordinary people who are able and empowered to act against injustice. These characterizations provide moral clarity for participants, as they distinguish them as people who take action when the norms they hold dear are egregiously violated.[37] In response to the injustices highlighted by the movements, SOA Watch and Plowshares activists are compelled to *do* something: they are not content to be "checkbook" activists; they are off the couch and out the door, working for a world in better alignment with their ethical and faith positions.

Being someone willing to go to prison, in both movements, is to occupy a glorified space. When prison witness was a cornerstone tactic of the SOA Watch movement, "prisoners of conscience" were hugely celebrated, presented as the most committed and effective parts of the struggle against torture and militarism in Latin America. Those who considered participating in direct action were well-assisted in their process; provided with nonviolence training, legal advice, and the massive support of the movement during the trial and through incarceration. In Plowshares, those who go to prison also occupy a special place. They are regarded as deeply committed to resistance, and as living Christ-like lives. In her book on the movement, Kristen Tobey writes of the "stratified community" within Plowshares, in which those who have served prison time are "somehow different" than other peace activists, they inhabit an "elevated status" as a result of their incarceration.[38] Many of the justice action prisoners included here insisted that they were no one special, but the reality is that to engage in resistance actions leading to incarceration is to become a stand-out in either movement.[39] This may not be intentional or welcomed by the participants themselves, but the recognition of one's commitment to the cause must be negotiated nonetheless.

The movements also play an important role in framing the issues that activists are concerned about, as well as in legitimizing the tactics they employ. SOA Watch works against U.S. foreign policy, and to stop U.S.-supported human rights abuses and torture. It was founded by a former Maryknoll priest, Roy Bourgeois, a gregarious leader who infused the movement with the social justice theology of liberation. From these roots, SOA Watch promotes an activist identity that is not specifically Christian, but one who is moral, responsible, and active. As U.S. citizens and taxpayers, participants are encouraged to feel accountable for the effects that U.S. policies have on the lives of others, and their participation in the movement is a way to make their positions against such policies clear.[40] The tactics permitted are nonviolent: protesting, lobbying, consciousness raising, and engaging in civil disobedience. Such actions take place at Fort Benning, in Washington, D.C., at the U.S./Mexico border—and also in affected countries. Acting "in solidarity" with others, activists travel to Latin America as part of delegations to learn about local and geopolitical issues, but also to educate and put pressure on local leaders and governments about the SOA.

SOA Watch is a large movement, attracting hundreds of thousands of people over the years, most of whom never take part in arrestable resistance. But activists' connection with the movement "feels good," in the words of justice action prisoner Lois Putzier, and offers them an opportunity to be better versions of themselves. During her interview, Lois recalled that when she was arrested at Fort Benning, "I was very good then," and that her participation "felt good." As an activist with SOA Watch, she was connected with "the nicest group of people," and being part of it was "fun."[41] Randy Serraglio remembered being part of the early organizing staff at SOA Watch as the "most fulfilling thing I've ever done," but also as extremely challenging. Randy cited the meetings, the dissimilar personalities, the duties to consensus—as well as the organization's determination to better address inequities in power and access, a challenge that was fraught, but was also "what we're all about."[42] Even in these challenges, Randy expressed a sense of satisfaction and alignment between his own values and those espoused by the movement.

Plowshares is a very different kind of movement. It is much smaller, and is fundamentally based on a radical reading of the gospel. The Prophetic

Tradition locates Plowshares as a Christian response to the sins of imperialism, "Lord Nuke," and militarism. It has a specialized vocabulary, as well as selective community in which its message deeply resonates. The symbolism of blood, for example, may be quickly understood within certain Catholic communities, but it does not necessarily translate across groups of other faiths, or within secular communities.

The Plowshares model of resistance includes the use of symbolism (blood, hammers, Catholic liturgy, banners), nonviolent civil disobedience, and the destruction of property. As John Heid explained, "Plowshares actions are at heart prophetic, given they flow from the texts of Isaiah and Micah . . . I felt our action did not originate in us, but came THROUGH us. . . . The moment spoke for itself."[43] In this, one is acting almost as a medium for God's message, one's actions are enabling a new form of communication and vision of the future. Importantly, the religious symbolism of a Plowshares action is not perceived by activists as only symbolic, it is real. In conducting a prophetic act, Plowshares activists are literally constructing a new and better world.

Plowshares founders Liz McAlister and Phil and Dan Berrigan were prolific writers and public speakers, and they have an outsize effect on movement identities. McAlister and the Berrigans jointly articulated the biblical supports required to understand the Plowshares philosophy and choice of tactics: nonviolence, including the destruction of property that "has no right to exist."[44] They wrote against the "idolatry" of nuclear weapons, and admonished the faithful to be more Christ-like through participating in resistance to imperial governance and atomic weapons. The necessity of going to prison is deeply rooted in Plowshares theology, which sees enacting "the cross"—crucifixion and suffering—as the true mark of a Christian life. Suffering (imprisonment), according to Liz McAlister and Phil Berrigan, is "the insurance policy, our only real credential, a guarantee, even, of discipleship."[45] From this perspective, time spent in prison is the only relevant evidence for demonstrating a life of faith and biblical commitment. Adopting this view—of Christianity, resistance, and the centrality of nuclear weapons as an omnipresent and systemic threat to all our lives—shapes activists' lives in defining ways. Participation in "regular life" becomes almost impossible, as participating in resistance becomes inevitable. The only question is *how* to engage, not if or whether.

To resist like this, one must be fully committed. Rosalie Riegle's interviews with various Plowshares participants show that there can be an ethos of "toughness" in the movement—an extolling for activists to be as committed to peace as soldiers are to war.[46] In other words, they should be willing to die for it. The clarity and force of this mandate leaves little space for hesitancy, or larger questioning of movement goals or strategies. Plowshares promotes the idea that resistance is what should be most prioritized in people's lives (trumping family obligations, other interests, career advancements, and so on). To be Christ-like, one should resist—everything else is secondary. This is a hard model to emulate, and is largely responsible for why the movement remains so small.

KNOWING AND FEELING: HOW MEN
AND WOMEN TOLD STORIES

I was told many wonderful stories of discernment across my year of research, and one thing that stood out quickly—and proved significant across time— was that a participant's gender (as male or female) shaped how they told their stories to me. When I analyzed their transcripts, I noticed that *how* men and women described what motivated and inspired them toward activism differed along binary gender lines, and in ways that can impact how the activists may be perceived by others as legitimate, political, and valid public figures. These findings deserve a moment of attention here.

The difference in men's and women's storytelling, most simply, was that men acted in resistance because they "know" something to be true, while women "felt" or "watched" or "responded" to the truth of something. Most of the men I spoke with said that they decided to cross a line or spill blood at a nuclear site because of what they "know." They rationalized their actions through explaining foreign policy and legal agreements, backed by relevant statistics and facts. Often, this process of legitimation was linked to a deeper analysis—describing the injustices in terms such as capitalist aggression, imperial politics, U.S. exceptionalism, and systemic racism. Ed Kinane, for instance, explained that he is an activist against foreign policy because "the U.S. has been so aggressively imperialist over the decades" and knowing this is "key to understanding so much of the world's problems."[47] For the men, the motivation to act came from an understanding of the "issues"—the real driving forces of U.S. policy and systems, while the impact of these policies on their own lives and feelings went unmentioned. Our discussions seemed to give the men a sense of satisfaction as they told me about what they did and why. In our interview, Karl Meyer said, "I admire Jesus, I admire Gandhi, but where they're wrong they're wrong, and where they're right they're right. I can tell the difference. I'm Karl Meyer."[48]

In contrast to such certainty, women described what they know in the language of feelings, perhaps mentioning the Geneva Conventions or a particular weapon system, but most often anchoring their stories in a sense of themselves—as a Christian, a mother, someone who cares about the future of the world. As Alice Gerard typically explained, "the reason I decided to cross, it was very personal."[49] Hence, and unlike the men, the specifics of particular policies (or even faith) was less important in what the women did. Instead, women—and especially lay women—spoke of their feelings, their experiences, and their personal motivations. These were expressed as core parts of why they did what they did, a relevant part of their discernment.

The difference in the two ways of telling stories can be subtle. For example, Kathleen Rumpf did not spell out the particulars of U.S. foreign policy when she told me why she participated in a Plowshares action. Her knowledge of the issues was demonstrated through acknowledging that a high chair in a soup kitchen is an (unacceptable) *consequence* of military spending.[50] As she watched "the face of the homeless change" in the 1980s, Kathleen personalized what she knew to be true politically. She acted in response to *this* knowledge; the personal experience and feeling of injustice. So, she acted "for" the homeless, but "because of" nuclear weapons. For women, it was often the emotional impact of particular policies that turned the tides, rather than the details of the policies themselves.

It is worth noting that the differences in the ways men and women spoke of their knowledge does not reflect a difference in what is actually known or felt by each group; the men *in general* are by no means more educated (or less feeling) about particular content than are the women *in general*. However, the valuation that the men gave knowledge and factual information was higher—they spoke to me as they would in a court of law: citing statistics, systems, and patterns—and they spoke with clear confidence. Women, on the other hand, spoke to me as a friend, a woman, a mother—reaching for emotional connection rather than factual mastery. (The difference may be most simply summed up as "I know this" versus "do you feel this?") Though both the men and women were deeply knowledgeable about the issues relevant to their action, *through how they told their stories*, women left open a potential to be criticized personally for their political actions, or delegitimized as "emotional" or "crazy" in their activism. By sticking to "the facts," on the other hand, men better closed off such pathways for argument or criticism. In this, unequal gender assumptions about who has legitimacy to act, who counts as knowledgeable, and who deserves attention and respect as a political actor may be subtly perpetuated.

In effect, the difference in the stories I was told reveals how the establishment of legitimacy can be a process that is itself gendered, as it furthers feminist observations around how women's access to power—and the forms of power that are accessible to women—are limited. Men, on the other hand, may easily claim power, and more diverse forms of power, readily.[51] Perhaps in their (seemingly unconscious) negotiations with this reality of gender difference, men portrayed themselves to be experts while women came across as "carers," each claiming power in a realm that is most accessible to their group. The nuns were more issue-oriented than the lay women, a pattern of difference between the women that holds throughout this research's findings.

Given the increasingly divergent paths that women and men experience from the moment of action onwards, this observation of gender differentiation marks an important nascent distinction, and merits notice.

PART II: THE DOINGS OF IDENTITY

Even when motivated by a deep faith life, alignment with a powerful movement, commitment to political and historical analysis and action, a sense of responsibility and privilege, and/or a conception of self that is suited to principles and rebellion, it still takes a lot of effort to align one's actions with one's ideals. The product of bridging what one knows with what one does is most visible in three sites: learning, the nonviolent lifestyle, and solidarity. In each site, justice action prisoners *do things* that demonstrate their commitment to identity-work, to living in alignment with their beliefs. This section explores more fully what comprises such work, as well as how such identities may be gained.

Learning: How They Know

Learning is a constant "doing" for justice action prisoners. Their worldviews are not mainstream, and the achievement of a counter-hegemonic knowledge is in and of itself evidence of a strong commitment to learning. As a group, justice action prisoners are committed to learning as a lifelong process. Knowledge and "the truth" are the backbones of discernment, and justice action prisoners are especially committed to staying updated around geo-politics and their faith.[52] Many justice action prisoners travel directly to sites of conflict, often on peace delegations, to learn about what is happening on the ground. Learning is also personal, and justice action prisoners come to know much about themselves—their values, capacities, and privileges, through their involvement in resistance.

What makes the information they gain radical and transformative is not necessarily revealed in the content itself, rather it is the way in which it is understood: the "counter-hegemonic" consciousness that makes sense of it. This way of knowing is required for high-risk activism, and may be gained in two ways: through traditional modes of learning (reading, attending lectures, taking college courses) and through experience (travel, work, belonging to certain communities, establishing personal contacts with like-minded others). Together, these can constitute an epistemology that is intentional, rather than based on social positioning. Indeed, very few of those I spoke with gained their social analysis through experience based on their own social location or traditional schooling, but rather achieved it through deliberate placement of themselves in alternative positions: geographic, social, and academic. Much of the work of gaining this analysis began during the process of discernment. It was consolidated, for everyone, through the experience of prison.

The learning that occurs happens as both a life-long process and as "ah-ha" moments. It is reinforced through experience. Current events, ongoing wars, prosecution of whistle-blowers, and political repression reinforce the analysis of justice action prisoners, while prison provides the ultimate validation that their analysis is correct.

Direct experience comprises much of the learning sought out by justice action prisoners. International travel to conflict zones (such as Nicaragua, Haiti, and Yemen) are key to their understandings of how U.S. policies affect people across the globe. Several participants spoke of their work among the poor in the United States, and of more fully realizing the daily challenges of the immigrant, the day laborer, or the homeless through spending extensive time with these groups. In such ways, justice action prisoners became more aware of the structural injustices (racism, capitalism, prejudice) that systemically perpetuate poverty and oppression within individual people's lives, which further readies them for resistance.

Kathy Kelly described the mandate to "know" through personal experience clearly. She told me that she needs to "stand alongside" those affected by U.S. policies to understand how they experience it. In places such as Gaza, Afghanistan, and Iraq, Kathy has lived in the refugee camps and villages of the working class and poor for months at a time, to learn the "real" effects of war and poverty in those places. She contrasts her approach with the "intelligence" gained by drones—information that is disconnected from human lives and, consequently, smooths the path for the dehumanization that is necessary for military interference. When she is home in Chicago, Kathy works tirelessly to share what she learns elsewhere, through prolific writing and speaking. Most basically, her activist project is powered by her commitment to grounded, human, and better understandings, for herself and for others.[53]

Experience is strengthened when people have a personal connection with someone affected by violence. Alice Gerard was galvanized to action by the 1989 kidnapping and torture of a woman she met at a language school in Guatemala—Urseline Sister Dianna Ortiz. Sister Ortiz was brutalized by SOA-trained military personnel directed by a North American officer.[54] Alice subsequently served 18 months for three separate SOA Watch actions, actions she carried out "for" Sister Dianna.[55] Similarly, Reverend Kenneth Kennon still feels angry when he thinks about the Nicaraguan woman he met in Tucson whose husband's body was returned to her street in hundreds of tiny pieces.[56] Such personal connections move people to action because they provide certainty in the underlining of what they know. After this sort of direct experience, justice action prisoners feel like they better understand the horror of what they protest. It is something that simply cannot be ignored.

Those with personal connections to those most affected make up the critical core of recidivist activists; only a few vowed religious in this research did not discuss personal experiences in their rationales for staying active in the movements over the long haul. Indeed, there are not many recidivists who are not clergy or otherwise involved in the lives of those they work with and for. Close and intentional experience with a dramatically different way of living is thus hugely correlated with the capacity to "know" like an activist ready to commit to prison.

Some participants described an "ah-ha" moment as key in their discernment process—a "moral shock" in the parlance of social movements.[57] In such a moment, various pieces of knowledge come together and the reality of a situation may become suddenly clear, making available a new course of action or life-path. Participant Tom Mahedy remembered that, for a time, he denied the links between the U.S. military in which he had served and the wars in Central America that he was hearing about through his church. In 1982, however, a few El Salvadorian Mothers of the Disappeared spoke at his church and he allowed himself to wonder, "what if they are telling the truth?"[58] Allowing himself to *answer* this question changed his life, and resistance became a matter of when and how to resist the SOA, as doing so became inevitable. Similarly, Jack Gilroy had an "epiphany" as a young soldier in Vienna, when he realized that he could not "hate" the young Russian soldiers meant to personify the epitome of evil to the American troops. After this moment, he was never a "good soldier" again.[59]

Whether through faith, reading, personal connection, travel, or a life-altering moment, at some point justice action prisoners begin to see differently, and they cannot go back to their "regular" selves afterwards. As Kathleen Rumpf explained, "I see the people who don't matter, I see through their eyes."[60] Seeing this way shifts justice action prisoners' understanding of the world as it mandates their resistance, and it fortifies them to stay involved over the long haul.

The Nonviolent Lifestyle

For many justice action prisoners, and particularly the religious, the primary labor of living in alignment is structural—it is in how they organize their lives. Social movement scholars refer to "biographical availability" as vital to enabling participation in social movements, and justice action prisoners are often strategic about prioritizing their own availability for action.[61] Indeed, a "nonviolent lifestyle" is foundational to being able to engage in prison witness; the risk of lengthy incarceration mandates that rent, childcare, work obligations, and so on are at least flexible. In a personal email, Ed Kinane wrote that "most of my discernment has come in shaping my lifestyle so as to be available for my style of activism." In other words, his life is organized to enable his activism, just as a Catholic Worker or member of the clergy has organized their life to maximize their potential for service. For Ed, this lifestyle involves not owning a car, keeping the heater turned down during the central New York winter, and earning so little money that he does not have to pay federal taxes (which simultaneously prevents his financial support to the war-state). For Fr. Bill Frankel-Streit, the commitment to resistance required leaving the priesthood in 1988, to "put my body where my mouth is, and join the Catholic Worker." For Sr. Dorothy Pagosa, it meant becoming a sister in her 40s, and adding a vow of nonviolence to her promises of chastity, obedience, and poverty.[62] Living in poverty, in community, as a Catholic Worker, priest, or sister is an intentional choice that facilitates more extreme methods of resistance and partly explains why there are so many vowed religious in these movements. The "nonviolent lifestyle," then, is not ancillary to resistance actions, but integral to it. For those who have done the organizing lifework of being an activist, the space between "regular life," radical activism, and incarceration is narrowed. For example, several of the priests I spoke with described their prison cells as did Fr. Louis Vitale, as a "monk's cell."[63] For the priests, incarceration is viewed as a seamless (if stressful) continuation of their life of service, their lives are structured to include high-risk activism.

On the other side of this, for those who are unable or unwilling to commit to such a lifestyle, the costs of participation in prison witness are higher. For those living more "mainstream" lives, going to prison, in particular, exacts a higher toll, and this is especially true for the parents (particularly of young children). For younger people working and with families, six months in jail is experienced as a significant sacrifice financially, emotionally, and professionally.[64] For vowed religious, those living in community, and those without young children, the same six months are typically smoother; with lesser impacts on family members and careers, and less traumatic challenges.

It is also easier for the priests, sisters, "professional" activists, and Catholic Workers to "step back into the same stream" upon release than it is for those for whom incarceration represented a total "break."[65] Voluntarily living in poverty or returning from decades as a missionary in Africa are ways of living that ease the disruption of prison, but it is important to remember that these are not inevitable ways of living. A nonviolent lifestyle is a choice—a serious, consequential, and daily choice—and at the core represents a labor of identity alignment.

Another way to align one's identity with one's values is to live in community, as in sharing living space with people other than family. According to my participants—and particularly among Plowshares activists—living in community provides the support necessary (religious, financial, moral, intellectual) to engage in resistance, as it facilitates the "social analysis" needed for direct action. Community is "the key to all of it," according to Ellen Grady.[66] Ellen's sister Clare explained that one's community is the group with whom one is "conspiring." She continued, "It's a dirty word, in the legal system, but it's actually quite beautiful. Con-spiring. Breathing together."[67] Community is "where we get the vision," according to Liz McAlister, and in the Plowshares tradition, community is considered essential for clear discernment.[68]

Living in community is also helpful for how it can provide personal nurturing and logistical support during incarceration. Sr. Carol Gilbert explained that living in community is a "mandate" for members of Jonah House, as resistance is simply "too hard" to keep up on one's own.[69] This insistence on community is supported by scholarship. In her study of Plowshares, Sharon Nepstad shows that community is the key element that enables activists to participate over the "long haul."[70]

Living in community does more than clarify thinking and provide childcare during periods of incarceration, however. It also tests one's capacity to live nonviolently, in the sense of right means contributing toward right ends. In community, individuals cannot escape the work of "disarming" their "own hearts." John Heid explained:

> Community. The image that comes to mind is, it's like the grist-mill. And it's a constant reminder, and I did get this from Phil (Berrigan), of all the things that we struggle with in a privileged first world culture. It's not exclusive to us . . . it's *dramatized* for us. . . . So the attachment that we have to ego and to power, to control my things, *my* laptop, *my* bicycle . . . that gets a regular workout and requires . . . a letting go. . . . Community is absolutely essential for the work that I want to do. . . . Intentional community is . . . an ongoing workout. (It is) a lot of work, and it forces you to work within yourself.[71]

Hence, community enables a lifestyle that is more consistent with one's (anti-capitalist, nonviolent, Christian) values. Living in community is both a form of resistance and a personal exercise—getting us closer to the world we want to live in, and providing ongoing opportunities to practice being the person we most want to be.

John explained the practice that comes from living in community simply, as "letting go" of attachment to things. Sharing communal values, items, and spaces is not easy. He laughed as he remembered Phil Berrigan saying, "Almost any one of us can be angelic in front of the Pentagon." John continued, "it is easy to be an exemplary model of nonviolent disarmament . . . on the picket line . . . and then go home and find something out of order and be apoplectic." Thus, community helps with consistency; it shows weak spots and provides opportunities to get better at nonviolence. This allegiance to being nonviolent involves every aspect of activists' lives, and requires constant effort. But community is also fun. Much of this "fun" comes from the people with whom one interacts—as Lois Putzier, explained, "you meet nicer people than you'd meet elsewhere, that's all there is to it."[72]

For the devoutly committed (and particularly for those inspired by a path of principled nonviolence), communal living is invaluable for the personal work that it facilitates and forces, as well as for the political stand that it makes. Fr. Steve Kelly thinks that the work of community is a deeper act of resistance, in the context of a capitalist status-quo, than are many acts of disarmament: it is radical and important to forego a culture of individualism, competition, and self-focus. In itself, then, living in community is resistant action.[73]

PART III: SOLIDARITY

Most basically, identity-work is the labor of aligning one's actions with one's ideals around "who I want to be." For most justice action prisoners, being a "good person" is meaningful only through implementation—through how one lives one's life on a daily basis. This is enacted through learning and experience, the "nonviolent lifestyle," and the development of community, and it is recognized in the activation of social privilege and responsibility—but everything comes together around acts of solidarity.[74]

Plowshares does not consider itself to be a solidarity movement, but rather works on behalf of all creation (its own form of working alongside and working for). However, SOA Watch explicitly names itself a solidarity movement, and strives to activate what Roy Bourgeois learned in La Paz, Bolivia, as a missionary priest there in the 1970s. In Bolivia, Bourgeois writes, solidarity 'meant to accompany' and 'to walk with.' To be in solidarity means to make another's struggle for justice, peace, and equality *your* struggle."[75] This form of solidarity is known as "accompaniment"—what archbishop Oscar Romero termed "acompañamiento." Accompaniment can occur when more privileged people live among those they are committed to protecting (as with the delegations from Witness for Peace or Peace Brigades International), and it can also mean doing supportive political work in the U.S. (such as protesting the SOA). The idea of accompaniment is for more privileged people to support the agency and agenda of those most affected by violence, but never to take a leadership role. Rather, one is acting alongside as a protective force, a warning, or a form of message legitimization and amplification.[76] One acts in solidarity with others when one is not the target of violence oneself, but *alongside* those who are its targets, and with whom one works *against* violence. Chandra Russo articulates "solidarity witness" as a "practice" to contest state violence, a way to make others see what is often obscured.[77]

Most justice action prisoners engage in solidarity actions as "advantaged group allies" (AGAs), in social movement parlance, people who work "for the benefit of a group to which they are outsiders."[78] In other words, they do not act to further their own individual or group needs, but to contribute as an ally—a helper or a friend. Most commonly, advantaged group allies are privileged in ways that movement beneficiaries are not, and are drawn to the work because of conviction rather than personal experience. They are not the most directly affected, but they participate because of their belief systems, their caring about the issues or the people, a specific experience, or their own self-concept. At its best, solidarity is not about doing something "for" another, but it is about building power, through relationships. For instance, through accompaniment one may "transfer" some of the "benefits of their privilege" to those who do not have it.[79]

Solidarity actions are appropriate in a world structured by inequalities, and they are complicated. Complicated because, in the same moment, they both rely upon *and* protest hierarchies that privilege and oppress different groups of people. By "using" privilege (such as whiteness) to protest violence (such as imperialism), activists may reify the racialized hierarchy. Feminists, Black, Indigenous, and people of color (BIPOC) activists, as well as many scholars, have argued that engaging in solidarity "on behalf of" others has the potential to magnify power differentials rather than to challenge them, as attempts at solidarity may replicate or strengthen the unjust colonial relations that have created these systems in the first place.[80] To be a self-conscious and accountable person, alongside "different" others, is hence its own form of labor—one that is intellectual, embodied, reflective, and intentional. The final part of "identity-work," then, is around what it means to be a good ally, in acts of solidarity with others who are dissimilar to (and usually less privileged than) oneself.

The fundamental challenge of solidarity is present in the very etymology of the word, which is defined as the "union or fellowship arising from common responsibilities and interests, as between members of a group or between classes, peoples."[81] So it is about working towards a common purpose, with other people who are "like" you. Herein lies the central difficulty of border-crossing solidarity work: what if the people you are working with are *not* members of your "group"? How, in a world structured by inequalities, do we cross borders (along lines of geography, but also lines of identity, status, and power) without relying upon and strengthening unequal relations? (How) can we act as allies when one group has access to resources, safety, legitimacy, and possibilities for resistance while those most affected do not? Questions around how to work together—across difference, towards common goals, without reinforcing the oppressive patterns that border-crossing work can often produce—are not limited to international solidarity work, but are daily present in coalitions of all kinds, and they spring partly from issues around identity.

For transnational feminists, theorizing solidarity in connection with identity has been critical scholarship, wherein solidarity is recognized as an essential but also dangerous undertaking.[82] At the same time, "coalition"—sisterhood, and community—are central feminist commitments toward liberatory trans-formation. Solidarity, then, *must* be deployed—but only through a "flexible" sense of personal identity, a sense of oneself as shaped by one's context and location within identity categories (race, class, gender, etc.), rather than essentialized categories such as "oppressed woman." Such flexible identities are "political"—i.e., changeable and strategic, and are crafted to be "equally accountable" to those near and far.[83] The coalitions that are built from such a notion of self are not built on "sameness" (we are all women!) but on shared struggles and experiences (we all experience oppressions of patri-archy) and through shared commitments towards common goals (we work together because we all care about such-and-such).[84] In these ways, solidarity is accomplished through who we *are* and what we *do,* as informed by what we *know*, but not through some fossilized idea of "us" helping "them."[85] Engaging in solidarity work, then, must be an iterative and reflective process: about oneself, one's compatriots, one's context and history, the effect (and not just intent) of one's specific actions, and a multi-layered understanding of whom one is working with and for.

Knowing that we live in an unfair world where "acting" as a privileged person risks enlivening inequalities is daunting. It is challenging, but it should not be a pass for privileged people to do nothing. The solution to eroding oppressive power hierarchies cannot be for those with the most power to feel helpless or afraid to act lest they mis-step; people of privilege must still do something. It is an imperfect tool, but when they do so carefully, people *can* use their privilege to help further justice-oriented goals. However, privileged people must proceed with a savvy understanding of what they are actually doing and activating in their efforts, both intentionally and not. In researching this book, I met many justice action prisoners who understood and accounted for the risks involved in engaging, as privileged people, in solidarity activism across borders of geography and power—and had decided to act anyways. They knew that they would invariably mess up. They also understood that only through their continual efforts, reflections, and *actions* could they help create change, and they were committed to learning better ways of doing things.

Solidarity is a deeply good idea; however, actually engaging in solidar-ity activism is individually, interpersonally, historically, and politically complicated. Specifically, one must understand the implications of "who" one is (in relation to those one is working alongside and in what context), and how this identity matters—but not to get too hung up on "me." Grounding solidarity activism in identity-work is thus a crucial first step to doing solidarity "well," one that justice action prisoners must undertake with clarity, tenacity, and their usual conviction.

SOA Watch and Plowshares Conceptions of Solidarity

Both the SOA Watch and Plowshares may be thought of as "solidarity" movements, in that they do work "on behalf of" others. Plowshares does not identify as a solidarity movement, but grounds their actions in phrases such as, "I do this for the world's children." On the other hand, SOA Watch explicitly protests on behalf of those most affected by U.S. policies (such as campesinos in Latin America) in intentional acts of solidarity. SOA Watch activists engage as U.S. citizens who feel responsible, and because those most affected are unable to safely lodge their own resistance; they need someone to "speak for" them.

Plowshares

For those involved in Plowshares, border-crossing solidarity is not a central organizing concept. Instead, it is a disarmament movement, struggling to clear the world of nuclear weapons. Plowshares actions are not carried out "on behalf of" a particular affected group, but as an all-out effort to save the planet and its inhabitants from total destruction. In this way of thinking, differences between people are less important than the fact of their human-ness, and their human vulnerability. Saving the planet from nuclear annihilation is bigger than the individual, or of one's specific (racial, ethnic, national, religious) group. We are all threatened by nuclear weapons and nuclear technology, and "all" must be protected.

This commitment to protecting humanity is centered in an identity shared by many Plowshares activists: as Catholics who are inspired to activism by principles of faith. From this perspective, solidarity is a Christian notion of "one-ness" that embraces everyone as part of the same human "family." Sr. Ardeth Platte explained:

> We really do believe deeply in a God that made a whole family of people across the world . . . a lot of people don't see it that way. They don't look at the Iraqi people as their brothers or sisters, or the Syrians as our brothers or sisters, or the Iranians. They *are* our brothers and sisters. They *are* the people we love.

Why would you ever consider doing this, severance of this community, within the family of God?[86]

Susan Crane reinforced this idea when she relayed a remarkable exchange with one of her prison guards from when she was housed at the Federal Correctional Institution (FCI) in Dublin, CA. A returned veteran from the second war in Iraq, the guard was interested in Susan's story and often engaged her in conversation. One day, he came to her and said, "I get it now," in reference to the difference in their thinking. He explained, "you think all life is sacred, and I think American life is more sacred."[87] This idea of "all life is sacred," of a shared humanity, underlies Plowshares philosophy. The philosophy argues that humanity will improve, as a whole, in a world freed from nuclear weapons via the enactment of principled nonviolence

With this focus on "one-ness," Plowshares activists are generally less thoughtful about the dynamics of power at play in their actions than are SOA Watch activists, a reality that reflects the principles of their movements. For Plowshares, there is reason for this: in the face of nuclear weapons, power differentials between people are really not that important—detonated bombs do not discriminate between the haves and the have-nots. This doesn't mean that Plowshares activists are unaware of power relations generally (indeed, several spoke carefully around issues of privilege and power in other realms); however, there is no need to center them in their actions.[88] As a result, solidarity remains a simple, core Christian concept of taking on others' struggles as if they were your own, entailing both empathy and action. In enacting it, Plowshares activists generally do not take on issues of identity, politics, and discrimination.

School of the Americas Watch

I interviewed Brian DeRouen during the 2011 conference at Fort Benning. In our few hours together, he shared stories that encapsulate much of the thinking behind SOA Watch notions of solidarity; as a practice, a method, a goal, and a way of being. Thus, I ground this section in his voice. Of his experience protesting the SOA, Brian said:

> How many actions in this country today can you take that will put you in solidarity with felons and their families, would engage your family . . . any classroom you walk into . . . with prisoners and guards, it's really a unique option. . . . And by crossing the line, folks are interested. They ask you, "what was prison like?" And 45 minutes later, they're still listening, but now you're talking about Gandhi in South Africa, and they are still engaged. Whereas if you just walked up and said "you want to talk about nonviolence?" They'd be like "hell no."[89]

Brian's words immediately expand common thinking about solidarity activism—and certainly stretch it beyond Plowshares notions. Yes, it is about the campesino in Nicaragua, but it is also about what happens *here.* It is a method of activism (working together), but it is also a goal in itself. For Brian, solidarity is an ongoing project that is about creating relationships with students in U.S. classrooms as well as the prison guards who hold him captive. For him, prison witness is a pragmatic nonviolent strategy that forges connection and keeps unlikely conversations going.

Brian's commitments are exemplified in his tattoo: his right calf is green with the ink of the word "nonviolence" in 27 languages. The tattoo is "another one of those tactics," he explains. It is a "way to connect with people" and allow them to learn without intending to. "They just want to know about tattoos, and 40 minutes later, they're learning about Cesar Chavez. . . . It's a human connection. You have a tattoo and they have a tattoo and they want to know about it."

Enabling unlikely connections is clearly one of Brian's strengths, and he sees himself as particularly well positioned to connect dots for residents of his suburban childhood home in Walnut Creek, CA with what he knows about prison. Through his own incarceration, Brian was able to see how "false" the "divisions" are between people, a schism he was able to make visible for his family and community:

> (My parents) got to . . . have their world turned upside down. . . . By (my mom) being in that visitation room . . . and becoming friends with a "real" criminal . . . she realized, but he's a father! . . . And he is just like me. . . . I think that's one of the hardest connections for our culture to make. I mean, "I'm good and they're bad." But when you're in that visitation room, it's impossible. It's impossible to maintain that.

In this way, Brian used prison as a strategy of translation, a way to "connect my whole upper middle class, suburban world" to what happens in America's prisons. People would have "never known" about it otherwise, but he was a messenger they could hear. Through his stories of "this is what I am eating, this is what I am thinking," he humanized incarceration for a segment of the public usually guarded from knowing about it.

Hence, for Brian, solidarity—in the sense of forging human connections—is the goal of activism, rather than its "method." Those he hopes to reach are not just those affected by the school whose existence he protests, but everyone he meets. Going to jail is a tactic, talking about a tattoo is a way to educate others about social justice issues, being a justice action prisoner is a way to be "sexy" enough to be published in the newspaper or listened to in a classroom—he uses the tools available to him to bond with people as he challenges what they know.

For others involved in the struggle to close the School of the Americas, solidarity is often the motivation for action. In this, SOA Watch mirrors Plowshares. When I asked her why she crossed the line, Lois Putzier said bluntly, "I really love these people, so it makes it easier to help them. You would help your own children."[90] Michael Pasquale's trial statement was framed around the idea that "if the most important commandment is to love my neighbors, these people are my neighbors. Therefore, we need to treat them as such."[91] The effect of such rationales is to narrow the genetic and geographic gap separating Lois and Michael from their family and neighbors, by *acting as if* blood-relation and proximity are not the crucial elements for what constitutes family and neighborliness. This move explodes the concept of whom we are responsible to, as it makes it necessary to resist institutions and practices that harm *anyone*.

The Liberation Theology proselytized by Fr. Luis Barrios further reinforces solidarity as a motivating reason for action. He said, "Solidarity is the most important sacrament. It's not going to church, it's not taking the communion, it's not baptizing, it's not marriage. No. It's how I deal with relationships with other people that can bring more people to the table instead of excluding them."[92] For those who protest the SOA, it is imperative that solidarity be a "way of living" rather than just thinking, which is why prison witness is their chosen tactic: it is a way to *do* something. In his travels, Ed Kinane explained, "I had seen the terrorism" caused by imperial U.S. policy, and so it seemed "logical to go upstream and see the source of where all those bodies were coming from." Going "upstream" led him to the SOA, and he ultimately served 18 months in prison, for three separate offenses, in consequence of protesting it.[93]

Often, the people I spoke with had some experience prior to activism in which they felt a sense of solidarity. Somewhere along their life path, they had met people who were different than themselves, and they were changed by the experience. This was most clearly revealed through a story told by Reverend Ken Kennon, a former pastor of the Christian Church of Disciples of Christ in Tucson, Arizona.

In 1980, Reverend Kennon's 23-year-old son died in an accident. The pain of this, he told me carefully, was "so wrenching, it shakes me today." After losing his son, Reverend Kennon began to work with Central American refugees traveling through Tucson as they fled the bloody U.S.-funded civil wars in their home countries. This work "completely changed my life," he said.

> It just boggled my mind that people could go on living, because my child had died by accident and theirs had been taken from them in such a horrible way.

So there was a way in which I was opened to their pain. . . . They became my teachers, they helped me to understand what it means to be a human being and what's truly important, and what isn't.[94]

The solidarity that Ken describes is based on a profound sense of connection with other people, forged in pain. He was "opened" to their pain—not "open" as in available, but "opened." Opened-up, laid raw: his pain and theirs not confined to their individual bodies but overflowing them, finding solace in relationships and recognizing the familiar in a new face. It is "solidarity in action"—fellowship arising from similar interests, and from a shared experience of pain. The road it paved for Reverend Kennon brought him directly through the gates of the SOA.

For SOA Watch participants, solidarity is a core commitment. It has been critically discussed within the movement since its inception. This depth of heartfelt and intellectual engagement shows in the ways people talk about it—it is an organizing principle of their experience. The scholarly work of Sara Koopman, a feminist geographer who has also been an activist with SOA Watch, demonstrates this commitment.[95] Specifically, Koopman is interested in white women prisoners of conscience (the term used by SOA Watch for justice action prisoners), women who are idealized as "good" but in their solidarity actions may reinforce a colonial role of "helper" that strengthens global patterns of domination. Koopman's prescriptions are reflected in this book's findings, which show many justice action prisoners in the movement to be consistently focused on challenging their own "imperialism within" (internal work and awareness that is at least partially a response to Koopman's scholarship). Of course this does not mean that everything is perfect—but the fact that such earnest work challenging hierarchies of power and self-identifications has been taken up demonstrates the movement's commitment to learning, and to doing better.

As the beneficiaries of empire, justice action prisoners involved in SOA Watch told me that it is precisely U.S. citizens who should protest U.S. policies that harm people in other parts of the world—their location mandates resistance "on behalf of" others. I was repeatedly told that privileged, white Americans are poised to do this: they have the power, the resources, and the responsibility, and their protest carries more legitimacy and force than would similar actions performed by more marginalized people. Sr. Megan Rice was typical when she told me, "I'm privileged and I've got to do it. This is my responsibility, and I'm free to do it."[96] At the same time, there were also expressions of awareness that such activism relies upon unequal relations and, in particular, colonial "white man's burden" gestures of "rescue."[97] Making space for two contradictory truths while maintaining the wherewithal to act is a notable accomplishment of the SOA Watch activists included in this book. The next section looks at one area in which this work specifically happens, the act of "speaking for."

Challenges of Solidarity: "Speaking For"

As privileged North Americans striving to make violence visible, justice action prisoners occupy an unusual position: through their activism, they can be legitimized as valid speakers for social and political issues, but they do not speak about issues that necessarily affect their own lives. This marks their work, immediately, as efforts of "solidarity"—and specifically, as acts of "speaking for" others. Many of the SOA Watch participants included here used the language of "speaking for"; it is a powerful trope in that movement, but it is also important for Plowshares. As Kathleen Rumpf explained, she took a hammer and banged on a B-52 "on behalf of the homeless," and from the space of the courtroom was able to speak "for" them, about the issues that most affect them. In this, she was the medium of action, but not the message.[98]

Embodying resistance as a speaker *for* others is riddled by the same dilemmas as border-crossing solidarity. As such, *how* justice action prisoners speak—on whose behalf and with what understandings—is a window into their understanding of the operations of power more broadly. "Speaking"—authentically, as oneself, on behalf of others—is a crucial doing of identity-work, and it is also one of the most complex. In this seemingly simple act of *talking,* "speaking for" brings together the tricky issues of privilege, border-crossing solidarity activism, and personal identity-work.

For whom and what one speaks, from the self-constructed platform of "valid speaker," differs among justice action prisoners. For some, "speaking" is personal, and is simply about making one's position known; to oneself, one's leaders, the affected, or God. For this cohort, speaking through action is about being in alignment with one's values. As Clare Grady explained, Plowshares activists are not "asking the government" to do anything, they are just "doing what needs to be done."[99] Those who took this position were primarily Plowshares activists motivated by principled nonviolence (the means determine the ends) and their religious beliefs. They were insistent that what they did, they did *for themselves*—to be in alignment, to be faithful, to *do* what their knowledge and faith compelled them to do.

More commonly, and widely among SOA Watch activists, "speaking" is interpreted in the sense intended by Archbishop Romero, who preached that "we who have a voice must be a voice for the voiceless."[100] As privileged Americans, justice action prisoners are taking responsibility by speaking on behalf of those most affected by U.S. policies, and they are speaking because they *can*. Sr. Megan Rice (who crossed the line at Fort Benning and was part of the 2012 Transform Now Plowshares action) explained that she conducts her actions for those who have more "urgent" things to do: as a U.S. sister, she is supported and "able" to act in resistance.[101] Karl Meyer explained that he "uses the powerful tools" of nonviolence and his own privilege to make visible the injustices under which others suffer, but not to "speak for" them.[102]

In his interview, Randy Serraglio told me that he works to close the SOA for "the same reason why I want some little snail to survive in the Santa Rita mountains," referring to a campaign for the Center for Biological Diversity in Tucson, where he now works.

> It cannot speak for itself. . . . And that snail is the campesino in Guatemala. No one is going to speak for the snail . . . and someone has to, or the snail will disappear, and that's an injustice in my book. I don't think we have to make species go extinct to live on this planet, and I don't think we have to torture campesinos in Guatemala to live on this planet as United States citizens. It's the same principle.[103]

As Randy so directly expressed, some people are in such a precarious position that they cannot be heard, and someone "has to" speak for them or like the snail, they will "disappear." Prison witness is one way to do this work: imperfect, imprecise, and potentially dangerous, but also powerful, informative, and potentially transformational.

Speaking, Listening, and Liberation

One of the chief tasks of transnational feminism has been to illuminate problems around issues of representation. As Linda Martín Alcoff writes, feminism—like SOA Watch—"has a liberatory agenda that . . . requires that women scholars speak on behalf of other women."[104] In this effort, Alcoff promotes a "speaking to" as a way to represent without fetishizing, distancing, or silencing those we seek to speak *for*. She suggests four steps for the Western, privileged feminist to consider, steps that are just as applicable to activists involved in solidarity movements, both domestic and international.

First, Alcoff writes, we must analyze our motivation to speak and represent others, understanding that sometimes the most helpful and liberatory thing we can do is *listen*. Second, we must analyze the significance of our social identity categories (our political location) on what we believe and say. Third, we must be accountable for what we say, as well as for the effects our words will have (one's good intent is not enough). Finally, as the litmus test for all representation, we must ask ourselves, "will it enable the empowerment of oppressed peoples?" With these cautionary guidelines in mind, Alcoff suggests that we may venture to speak *for* others.

The first step in speaking-for comes in analyzing one's intent, and in listening.[105] Among the SOA Watch participants represented in this work, there was widespread commitment to "listening." Randy Serraglio told an exemplary story from his time as an organizer with the SOA Watch in the mid-1990s. At that time, the movement was working to "diversify" its participants, ensuring that people of color, women, and people from Latin America were put in positions of leadership. This meant having people affected by the school's policies speak prominently at the November vigil:

> Even if it was a pain in the ass to translate what they were saying, we were going to do it because that's what we're all about. We can speak for these people as long as we want, but the real point is, they need to be able to speak for themselves, and they need people to fucking listen to them. That's what we're aiming for here, right?[106]

Here, Randy shows that activists must close their mouths as they open their ears, and commit themselves to learning. Sr. Kathleen Desautels further explained that listening must happen in such a way that speakers can be truly heard, listening is not passive.[107] Hence, SOA Watch needs to get the people most affected by the school speaking, but *also* to ensure that the power dynamics underlying the relations between "activists" and "affected" are negotiated so that it is not just a "pain in the ass" for those most affected to speak. Rather, the goal is for activists (and others) to actually *hear* what they have to say.

Another way to center affected people's voices is through trial statements. SOA Watch activists have often used their opportunity to be memorialized in the public record by reading the words of those who have been harmed by the SOA. Decentering oneself, as one places another person's story and voice in the public record, is an innovative way to meet Alcoff's first mandate. Indeed, the SOA Watch activists included here largely seemed to understand that the acts of listening-to-learn, amplification, centering other people's voices, and decentering oneself are crucial to power-shifting solidarity work.

Alcoff's second and third steps mandate locating ourselves contextually; knowing where we "stand" in terms of geography, class, race, nationality, gender, etc.—and being accountable for the effects of our speech acts more broadly. These are precisely the questions that justice action prisoners struggle with when they take up issues of their privilege. In answering them, they find prison witness the required response to being "accountable" to their "location." In other words, they go to jail because they *have* asked these questions, and answered them in a way that expresses their culpability.

Sara Koopman offers several other concrete ways to enact Alcoff's recommendations around self-identity and accountability for activists with SOA

Watch, ideas that resonate with what I heard from many participants during interviews. These include an emphasis on accountability rather than guilt, using terms such as "those most affected" rather than "victims," striving toward being "true" rather than being "good," and being better "compas"— companions, comrades, and colleagues—rather than "helpers."[108] Koopman does not claim that hers is a sufficient recipe for responsible solidarity. Instead, what she finds essential is to begin one's border-crossing activism in one's own body: to confront the "imperialism within" as an ongoing challenge, rather than jumping in and "saving" others without attention to historical precedent, context, and entrenched relations of power.

In answer to Alcoff's important fourth question "will it enable the liberation of oppressed peoples?" the answer from SOA Watch—from a practical standpoint—must be "yes." Millions of people *are* now aware of the school and, to date, seven Latin American countries have ceased sending military personnel to the SOA. While the school itself remains open (and others like it operate un-hindered in covert locations around the world), there is no doubt that the pressure generated by the movement has been transformative to both the school and the activists involved. Though of course reliant on the "master's tool" of privilege, justice action prisoners do speak on behalf of others in the aim of liberation, and the movement consistently prioritizes the voices and experiences of those most affected.

For all privileged activists who are self-reflective in these ways, it is a continual challenge to negotiate one's privilege with one's responsibility to act. Sara Koopman is helpful in reminding us that our sphere of action is inherently imperfect, but that we still must start. She writes, "The master's house is taking up all of the land. If we are going to build a new house it has to be on this same plot, and most of our building materials will be recycled from his house. We cannot ignore his tools, or we will constantly trip over them; but we can dismantle and rework them."[109] In other words, the goal is not to continue speaking-for, but to go about the work of constructing another world—a world in which everyone may be empowered to speak (and be listened to) as themselves. From the framework of transnational feminism, justice action prisoners seem to be on the right track, where the work begins, but does not end, with "me."

Experience of Solidarity

Across both movements, I was repeatedly told, it is important to *experience* solidarity: to translate one's ideas and ideals into concrete action. For Kathy Kelly, solidarity means standing alongside people. "Real security," she explained during her interview, "is Afghans knowing other Americans. . . . It is important to be alongside ordinary people in times of war." For Kathy, this conception of "war" also describes the war "against the poor in the United States," hence going to prison is one way to be in solidarity with this nation's poor. "It's one thing," Kathy explained, "to feel a solidarity type relationship to someone who's been packed off to jail, but it's another to sit on the same bunk with the person . . . see the kids' pictures . . . this is a very, very different approach."[110] Kathleen Rumpf agreed. The women in U.S. prisons, she explained—connecting abuses across geographic lines to the same policies— "are the disappeared in this country."[111]

Solidarity can also be experienced during the direct actions themselves. For Derrlyn Tom, whose trespass at Fort Benning was inspired by her migrant students at Mission High School in San Francisco, the base fence symbolically represents the border fence. Hence, crossing the line gave her a deeper, more embodied understanding of what that fearful crossing meant for her students and their families. "It was just too tempting," she said of sneaking through the fence at Fort Benning, a temptation that was followed by the sense that "this is nothing . . . I'm risking nothing" in comparison to those who cross the U.S.-Mexico border.[112]

CONCLUSION

The decision to engage in prison witness is not a decision made easily, but is instead the result of lengthy processes of "discernment"—deciding what to do and where, and how to act in a way that resists injustice as it activates one's best self. The work of aligning one's identity with one's actions is not simple, and for most people in this book entailed life-shaping decisions, such as deciding to join the Catholic Worker, taking (or breaking) religious vows, or choosing a "nonviolent lifestyle"—perhaps in community with others. These decisions smoothed the way for people's significant decisions to act in resistance, acts intended to translate their faith life and intellectual knowledge into bold, embodied, and risky doings—performed with the expectation that they would lead to criminal trial and incarceration.

In their efforts to be good allies to others, and to use their privileged positions responsibly, justice action prisoners are active in a realm that is fraught and challenging: crossing lines of geography and power, using their positions of privilege to "help" and "speak for" those less able to do so, and engaging in a strategy that is personally challenging and dangerous. Of course, they do so with varying levels of sophistication and nuance. Overall, however, the participants in this book—and especially those from SOA Watch—expressed careful understandings of what it means to act in solidarity, with and for others. The work begins in identity-work and a real understanding of one's political location in a hierarchical world. Specifically, justice action prisoners explained their thinking around the politics of "speaking for," as well as their need to "experience" solidarity alongside others—to learn, understand, and amplify other people's stories, using the power of their privilege as a tool to do so.

To do this work—and to keep it up—is an ongoing and substantial personal labor. Prison witness is the chosen tactic of only a select few—hundreds of people in the U.S., not thousands—and the "work" that they do significantly begins at the level of identity. Indeed, this research finds that people participate in prison witness only after much learning, experience, and long thinking, about both who they are and what they know. Bringing their self-concepts into line with what they know about faith, history, and politics ultimately mandates resistance. Such interior and intellectual work is essential for effective and systemic nonviolent change, and is a critical piece in our understandings of the border-crossing, justice seeking, solidarity activism of justice action prisoners more broadly.

NOTES

1. Quoted in Riegle 2012a, 208. In the same book, John Dear explains the Christian version of discernment, which entails puzzling through "where the God of peace wants me to be." Discernment wonders "where is that place?" and what is that work? (Dear, quoted in Riegle 2012a, 105–106).

2. In determining whether or not to be arrested at the SOA, participant Michael Pasquale spent an academic year working through the ethics of civil resistance with his students at Le Moyne College, simultaneously committing his own Jesuit practice to the question (Interview by author, Syracuse, NY, March 27th, 2010). Sr. Mary Kay Flanigan "stared down" her fears for two weeks, and then realized "there's so much on the other side" (Interview by author, Chicago, IL, March 8th, 2012). In a private email dated July 4th, 2013, Fr. Steve Kelly explained that "99% of the witness is in the months preceding the action," wherein activists use "scripture and current assessments, evaluations of our culture" to determine how "one has to act in concert" with others and be "part of the solution." Discernment is the work of figuring out how to "embody where we are going."

3. David Snow and David McAdam, "Identity Work Processes in the Context of Social Moveents: Clarifying the Identity/Movement Nexus" in *Self, Identity, and Social Movements*, ed. Sheldon Stryker, et al. (Minneapolis: University of Minnesota Press, 2000), 46–47.

4. For example, see Kenneth Kennon, *Prisoner of Conscience: A Memoir*. Xlibris Corporation, 2002; Ed Kinane's articles on TruthOut, https://truthout.org/authors/ed-kinane/; Kathy Kelly's *Other Lands Have Dreams: From Baghdad to Pekin Prison*. Petrolia, CA: CounterPunch and AK Press, 2005, as well as her prolific articles for Voices in the Wilderness, https://www.marquette.edu/library/archives/Mss/VITW/VITW-sc.php; Karl Meyer's writings for *The Catholic Worker,* https://merton.

bellarmine.edu/collections/show/25; Liz McAlister's articles and letters, including for Jonah House, http://www.jonahhouse.org/archive/reflections.htm; and Brian Terrell's articles for Common Dreams, https://www.commondreams.org/author/brian-terrell.

5. McAlister, Kelly, and Grady Interviews. Also Sr. Ardeth Platte, interview by author, Baltimore, MD, April 13th, 2012.

6. Rumpf, interview.

7. Platte, interview; Elizabeth Deligio, interview by author, Chicago, IL, March 6th, 2012.

8. Gwin, interview.

9. Nepstad, *Catholic Social Activism*, 2019.

10. Jack Gilroy, interview by author, Interlaken, NY. February 8th, 2012.

11. Distantly seconded by Gandhi and Saul Alinsky—organizing texts that are more common among nonviolent activists globally.

12. Nepstad, *Plowshares,* 2008.

13. See Murray Polner, *Disarmed and Dangerous: The Radical Life and Times of Daniel and Philip Berrigan, Brothers in Religious Faith and Civil Disobedience* (Routledge, 2018); Philip Berrigan and Fred Wilcox. *Fighting the Lamb's War: Skirmishes with the American Empire* (Wipf and Stock Publishers, 2018); Philip Berrigan and Elizabeth McAlister, *The Time's Discipline: The Beatitudes and Nuclear Resistance* (Eugene, OR: Wipf and Stock Publishers, 2010).

14. Quoted in Ron Dart. "The Christian Prophetic Tradition." *Clarion Journal of Spirituality and Justice,* 2006. http://www.clarion-journal.com/ clarion_journal_of_ spirit/ 2006/06/the_christian_p.html.

15. Guenther Roth. "Socio-historical model and developmental theory: Charismatic community, charisma of reason and the counterculture." *American Sociological Review* (1975): 148–157.

16. Berrigan and Wilcox, *Fighting the Lamb's War*, 1996, 214.

17. Berrigan, interview.

18. Fr. Bill Frankel-Streit, quoted in Amy Biegelsen "Divining Providence: Bill and Sue Frankel-Streit are parents, Catholics, felons and anarchists. It's all part of their mission to serve God," *Style Weekly*, Richmond, VA. 05/05/2010, http://www.styleweekly.com/richmond/divining providence/ Content? oid=1369974.

19. Fr. Bill Frankel-Streit, interview with author, Camden, NJ, September 6th, 2010.

20. Quoted in Biegelsen, "Divining Providence," 2010.

21. Platte, interview.

22. Roy Bourgeois, "Excommunicated for 'Grave Scandal' of Ordaining Women," *Religion Dispatches*, 08/06/2013, http://www.religiondispatches.org/archive/ sexandgender/7237/.

23. Fr. Barrios, interview.

24. Tiffany, interview.

25. Meagan Doty, interview by author, Columbus, GA, November 19th, 2011.

26. Deligio, interview.

27. Fr. Frankel-Streit, interview.

28. Susan Crane, interview by author, Camden, NJ, September 5th, 2010.

29. Barrios, interview.

30. Nancy Gwin, interview by author, Syracuse, NY, March 13th, 2013.

31. Clare Grady, interview.

32. John Heid, interview by author, Tucson, AZ, May 15th, 2012.

33. Clare Grady, interview.

34. Rae Kramer, interview by author, Syracuse, NY, March 31, 2010.

35. Randy Serraglio, interview by author, Tucson, AZ, May 13th, 2012.

36. Julienne Oldfield, interview by author, Syracuse, NY, August 4th, 2010.

37. Sharon Nepstad. *Convictions of the Soul: Religion, Culture, and Agency in The Central America Solidarity Movement.* New York: Oxford University Press, 2004a; See also Nepstad 2008; Tobey, 2016.

38. Tobey 2016, 17.

39. Plowshares activists are sent off to prison after a "Festival of Hope," a celebration of their witness. SOA Watch POCs are regarded as celebrities in their movement.

40. Koopman, 2012a.

41. Putzier, interview.

42. Serraglio, interview.

43. John Heid, personal email, June 26th, 2021.

44. Liz McAlister, interview by author, Baltimore, MD, March 13th, 2012.

45. Quoted in Tobey, 2016, 89.

46. See Riegle, 2012a.

47. Kinane, interview.

48. Meyer, interview.

49. Alice Gerard, interview by author, Grand Island, NY. February 13th, 2012.

50. She remembered, "I came into a soup kitchen in Washington, DC, and there was a high chair in the kitchen. And I was like 'What? Wait! Wait!' Now it's commonplace, but I said, 'when did it become acceptable *in America* for children to be in soup kitchens and shelters and homeless?!'" (Rumpf, interview).

51. See Bertham Raven, "The Bases of Power: Origins and Recent Developments," *Journal of Social Issues* 49, no. 4 (1993): 227–251; Paula Johnson, "Women and Power: Toward a Theory of Effectiveness," *Journal of Social Issues* 32, no. 3 (1976): 99–110.

52. Plowshares actions are directed by what Sr. Carol Gilbert described as a profound "social analysis." The women at Jonah House read about and stay current with U.S. weapons policy, but they also watch *ABC News* together every night (to be "connected to the public"), and listen to Amy Goodman's radio program "Democracy Now" (to get the "real story"). From this variously and well-informed place, Carol explained, they discern appropriate resistance actions. (Gilbert, interview). Similarly, the annual vigil at the SOA has traditionally been preceded by two full days of conferencing, including seminars, trainings, and film screenings on subjects such as U.S. foreign policy, drones, the drug war, and nonviolence.

53. Kathy Kelly, interview by author, February 25th, 2012.

54. Katherine Seelye. "Dianna Ortiz, American Nun Tortured in Guatemala, Dies at 62." *The New York Times.* February 20th, 2021. https://www.nytimes.com/2021/02/20/us/dianna-ortiz-dead.html.

55. Gerard, interview.

56. Reverend Kenneth Kennon, interview by author. Tucson, AZ, May 13th, 2012.

57. Sharon Erickson Nepstad. "Oppositional Consciousness among the Privileged: Remaking Religion in the Central America Solidarity Movement." *Critical Sociology* 33, no. 4 (2007): 661–688.

58. Thomas Mahedy, interview by author, Columbus, GA, November 18th, 2011.

59. "I thought, 'what is this all about? I'm supposed to hate this kid?' . . . After that, I was no longer the good soldier." He has been an activist against American "imperialistic policies" ever since. (Gilroy interview)

60. Rumpf interview.

61. McAdam 1986; Kraig Beyerlein and Kelly Bergstrand. "Biographical availability." *The Wiley-Blackwell Encyclopedia of Social and Political Movements.* Edited by David A. Snow, Donatella della Porta, Bert Klandermans, and Doug McAdam (Oxford: Blackwell Publishing, 2013).

62. Kinane, Frankel-Streit, and Pagosa interviews.

63. Fr. Vitale interview.

64. The experience is different for lay women with families than it is for lay men (with or without families)—not to mention the vowed religious. At least nine of the twenty men I spoke with are fathers. Tom Mahedy, Ken Kennon, and Dan Sage spoke specifically of how their fatherhood role impacted their experiences. The ten mothers included described their children as painful to separate from, and as challenged by their activism. It is quite logical, then, that the "nonviolent lifestyle" (childless by choice, or waiting till the kids are grown) is an important piece of what makes resistance possible (assorted interviews).

65. Kinane interview.

66. Ellen Grady, interview by author, December 16th, 2011.

67. Clare Grady, interview.

68. McAlister, interview.

69. Sr. Carol Gilbert, interview by author, Baltimore, MD, April 13th, 2012.

70. Nepstad, *Religion and War Resistance*, 2008.

71. Heid, interview.

72. Lois Putzier, interview by author, Tucson, AZ, May 13th, 2012.

73. Fr. Kelly, interview.

74. Solidarity is a buzzword in activist circles today, but it is not a new idea or activist practice. From the Abolition Movement to Freedom Summer, the Sanctuary Movement to the Movement for Black Lives, solidarity has always been present in American activism, and has been crucial in the achievement of many progressive goals.

75. Roy Bourgeois. *My Journey from Silence to Solidarity.* Yellow Springs, OH: fxBear, 2013.

76. Accompaniment often relies on the protective presence of a person of privilege (a white citizen of the U.S. living alongside an indigenous human rights worker in Guatemala, for example) and works via deterrence. Though it relies on entrenched inequalities to be effective (white and POC, north and south, wealthy and poor), this form of solidarity can also cross lines of access and power well. In this form of solidarity action, the privileged member is present as a protective force, never an agent

of change. See Patrick Coy, "Shared risks and research dilemmas on a Peace Brigades International team in Sri Lanka," *Journal of Contemporary Ethnography* 30, no. 5 (2001): 575–606; and Coy, "We Use It but We Try Not to Abuse It": Nonviolent Protective Accompaniment and the Use of Ethnicity and Privilege by Peace Brigades International." In *Annual Meeting of the American Sociological Association, Washington, DC, August* (Vol. 13) 8/2000.

77. Russo, *Solidarity in Practice*, 2018, 21.

78. Daniel Myers. "Ally Identity: The Politically Gay" in *Identity Work in Social Movements*, ed. Jo Reger, Daniel Myers, and Rachel Einwohner, vol. 30 (University of Minnesota Press, 2008): 167–187.

79. Holiday Phillips, "Performative Allyship Is Deadly (Here's What to Do Instead)," *Forge*, 05/10/2020, https://forge.medium.com/performative-allyship-is-deadly-c900645d9f1f. For example, white allies who are part of native struggles have been reminded that they have more "leeway" with the police than do native people, so they should step forward when things get heated. White allies in other BIPOC struggles have been asked to "leverage" their privilege—to confront members of their in-group, as well as any social institutions that oppose social change. (Droogendyk).

80. See Ancestral Pride. "Everyone calls themselves an ally, until it is time to do some real ally shit." https://warriorpublications.files.wordpress.com/2014/01/ancestral_pride_zine.pdf; Ivan Boothe and Lee Smithey. "Privilege, Empowerment, and Nonviolent Intervention," *Peace & Change* 32, no. 1 (2007); Droogendyk, Lisa, Stephen C. Wright, Micah Lubensky, and Winnifred R. Louis. "Acting in solidarity: Cross-group contact between disadvantaged group members and advantaged group allies." *Journal of Social Issues* 72, no. 2 (2016): 315–334; Alicia Garza. "Ally or co-conspirator?: What it means to act #InSolidarity." 9/26/16. *Movement to End Violence*. https://movetoendviolence.org/blog/ally-co-conspirator-means-act-insolidarity/; Russo, Chandra. "Allies forging collective identity: Embodiment and emotions on the migrant trail." *Mobilization: An International Quarterly* 19, no. 1 (2014): 67–82; and Russo, *Solidarity in Practice*, 2018; Luna, Zakiya. "Who speaks for whom? (Mis)representation and authenticity in social movements." *Mobilization: An International Quarterly* 22, no. 4 (2017): 435–450.

81. "Solidarity." http://dictionary.reference.com/browse/solidarity

82. Linda Carty and Chandra Talpade Mohanty, eds. *Feminist Freedom Warriors: Genealogies, Justice, Politics, and Hope*. (Chicago: Haymarket Books, 2018); Anna Carastathis, "Identity categories as potential coalitions," *Signs: Journal of Women in Culture and Society* 38, no. 4 (2013): 941–965; Elizabeth Cole, "Coalitions as a model for intersectionality: From practice to theory," *Sex Roles* 59, no. 5–6 (2008): 443–453; Elizabeth Cole and Zakiya Luna, "Making Coalitions Work: Solidarity across Difference within US Feminism," *Feminist Studies* 36, no. 1 (2010): 71–98; Brenda Lyshaug, "Solidarity without 'Sisterhood'? Feminism and the Ethics of Coalition Building," *Politics & Gender* 2, no. 1 (2006): 77–100; Mohanty, *Feminism without Borders*, 2003; Bernice Johnson-Reagan, "Coalition Politics: Turning the Century" in *Home Girls: A Black Feminist Anthology*, ed. Beverly Smith (New Brunswick, NJ: Rutgers University Press, 1983).

83. Cole and Luna, "Making Coalitions Work," 2010.

84. Chandra Talpade Mohanty, "Social Justice and the Politics of Identity" in *The SAGE Handbook of Identities,* ed. Margaret Wetherell and Chandra Mohanty (London: SAGE Publications, 2010).

85. Cole and Luna, "Making Coalitions Work," 2010, 84. In a study of activists who work on solidarity projects, Elizabeth Cole and Zakiya Luna questioned twelve feminist activists about how to mitigate the risks involved in working in coalitions with others. The twelve advocated for feelings of "connection" with the oppressed combined with feelings of "accountability" as privileged individuals. What was needed among privileged activists was a broadening of recognition for "who" is recognized as part of "our" community. Scholar Andrea Smith, one of Cole and Luna's respondents, advised for feeling in "solidarity" with people in the third world "paired with a feeling of being culpable" as U.S. citizens.

86. Platte, interview.

87. Crane, interview.

88. For example, participants voiced a clear understanding that privilege is a *prerequisite* for the type of actions they conduct. As Sr. Ardeth said, "these are actions for privileged people to take." She told me that she engages in Plowshares actions—which benefit everyone on the planet if successful—because she is *able* to do so. She is not oppressed in ways that make her "daily struggles for survival," recognition, or safety take her daily attention. Nor is she oppressed in a way that makes the force of that oppression the necessary target of her activism; she is privileged enough to choose what to focus on. As a result, she has the "luxury" to work against nuclear weapons. Her ability to engage is predicated on her compound privilege, and she has no expectation that those who are less privileged should participate. (Platte, interview).

89. Brian DeRouen, interview by author, Columbus, GA, November 18th, 2011.

90. Putzier, interview.

91. Pasquale, interview.

92. Barrios, interview.

93. Kinane, interview.

94. Kennon, interview.

95. Sara Koopman, "Cutting through Topologies: Crossing Lines at the School of the Americas," *Antipode*, vol. 40, no. 5, 2008b: 825–847; Sara Koopman, "Field note: Columbus, Georgia, USA," *Americas* (2004).

96. Sr. Megan Rice, Solvay, NY, February 29th, 2012.

97. "I use it but try not to abuse it," Sr. Kathleen Desautels explained, while Sr. Dorothy Pagosa realized, when she did accompaniment work in El Salvador, that she needed to go home because "my role was to try and change U.S. policy." (Sr. Kathleen Desautels, interview by author, Chicago, IL, March 6th, 2012, and Sr. Dorothy Pagosa, interview by author, Chicago, IL, March 7th, 2012).

98. Rumpf, interview.

99. Clare Grady, interview.

100. Attributed.

101. Rice interview.

102. Meyer, interview.

103. Serraglio, interview.

104. Linda Alcoff. "The Problem of Speaking for Others," *Cultural Critique* 20 (1991): 5–32.

105. This idea is reinforced by activists involved in the Movement for Black Lives, in which white allies are asked to show up, to use their privilege to protect others, but also to "stay off the megaphone." See Ann Thurber, et al., "Staying Off the Megaphone and in the Movement: Cultivating Solidarity and Contesting Authority Among White Anti-Racist Activists," *Understanding and Dismantling Privilege* 5, no. 2 (2015): 1–20.

106. Serraglio, interview.

107. Sr. Desautels, interview.

108. Koopman 2008a.

109. Koopman 2008a, 299.

110. Kathy Kelly, interview.

111. Rumpf, interview.

112. Derrlyn Tom, interview by author, Washington, DC, April 14th, 2012.

Chapter 4

Embodiment, Privilege Power, and the Experience of Action

I was lying in bed one night, crying, and it got to the point where even that felt selfish to me. Because I still had a bed. . . . And I just realized, it's selfish even to cry in my bed. I have to start going out and crying in places where injustice stems from. And I started going to the White House. . . . I started going to prison and I was fearless, because it was very freeing for me to go to prison . . . I felt strength . . . I was speaking up for the people I loved, and cared so deeply about.—Rumpf (interview)

In nonviolent resistance, people use their bodies to protest the state. As Berkeley free-speech activist Mario Savio famously explained in 1964, when the "machine becomes so odious . . . you've got to put your bodies upon the gears and . . . and you've got to make it stop."[1] Nonviolent tactics, essentially, are ways of interfering with the smooth running of the "machine," ways to say "no" physically, with your body. The most wonderous thing about nonviolence is that *any* body can work in the effort. You do not have to be a young man to participate (as you do in most forms of military service)—or even an adult. You can be a grandparent, a child, a laborer, or an immigrant. In nonviolence theory, *every* body has power, for nonviolence works via the personal, anonymous, and voluntary "suffering" of those who resist.[2] In this understanding, the body is a neutral site and mode of political power, and transformative change occurs through what is called "people power"—the power of "regular people" *doing something* in the face of oppression and violence.[3] Nonviolence is hence theorized as a method of action for the powerless: it shuffles the cards and changes the game. Through the moral ju-jitsu of disciplined nonviolence, students can topple dictators.

While it is true that *any* body can participate in nonviolence, in a context of inequality—and especially for a technique as individualized as prison witness—it is misleading to say that "who we are" does not matter in what we can do, or that all bodies can work in the same ways. Instead, identity matters—easily evidenced by celebrities using their fame to bring attention to issues that they care about.[4] In the case of prison witness, which relies on individual action and a notion of "goodness" (for if we do not believe someone to be "good," their incarceration will not strike us as troublesome), "people power" is an inadequate analytic for understanding the actual mechanisms at work. Instead, we must include an evaluation of identity and, specifically, what I call "privilege power" to understand the dynamics of the protest action.

Privilege power is a potent mix of white skin, middle/upper class position, high levels of education, Christian/Catholic faith, heterosexuality/chaste status, and professional achievement that combine to make a person largely un-objectionable within the mainstream United States. Through their participation in high-risk activism, justice action prisoners' animations of privilege are revealing of how they understand and negotiate aspects of their own identities. As a group of predominantly white, well-educated, American citizens, the participants in this book often use privilege power intentionally, as a strategic part of their activism. They will strategically employ the status of the priestly collar, for example, to buy time and increase media attention toward movement goals. In this, one's privileged identity is deployed as a source of power and tool on which activists may rely.

A privileged identity is not only a resource that may be pulled from, it is also a filter that shapes and determines experience. This research shows that engaging in the same activities (action, arrest, trial, incarceration) can result in vastly different experiences for different people, ranging from pleasurable to terrifying, empowering to devastating. Of course, how activists make sense of their experiences is partly shaped by the movements to which they belong, as "good people," activists, Catholics, and so on. However, participants did not highlight these belongings. Neither did they discuss their own gender or religious identity as important, though these markers proved significant under analysis. Lay women described experiences that were similar to one another, while the vowed religious women, and most of the men, described a different form of similar experiences. Hence, we can say that "who we are" is partly formed through what we *experience* as real, as shaped by our visible identities.

This chapter has three parts, all connected to a conception of identity as it relates to nonviolent activism. The first part explores some of the ways in which justice action prisoners use their bodies in their actions—what it actually means to say that nonviolence is "embodied." The second part focuses on how a concept of social privilege shapes and motivates resistance for justice action prisoners, as well as how they may strategically use their own privilege to bolster and broaden the impact of their actions. The last part examines how identity matters through some of the ways it affects the activist experience itself. Specifically, the actual "moment of action" is found to be an experience that is shaped by identity and, in particular, gender and religious identity. The stories lay women told of the moment of action are most often personal, expressed as a "conversion" moment and contextualized within a culture described as patriarchal and unjust. In contrast, men and the vowed religious remain focused on the issues that drive them: militarism, imperialism, and God. The stability of these differences across participant identities reveals the ongoing role of systemic forces (and most significantly, patriarchy) in shaping both what we do and how we experience it, as well as how particular identities and communities of belonging can mitigate such forces.

PART I: EMBODIMENT

No matter which way you kind of dress it up, it comes out the same thing. You're putting your body, basically your political body, against the body politics. So you're just putting your body in the way, and that's what some nonviolent activists say is really your only weapon, the only weapon that you have.—Fr. Frankel-Streit (interview)

Nonviolent direct action is fundamentally a politics of the body; one puts one's body in a public space to express dissent, making the dissent visible and undeniable ("you can't ignore bodies," participant Ken Crowley explained).[5] Nonviolence theory takes account of what some activists call "somatic politics"—basically everything we communicate in forms other than words—as a form of power.[6] Through everyday people engaging in resistance, power is generated, shifted, transformed, and confronted. The body and power are thus already always connected: the body is an instrument of power, the medium that makes power visible, and the force that persuades change.

For the strategy of prison witness, in which a person performs an illegal action to be a witness against state violence, the centrality of the body is essential. Activists act symbolically, they sit, stand, "die in," "lie in," and walk. By putting their bodies where they do not ostensibly belong, the nonviolent actor highlights their own body's insecurity in an effort to make it (and others') more secure in the future.

This re-articulation of security at the level of the body is especially visible in Plowshares actions. Most often, Plowshares are enacted by elderly people—people in their 70s and 80s, often people with health problems— these "bumbling, bumbling people" in Ellen Grady's terms, who still manage to reach some of the most protected sites in the U.S. military.[7] For example, it took all night for the participants of the 2009 "Disarm Now" Plowshares action to reach their destination at SWFPAC, just a few miles into the base.

The group had to stop frequently for then 81-year-old Fr. Bix Bichsel to rest and take glycerin tablets for his heart problems. At 82, Sr. Megan Rice, along with Michael Walli and Gregory Boertje-Obed, were part of what nuclear experts called "the biggest security breach in the history of the nation's atomic complex" at Oak Ridge, TN. In this action, the three found their way to the U.S. "inner sanctum" of nuclear bomb parts and fuel. The *New York Times* reported:

> With flashlights and bolt cutters, the three pacifists defied barbed wire as well as armed guards, video cameras and motion sensors at the Oak Ridge nuclear reservation in Tennessee early on July 28, a Saturday. They splashed blood on the Highly Enriched Uranium Materials Facility—a new windowless, half-billion-dollar plant encircled by enormous guard towers—and hung banners outside its walls. . . . The plant holds the nation's main supply of highly enriched uranium, enough for thousands of nuclear weapons.[8]

The "Transform Now" action was an "embarrassment" for the Obama administration, and the trespassers were charged with destruction of property and sabotage. What most startled officials was Sr. Megan's presence, for what an 82-year-old nun's presence meant about militarized notions of security. By putting her body where it did not belong, Sr. Megan exposed the greatest military superpower on earth to be essentially insecure.

Quite basically, the activists' presence in such restricted (and dangerous) spaces highlights the *insecurity* brought about by nuclear weapons.[9] The strategy of nonviolence, in this sense, works by making the violence of the system, as well as the vulnerability of the body, visible. Remarkably often, the state (or other authority) responds to such nonviolent acts with force. This forceful response—to ordinary human beings asking for more secure lives—is itself part of what makes nonviolence "work." Indeed, provoking a violent response through nonviolent action is a powerful method in the nonviolent toolkit.[10]

As an embodied technique, nonviolent direct action includes "body stories."[11] These stories are about what happens to one's body in resistance, as well as how activists use their variously-identified bodies in symbolic ways to intensify their acts of protest. Activists often use their identities strategically. For example, they might rely on their motherhood, religious or professional status, appearance or costume, and so on to propel their messages, strengthen their moral legitimacy, and connect more fully with others.

Such identities are resources from which activists may gain power, and they may also create spaces to act in otherwise restricted contexts. Selina Gallo-Cruz has written about how their very "invisibility" as political subjects has allowed women in oppressive, conservative contexts to effectively act in resistance: because they are not perceived to be political subjects, their resistance goes unseen or unpunished. The Mothers of the Disappeared, for instance, is a movement that shows how women, through enacting their (traditional, mainstream, conservative) roles as "mothers," were able to organize and protest during the dictatorships in Chile and Argentina, while the men in their lives were being tortured, killed, and disappeared.[12]

Some of my favorite "body stories" came from Kathleen Rumpf, a septuagenarian member of the Catholic Worker now most active in the field of prison reform.[13] Kathleen has been arrested over 100 times ("so far"), for violations including those against the SOA, hammering on a B-2 bomber, and participating in the Killer Drone protests in Central New York. Liz McAlister once described Kathleen as "a one-woman crime wave"; she is a busy activist.[14] Kathleen uses humor as a way to break down barriers between herself and others. She often pleads innocent, "on behalf of governmental insanity." At the SOA, she "commits art." As a prisoner, she is part of the "injustice system," and her often raunchy jokes catch those of us expecting her to act the part of an old Catholic lady delightfully off-guard. She laughed when she told me about being arrested at Griffiss Air Force Base, where she asked one of the soldiers why the B-52s were called BUFFS. "He said, 'it means Big Ugly Fuckers.' And I looked at him and said, 'don't you ever call me that!'" Living as an over-400-pound woman for much of her life, Kathleen has been known to threaten arresting officers with the phrase "be nice, or I'll go limp!" Sometimes she plays the coquette: "I told you this is not my first time," she once teased an especially handsome officer who was surprised at the length of her rap sheet. At the Nevada Test Site, she led a group of women in the Hokey Pokey. She was a member of the 1982 Greenham Common/Seneca Peace Camp, an all-woman action that relied on symbolism of womanhood such as knitting, dancing, and singing to express their view that the presence of nuclear weapons makes women and children less safe, not safer, as the government claimed. In all of these ways, Kathleen consistently *uses* who she is—a fat, white, poor, American, Catholic woman, authentically and with purpose, to protest the state and its violence.

Her actions are personalized responses to what she experiences—living with the homeless on the Bowery, working with prisoners, being part of the working poor. They are symbolic and creative, and true to who she is. As such, they are inherently gendered. To protest state violence, she will cry in public. She dances, she sings. She pours blood, fasts, and uses her quick wit and gentleness to surprise, disarm, and connect with authorities. At the SOA in 1998, she helped spray-paint the entrance sign to read "School of the Americas, School of Shame." When the arresting officers arrived, she began singing to them, calling out "It ain't over till the fat woman sings!" In such ways, she plays with who she is to challenge, upset, lighten, and humanize the dark spaces she has dedicated her life to illuminating and transforming.

Not surprisingly, public responses to her actions are also personalized, as well as gendered. Most tellingly, she is discounted as a "crazy lady." For example, late one night during a 2010 action at the Syracuse Justice Center (she lived in a metal cage for a week to protest the jail's conditions), mounted police called in a 5150—the code for someone experiencing a mental health crisis, as an intentional form of harassment. During our interview, Kathleen recalled an action in the early 1980s, when she sat by herself for a weeklong hunger strike on the steps of the Pentagon. Vulnerable, alone, and hungry, she held a sign reading "It is a sin to build a nuclear weapon." After several days, the "meanest general" quipped to her, "it is a sin to be a glutton." She wept, because "he had thought for a week about what to say, to hurt me. And he did." These reactions—like the actions themselves—are not directly "political," but personal. However, the fact that they "work" as political protest, *as well as* messages of harm, exemplifies the feminist dictum that "the personal is political." They cannot be pulled apart.

In retrospective, the life-work of Kathleen Rumpf shows that her protest is always embodied; it looks the way it does because *she* looks the way she does. The form of her resistance, as well as how it has been understood, publicized, and criticized, reflects the authentic use of her identity—and very literally, her body—as messenger, medium, and message.

Ellen Grady described another variant of the strategic use of (gendered) identity in resistance action, and what it means to protest nuclear weapons as a woman in the United States. She recalled a 1980 action at the Pentagon:

> We watched the film Hiroshima Nagasaki. (My mom) was devastated . . . she felt . . . that she needed to make amends. Seeing the women, and their hair falling out in these clumps—my mom had really really long hair at the time . . . beautiful thick hair. She said, "I just want to cut my hair off. I just want to cut it off there at the Pentagon." And so we went. In those days you could go inside the Concourse. . . . We thought, well let's show this film. And so we brought a generator in there, and we showed the film . . . we made a banner that said "How many Hiroshimas before we understand?" We stood under the banner after the film was over, and then this woman who was dressed as Death came to each person and . . . cut our hair. . . . And it was cut in such a way so that it looked like it had come out in clumps. And then they left the hair on the floor. And we had blood, so we put blood on our faces and we just stood in silence. . . . The crowd was just stunned and silent. And there was . . . nothing. There was just silence, and then this Japanese tour group was there, and they just started *crying.* It was quite a moving action. And then all of a sudden, the police came . . . and the police said "you can't just leave this hair here!" And we said, "we are not taking

it with us!" And they arrested . . . the Death Spectre. And then my mom dipped her hands in the blood and put them on the wall, so they took them both away.[15]

This action used the women's bodies: their hair, their blood, and their presence in a site of (male) state power to connect with other women across time and space (the Japanese tour group, the victims of the bombings). For those at the Pentagon that day, the emotional impact and spaces for new thinking were facilitated by people's easy recognition of the body as messenger. The action "worked" as a symbolic and emotional protest because it was founded on women's generalized identities "as women"—women who stand out for their willingness to cut their beautiful hair "in clumps"—to look ugly on purpose, to be vulnerable, and to go to jail to make more visible the horror of nuclear weapons.

PART II: STRATEGIC USES OF IDENTITY

We are all shaped by "who we are," and particularly by our visible identities of race and class.[16] In choosing to carry out prison witness, justice action prisoners are both motivated and shaped by their various categories of belonging—by their race, class, gender, and so on, but also by their personalities, quirks, and strengths. The experience, and arguably the efficacy, of prison witness is impacted by participant's belongings in various categories of privilege, including the social privileges of white skin and so on, but also their ascriptive characteristics such as having the resilience, courage, and resources of faith and intellect to make incarceration a strategy that may be chosen freely, and endured. Awareness of their privileges often motivate people to act in resistance, and they also propel the actions forward in particular ways.

Experiences are also shaped by participants' professional and family identities, such as one's identity as vowed religious or parent, and sometimes these roles have profound effects (mothers, for example, all leave prison talking about motherhood). A person's movement affiliation matters too, so whether one is buoyed by Plowshares, SOA Watch, or another movement—or one acts alone in solitary witness—influences what happens to people, how they feel about it, and how they (and their action) are received by others. For those included in this research, one's identity categories prove most important in the decision to act in resistance, how it feels to do it, as well as being resources from which to draw power, strength, and clarity of purpose. For several in this research, an important part of navigating identity through the course of resistance entailed thinking about their privileged status. How to "use" their privileges well—responsibly and effectively—on behalf of others, was recognized as both a powerful and dangerous tool upon which they relied.

Privilege in Action: Using "Who I Am" for "Good"

"Using" privilege toward activist aims has many advantages; it can provide safety for movement participants, it can increase the efficacy and awareness of an action, and it can invite a larger audience to learn about something they may otherwise remain ignorant of or purposefully avoid. For those without fame or fortune, using privilege most often entails taking advantage of one's position within a community (one's status or profession) to strengthen the impact of one's activism. However, using privilege can also mean using whiteness and social class, especially, as stand-ins for integrity, accountability, goodness, or seriousness of intent.

No matter what, relying on privilege to further movement goals is fraught. In his analysis of *Freedom Summer,* social movement scholar Doug McAdam explains that using privilege, and specifically white privilege, is inadequate in the effort of social change—it must be paired with intentional efforts to undermine it.[17] In their article on the subject, social movement scholars Boothe and Smithey argue that privileged allies can access their power, resources, and skills to benefit the causes they care about, but that without adequate knowledge of how their dominant status impacts their work and organization, life can be breathed into hierarchical patterns while affected groups are further disempowered.[18] Hence, it is not just self-knowledge that is needed, but knowledge of the context from which that self arises. Further, one must understand the effects of one's participation within this space—for instance, what does it mean to employ one's status as a stand-in for integrity or morality? What does it rely upon and reinforce? Otherwise, mobilizing whiteness, for example, to convey "goodness" (and with it, the assumption that one "doesn't deserve to go to jail"—the thinking that is required from outsiders to understand resistance goals) works to keep hierarchical systems in place, rather than to disrupt them.

Many of those I interviewed are engaged in the work of using privilege intentionally, and even strategically, for "good." In her interview, retired health professional; white, married mother; and convicted felon Rae Kramer explained how privilege works in nonviolent resistance. She said:

> The power of the prison witness more publicly was . . . the more that you are connected to mainstream life, the more effective and powerful is the witness. . . . I am a soccer coach. How do I tell these families that this woman who they have entrusted their children to . . . is going to jail? Wait a minute, bad people go to prison! The cognitive dissonance right there—that was the magic moment.[19]

Rae explained that it was her *status* that made her line-crossing at Fort Benning effective. It was her "connection to mainstream life" that enabled wide-scale critical thinking about the SOA in her community.

In blunter terms, prison witness partly works because the people going to jail are not those who *usually* go to jail. Rae knows that when so-called "good" people are incarcerated, it makes other people *think*—and this thinking propels change. Quite simply, when high-status individuals engage in prison witness, more people are given information to know about—and think critically about—the issues of activist concern. The scrutiny that prison witness activates, however, relies on engrained colonial assumptions about whiteness/wealth/high-status corresponding with virtue and worthiness. So at best, *using* privilege is a double-edged sword. On the one side, the mechanism Rae describes is politically and culturally powerful, and she is correct to acknowledge it so clearly. On the other side, the underlying structural violences that activists like Rae are so keen to uproot may be reinforced through their actions.

In general, the people represented in this book have determined that, on balance, the potential benefits of using privilege are worth the risks they entail. For these participants, their privilege was a key factor enabling their action. For example, more than half of those I spoke with explained that their white skin provided not just motivation to act, but relative safety in doing so. Their activism was also enabled by their U.S. citizenship, having an identity (priest, mother, professional) that makes others "think twice" about their action and subsequent imprisonment, the "inner strength" to bear lengthy incarceration, the financial security to "step away" from day-to-day life, as well as assuring the "privilege to explain my legal record" after release.[20] In this research, a basic awareness of the power of privilege was found across all axes of identity, with no great differences among men, women, lay people, or the vowed religious.

The majority of participants made a direct connection between their structural location and their need to take on disarmament or human rights work. For some, their awareness was simply around the fact that they were uniquely able to participate in resistance because of their position (economically able, the children were grown). More often, the awareness was also tied to the political: Professor Bill Houston explained that being accountable as someone whose life "benefits from the oppression of other people" propelled him to cross the line at Fort Benning.[21] Liz Deligio said that not only did her U.S. citizenship protect her, it also made her "liable."[22] It was her particular position—as a then-28-year-old, white, theology graduate student from Chicago—that enabled but also *required* her action. Hence, negotiating one's privilege is an ongoing project for the justice action prisoners represented in this book. This process involves not only an accurate self-assessment of their subjective and ascriptive identities, but also an understanding of what these identities mean both personally and politically, as well as what they mandate that activists *do*.

What Do You Wear When You Get Arrested?
Using Privilege Strategically

Though complex and difficult, many justice action prisoners have determined that using privilege strategically is the best of their available options for effective resistance. To get at notions of privilege without leading the way in my interviews, I asked many participants the follow-up question, "what do you wear when you plan to be arrested?" For a goodly number, the response was logistical: dress warmly, wear layers, a scarf works nicely as a pillow while you wait in a holding cell. For others, the question opened up their understandings of privilege, their responses revealing what they know and think about in terms of their own privilege, as well as how they consciously negotiate their own visible identities.

Ten participants—three Catholic Sisters, three lay women, one Anglican priest, and three lay men—spoke clearly of using privilege intentionally, as an integral method of nonviolent protest. Nancy Gwin, a retired teacher, told me that she always dresses up when she goes to a protest. "There's Nancy, in her flats!" other activists say—but she wants onlookers to see that there are people "like them" (white, middle class, and professional) who are interested in issues of disarmament and human rights.[23] Ann Tiffany explained that she likes to "present as a middle-class white woman" in her actions. She recalled one instance where she turned herself in to the local jail in a grey suit and pumps, and the woman checking her in thought she was there as a lawyer.[24] Creating opportunities for such cognitive dissonance is tactical; it is a way to force critical thinking, aimed at dismantling false divisions between inmates and lawyers, good people and bad, activists and professionals. Through "performing" their mainstream identities so specifically, Nancy and Ann hope to appeal to others who are "like" them, using who they are intentionally to increase their potential audience, gain legitimacy, and widen their scope of impact.[25]

Viewed in another way, performing mainstream acceptability is a way to make oneself *less* visible in one's actions—and to move the focus away from oneself and toward one's messages. For example, one of the realities of being an older white woman in the United States is social *invisibility*; it is a strange truism that elderly women are not noticed for their identities.[26] Hence, by dressing as "respectable old ladies" rather than somebody's idea of radical, Ann and Nancy may keep the focus more directed on the message than the messenger. In any case, for these two women "dressing up" is an intentional, personal, and political act, and it carries significance well beyond their choice of shoes.

In contrast to Nancy and Ann, Catholic Worker Brian Terrell tries to downplay the impact of his white and male privilege through how he dresses—both during his actions and in court. I asked him what he wears when he is inviting arrest. He answered that he doesn't "dress up," because:

> I get enough preference as it is. Just being a white, now middle-aged, man. I don't need to claim that. In fact, I need to do the opposite. I need to practice downward mobility. . . . And I think in a system where it matters, in a system where someone wearing a suit and tie gets better treatment, I'll wear blue jeans and a T-shirt.[27]

Brian's intention is to level the playing field, to distance himself from his privileges so that he may be treated as no-one special—just another poor person coming through the courtroom doors. In practice of course, distancing oneself from one's privileges may be an impossible task. The effort, however, shows that Brian is aware of the structural context in which he acts, and that he is working to be accountable to his identities (across a variety of contexts) in the most active and concrete ways he can.

Father Luis Barrios, a Puerto Rican priest and professor of Forensic Psychology at John Jay College of Criminal Justice, deploys his privilege as a priest strategically during resistance actions. As a person of color, his priesthood is his most visible privileged identity. When asked if he wears his collar when he knows he is going to be arrested, he replied:

> Yes, I like to do that. It's a power struggle, and because it's a power struggle, I take advantage of that. So uniform to uniform. . . . We did *Occupy Wall Street, Occupy Faith*. So it was about 18 religious leaders, Muslims, Jewish, Christian, Buddhist. And the police have a lot of difficulty. 'Cause everyone says, let's do what we all know how to do. Let's pray. We all prayed. Every religion prayed. . . . I remember, the Lieutenant came to me and says (whispers) "excuse me Father?" I say "Yes?" "We need to do the arrest." I say, "I am praying to God!" He said, "Oh I'm sorry. Let me know when you are finished." (Laughs.) So he just stood there, he doesn't know. He said "Are you finished talking to God?" I said "No, not yet! I'm getting there." (Laughter.) I'm just waiting for the media to get there. Okay. Then I got a police officer, Italian, he'll say, "Oh, my mother, my mother's gonna kill me, when I tell her that I arrested a priest. She's gonna kill me. She's not gonna talk to me. I don't know why I do this!" The police always . . . say "I'm sorry I have to do this. It's my job." I say, "I know this is your job. This is my job, this is why I'm here! So you do your thing. I'll do mine." So, yes. I take advantage of the collar.[28]

In this story, Fr. Luis illustrates how he intentionally uses his collar to buy time and arouse feelings of guilt or moral quandary in others—in the aim of furthering movement goals.

The status attached to the priestly collar is important whether or not the actor uses it intentionally. Fr. Steve Kelly spoke of his experience as part of the 2009 *Disarm Now* Plowshares action in Washington State. As the five activists walked across the military base early in the morning, the first guard who spotted them saw Fr. Steve's collar and communicated to military personnel that "protesters" had trespassed onto the base (and not criminals, terrorists, or some other word). "So right away they knew we were protesters," Fr. Steve explained, "they could see my collar . . . so in some cases it can diffuse it a little bit" though "it's not guaranteed."[29] In this instance, however, where he was present in a "shoot to kill" zone, being quickly recognized as a priest assured safety for himself and his companions. Interestingly, very few American nuns wear the habit, so the benefits of this visible identity are not similarly bestowed upon them.

Participants also described using their privileged identities as catalysts to "make space" for others. Sr. Dorothy Pagosa explained how this works when she told me that "privilege gives us entrée" during actions, an opening she can use to "let the people who really know what they're taking about talk."[30] Similarly, Sr. Ardeth Platte explained that when she was the mayor of Saginaw, Michigan, she would tell "everything that was going on" in local politics to the "disadvantaged community" so that *they* could be "the ones who came to city hall and put the pressure on *us*."[31] As their representative, Sr. Ardeth was not speaking-for this community, but empowering them to speak for themselves. In these cases, the intent is to use the privileges provided by race and status to create a space for others to fill, but not to fill the space oneself. For sisters Ardeth and Dorothy, "making space" does not challenge traditional hierarchies, but it can create opportunities for others to galvanize deeper change.

Of course, spending time in prison as a result of nonviolent resistance is not a ticket to "wokeness," and indeed, a handful of participants did not seem to recognize that they were using privilege in their activism at all.[32] This is a problem, and by employing an inherently complex and power-laden technique, both movements and individual activists must critically and reflexively learn, and learn more, about what "using" privilege in their activism relies upon and means. This is necessary for those whose deepest wishes are to transform the systemic inequalities that produce violence in this world, and must be attended to earnestly and persistently.

In the realm of prison witness, privilege is activated as a platform of connection with others, intentionally disavowed in an attempt to dismantle hierarchies, used as a source of power to further movement goals, utilized to create space for those with less privilege to fill, and both not well understood and completely misunderstood.[33] Acting in relationship with privilege will always achieve imperfect results. But justice action prisoners are among those who believe that people must act, even when their privilege insulates them so that their most strident acts are relational privileged experiences.

PART III: THE MOMENT OF ACTION: GENDER, POWER, AND FAITH

The first two parts of this chapter focused on how identity (and specifically, the visible and privileged identities of race, class, and status) is understood and deployed to further movement goals. This third part examines the impact of identity in a different way—not as something that may be negotiated intentionally or that exists "out there," but as something that shapes activist experiences. The justice action prisoners I spoke with were seemingly not aware of these patterns, but the differences in their stories strengthen postpositivist arguments about our structural identities working as filters that determine experience and meaning-making. Specifically, the "moment of action"—the spiritual, exhilarating, and occasionally terrifying moment in which a justice action prisoner crossed a line, hammered on a piece of weaponry, or poured their own blood—was crucially impacted by gender, as well as by religious identity and age. Interestingly, one's movement affiliation or status within a movement (a first-time offender or decades-long recidivist) did not seem to affect the quality of one's experience, other than sometimes to make it a bit easier (or less profound) for those with more experience or closer movement ties.

For lay women, participation in resistance was most often experienced as personally transformative, and as specifically feminist, action. Men and vowed religious women, on the other hand, described participation in disembodied ways, having more to do with God and strategy than self and community. These fissures make visible how patriarchy continues to form the activist experience, as well as how religious beliefs and belongings can affect the significance of deeply rooted structural inequalities.

Empowerment: A Gendered Experience

Nonviolence scholar Michael Nagler writes that nonviolent action is a "peak experience" for its actors. Participation in protest can feel "effervescent," according to Mathew Kearney, and Jeffrey Juris describes "moments of freedom, liberation, and joy" in resistance actions.[34] Among social movement scholars, there is wide recognition that it *feels good* to participate in protest and collective action. Resistance was often remembered by participants in this study as a positive and enjoyable experience, and many justice action prisoners explained that the actual moment of action was "empowering." They described emotions ranging from feeling like one's most authentic self to excitement about producing political changes. Others, however, never mention how it felt to participate. How and *whether* empowerment was described varied neatly between men, women, the laity, and the vowed religious.

The Empowerment of Lay Women

As Ann Tiffany told her story, I heard a coming-of-age narrative. Ann married young, and soon realized that her marriage was a mistake. "Alcohol and other women" were a part of her husband's life, but divorce was discouraged in the 1950s and it was "me that was going to have to change," not her husband or his behaviors.[35] Ann had four children when she finally left her marriage, and its many constraints. She recalls crossing the line at Fort Benning in 1997 at the age of 63 as crossing a threshold into adulthood. Speaking about that day, she remembered:

> It was one of the most empowering things I've ever done. . . . I wasn't really very good at speaking up to authority. . . . But when I was arrested the first time at Fort Benning . . . I just felt so, I felt powerful. I felt, "You've done it, Ann. You've stood up for what you believe in, and you've been confronted and you still stood. You didn't leave." And that, that was good for me.

This was not simply because she was saying no to U.S. imperialism, or to the violence of the school, but because:

> I think that probably (being a woman) was where my feeling of power came from. That *as a woman* I stood up. Because most of the authority that you stand up to is male. I stood up to my husband a couple of times but it was really, really difficult . . . there was definitely some relief and I just felt very good about myself. Each time it made me stronger.

For Ann, there was something deeply satisfying about resisting what she had struggled so long against—a power that was militaristic, yes, but also a power that was male.

Ann's story is typical of the way that lay women spoke of the personal empowerment that comes through action. Like Ann, 14 (of the 16 lay women interviewed) described their actions as pleasurable moments of personal power. Their resistance worked against both the particular instance of militarism they were directly confronting and against their position as women in a patriarchal culture—both broadly and within their nuclear families.

A goodly number of these women (who came of age during feminism's second wave) acted without the support of their spouses, families, or communities. Indeed, there was a specific way that lay women in their 50s, 60s, and 70s explained the feelings of empowerment derived from their action—as something that was personal, but also related to facing one's position within the gender regime and *doing something* about it. Ann and her peers recalled their resistance as a moment of personal power, conducted within a broader context that, because they are women, constrained them.

Julienne Oldfield's story exemplifies this.[36] Telling me about crossing the line at Fort Benning, Julienne explained that her husband was adamantly opposed to it. She would have done it "years before," she told me, if she were "selfish." In the end, Julienne crossed without his support, even becoming a U.S. citizen to do so. Her husband was so angry that he refused to talk to her during the months between her action and her incarceration. For several months, they lived together silently, in the same house. "It was dreadful," Julienne explained. However, she was emboldened to act by the SOA Watch community and her faith life, which together—in contrast to her husband— supported her "to be" who she "already was."

For Julienne, crossing the line was an act that transgressed the school, but it also transgressed the limits of her identity within her marriage. Those few steps effectively marked her, to herself, an independent woman. She was a person who did what she believed to be right, regardless of her husband's support. Julienne's interview included a lengthy history of how her family had moved to Syracuse for her husband's job at the university decades earlier, and everyone felt miserable. They had been uprooted from a happy life in England, where Julienne was an elected official in her community and their extended family was nearby. Moving to the U.S. was clearly felt as a sacrifice made by the family to support her husband's career, and my knowing this seemed important for understanding the significance of his not supporting Julienne—years later—in her own bold act.

The personal and emotional work required to get Julienne across the line remained primary in her recalling of the experience, and for the lay women like her, the result of acting in resistance was shared as a tremendous feeling of personal empowerment. This was not just through making their positions about the school clear, but also through cementing their identities as independent and autonomous women and activists—in alignment with their values, but not necessarily in their relationships with others.

In short, the theme that emerged among lay women was that acting in resistance felt empowering for them *as women*. The moment of action was frequently described as a conversion moment: a moment of anchoring themselves in their own chosen identities, as well as publicly identifying themselves as women who are against torture and nuclear weapons, but also against patriarchy and perhaps even their own limited roles in their own families. It was important for these women to act politically, through the judicial system, and in public. Equally important, however, was Ann's feeling that "as a woman I stood up."[37] Such experiences were not similarly described by the men or the Catholic sisters.

Powerful Men

A handful of male participants described their moments of action as empowering, but other than John Heid, this "empowerment" was expressed in a very different sense than that expressed by the lay women. John was unique when he described how it felt to participate in resistance. Of his first arrest, he said it was "as liberating and wonderful a moment as the day I got married. I just felt, oh, free. Free to be who I really was. Nothing could hold me back. . . . And if I didn't do it, then I'm my own jailor. I am my own prison cell, and it's a supermax."[38] Participating in resistance was a way to feel exactly who he was meant to be, doing just what he was meant to do—and anything else would have been experienced as an insult to his liberty, a restriction to his deepest sense of self.

For the other four men who discussed something like empowerment during their interviews, it was meant in a very different sense. For these men, empowerment meant generating new power toward political change rather than as an experience of personal empowerment. In other words, efficacy. Randy Serraglio, a self-described "hot-head" who grew up "looking for trouble," was able to "channel a lot of rage" through his nonviolent resistance to the SOA. He explained that carrying a cross with a person's name on it onto a U.S. military reservation was "power. That's the power of the life they gave, which is not extinguished." Getting arrested later that day "was exhilarating. . . . We made millions of people aware of the School of Americas. . . . And we forced the Pentagon to change the way they do things even if we didn't actually close the place, and we brought a lot of light and heat on them for this counter insurgency-stuff. And we did the right thing."[39] Randy's action felt good because it was politically effective, but not because it transformed how Randy felt about himself or his relationships. Rather, it was powerful, and the "right thing" to do. For this reason, it felt good to be part of.

Karl Meyer also described the moment of action as empowering. In our interview, he remembered the day in 1955 when—with Dorothy Day and 25 others—he disobeyed an air raid drill simulating a nuclear attack in New York City. He "became a radical" that day. By getting arrested, he "crossed the Rubicon," as he aligned himself with those he admired: Joan of Arc, Socrates, and Gandhi. Doing so felt "wonderful," and brought him the respect of the peacemakers of the time. (In 1955, prison witness was met with more media attention than today's actions generally are, and this particular action was heavily publicized.) Choosing to break the law "skyrocketed" Karl to national fame, as it confirmed him as a trustworthy fellow within the peace movement.[40] Resistant action was empowering for Karl in the sense that it made him *more powerful* (i.e., *effective)*—while the personal effects of the action were less relevant to his experience overall.

The other men who spoke of empowerment during interviews intended a similar meaning; participation was empowering because it shifted things structurally. Prison witness was recognized as a tool that worked, and it resonated with their values. Their actions did not seem to create or validate their senses of worth as political or private subjects (as they seem to for the lay women), but rather allowed them to be better men, better Christians, and better positioned to work for the causes they care so much about.

It's Not About Me: Using Power Effectively

For the Catholic sisters, priests, and most of the lay men, resistant action may have felt good (along the lines of enjoying the day), but this was unimportant in how their stories were recalled. The majority of these participants discussed their resistance without referencing their personal experiences or feelings at all, or they discussed their experiences somewhat obliquely, as an instance of nonviolence or God "working." Certainly, they did not speak of personal empowerment. Instead, the emphasis in this group's storytelling was on relationships with God, "right action," and as instances of good strategy. None spoke of their own experience as particularly significant; it was simply not the story they chose to tell. For them, the personal effects of participation (including potential references to feelings of joy, fear, or pride) seemed beyond the point.

For those in this group, the moment of action was recalled as a series of steps: we cut the fence, we prayed together, the arresting officers arrived. When extraordinary things happened, they were credited to grace or described as miracles. For example, Sr. Ardeth Platte told a story of a heavy-duty lock on a gate "cracking open, it shouldn't have done that." Her explanation for this was that "there are miracles in these things." She went on to dismiss the attention her actions gain as un-sought: "We don't call the press or anything," but people hear of what they have done and "it resonates."[41] Sr. Ardeth's personal experience is clearly not what she wants to share. Especially for the vowed religious women in their 60s–80s, the lack of personalization exists in sharp contrast to the way lay women discussed their resistance and its aftermath.

With their strong emphasis on God, for the people in this group the interpretation of personal events—what it actually *feels like* to engage in direct actions—is impersonal and disembodied, at least in the stories they choose to tell. Though engaging in the same types of actions (and sometimes, the very same actions), the experience of resistance is different for men and vowed religious women than it is for lay women, and this is true across movements. This makes it evident that how the action is experienced—whether or not it feels effective, pleasurable, scary, or otherwise—is dependent on the identity markers, and specifically the gender and religious status, of those doing the resistance.

Analysis of the Different Experiences Described

The ways that men, women, the laity, and the vowed religious told their stories of action differed in remarkably similar ways. While there is no simple accounting for these patterns, some of the differences in story are methodological and must be attributed to the identity of the listener, i.e., me. I conducted interviews the year that I became a mother, and I often travelled to activists' homes with my husband and new baby. Surely, my similarly-privileged identity to those I was studying impacted the stories told, and specifically the men's consistent emphasis on strategy and righteous Christianity (positioning themselves as experts) and the lay women's intimate narrations of family and community (positioning themselves as moms and fellow feelers-of-emotion).

However, the differences in story exceed method. Essentially, when describing their actions, the men and sisters explained that they did something that "worked." They did something strong that had to be taken seriously, in response to conditions that they know to be true. They felt comfortable with the strategy, and enacting it confirmed their sense of themselves as valid political subjects and content experts. They were confident that they would be taken seriously as such. Their actions, as well as how they experienced them, were discreet and focused, though perhaps in line with a nonviolent lifestyle already chosen. For this group, the moment of action did not represent a "break" or a revolutionary moment that permeated their personal lives, as it so often did for the lay women.

The sisters' and men's stories were not about themselves or their feelings, in part because there is a legacy of political action that makes space for men, in particular, to speak as valid political actors. In this tradition, men (as well as the vowed religious, who are better imbued with the power to "speak" as moral leaders) do not need to explain themselves, they can just *act*. The political and ethical space for doing so already exists. For these groups, then, it is not radical to participate in the public sphere. What *is* radical is *how* they participate.

The easy assumption of political legitimacy and belonging expressed by the men and vowed religious is not something to judge negatively or to view as conceit. On the contrary, everyone should feel entitled to legitimately participate in the public sphere. What is remarkable is not that men, generally, feel entitled to act publicly, but that even some of the most privileged, well-known, and radical lay women activists in the United States today do *not* feel this way. In their stories, lay women fundamentally do not share claim to political activism or nonviolence, they do not construct themselves as subject experts (though they most often are), and being a core part of a nonviolent movement or legacy is far less important to their experience overall. Certainly, the movements could do better at enlarging the space of political legitimacy for participating lay women, but from the stories told in this research, the issues are far larger than the movements: it's a problem rooted in living in a patriarchal culture; it is not simply about belonging to a movement that reflects these patriarchal values.[42]

In their stories, the lay women included in this research spoke to me as a wife, mother, and "feeler" of emotion, oppression, and power. Their moral legitimacy (as "carers") was where their feelings of power sprang from, a typically "feminine" (non-transgressive and safe) way for women to express power in Western culture.[43] Some of the most important pieces of lay women's stories included their own biographies and emotions. These are noteworthy parts of what it means to engage in nonviolent resistance, and these are histories that the sisters' and men's stories leave out. But their presence also shows that women's power and legitimacy is not experienced as coming from their actions themselves, but rather from their status as moral authorities in their communities; as wives, mothers, and friends. How power is distributed and experienced, then, is neither neutral nor similar across various identity groups. Instead, structures of gender oppression define different people's experiences, from the level of feeling through expression itself.

Within this, it is significant that religious identity trumped gender in the ways that actions were experienced; the Catholic sisters included in this research were as silent as the men on issues of "empowerment." Indeed, the sisters' interview transcripts read with very few references to *I, me,* or *my*, their senses of self are simply not principal parts of their stories. Part of this may be credited to their very clear motivations for action (faithfulness rather than efficacy), the communities they felt responsible to (faith communities, the world's children), as well as who they felt accountable to (God, never the state). Hence, "what happens" to the sisters—to their bodies and in their communities—is simply less relevant than it is to the lay women.

However, the differences among women are most clearly explained through the types of communities different women belong to.[44] Lay women's stories show that being a part of an activist community that validated and "saw" them as powerful subjects was experienced as new, and for almost all of them, being part of this was transformative. Beyond the political statement they made, when they "crossed the line," lay women experienced personal power *as a woman* in a way that was deeply meaningful. For the vowed religious women, on the other hand, this "line" had already been crossed. As Sr. Kathleen Desautels explained, "The best gift of the church is to help me understand what it means to be a little bit on the fringe. As a woman in the Catholic church."[45] Being on the "fringe," Kathleen had already carved out her place among a community of activist-sisters in a traditional, patriarchal church. In other words, American Catholic sisters have, by and large, already made radical connections within an intellectual, spiritual, activist, and often feminist community: the sisterhood. They are already alternative leaders within a conservative and masculinist institution. The voice they have found, as moral "leaders," is one they have gained through community, but not through institutional power. Hence, the sisters, like the men, were able to engage in actions from an already-constructed place of support and belonging, thus allowing the experience to be more directly political than personal.[46] (This explanation may also illuminate the cases of the two lay women who did not discuss empowerment: both were aligned with Plowshares, and had close ties with Jonah House—fulfilling a similar role in terms of community and belonging.) The significance of this radical network and sense of belonging provides further support for the centrality of community within such high-risk activism: not only is it part of what makes it possible to participate as political actors, it is also what helps women to *feel* like political actors.

Examining women's roles in the U.S. peace movement historically provides further insight into the different experiences of action that lay women and men describe. Women have always struggled to find a foothold as "valid" political speakers in the peace movement—and not just outside of it. In her book, *Radical Pacifism in Modern America*, historian Marian Mollin shows that being a woman in the U.S. peace movement between 1940 and 1970 meant navigation of a hugely patriarchal world.[47] Plowshares is a particularly masculinist movement historically (now principally led by women), inspired by two Catholic priest-brothers. Philip Berrigan was known to pressure people to participate in resistance using phrases such as "having no balls" and "becoming a man."[48] Traces of these histories are still visible in the men's and women's stories told here, though these themes were never directly discussed among my participants.

What the different "gender stories" make evident is that, even in the most progressive movements, we cannot expect patriarchy (or other forms of structural violence) to "disappear" simply because the cause is just. Patriarchy is the water that we swim in, and our most radical movements will perpetuate it unless they work intentionally and specifically against such inequalities. This is precisely why activism, as described in Chapter 3, must be grounded in work that is personal and reflective: regardless of intent, systemic change will not be achieved without confronting one's own or one's movement's roles in structures of oppression.

The different experiences recalled by lay women, men, and the vowed religious reveal the ongoing ways that people experience power and empowerment. The men commonly conveyed the sense that they "use" power impersonally, toward a directly political goal. Lay women did something that made them "feel" powerful as women, in relationship to others and through previous experiences. By engaging in a dangerous, risky, political (i.e., male) strategy, the men were doing something that—though extreme and perhaps even thrilling—felt authentic and natural to their conceptions of who they are. For the lay women, the very act of participation felt to be a transgression: a transgression that was exciting, courageous, rebellious, political, powerful, and personal. Such differences confirm that patriarchy plays an important role in shaping both resistance and its experience, while the stories recalled by the sisters show that the extent to which this matters remains negotiable, and is impacted by intellectual and faith communities.

CONCLUSION

Prison witness is an embodied form of protest that means different things to different actors, and is experienced differently across groups. This chapter shows how identity is a driving force in resistance actions, whether consciously understood and deployed or not. Almost all of the justice action prisoners represented in this research know that their identities are tools that may be used to propel their activist messages, as well as stumbling blocks that can obstruct or even deepen the broader structural changes they seek to achieve. Less well understood is that identity not only shapes how their activism affects and is perceived by others, it also shapes how they experience it themselves.

Men's and women's experiences of prison witness were profoundly impacted by gender and religious identity, not only through what happened to them but also through what ultimately emerged as important in their experiences of resistant action. In this way, identity is not simply something to be negotiated carefully, but something to understand as fundamental and determining. We are affected by our context and its meanings—in ways that we can understand and navigate, but also in ways that feel deeply personal and essential to "who we are," what happens to us, and what emerges as significant from what we experience and believe.

NOTES

Note: An earlier version of part of this chapter, "Prisoners of Conscience in the Plowershares and School of the Americas Watch Movements," was published in *Social Movement Studies*, 18, no. 5 (1029): 535–549. Reprinted with permission.

1. Public Affairs, UC Berkeley: "Words of Freedom: video made from Mario Savio's 1964 'Machine Speech.'" September 30th, 2014, https://news.berkeley.edu/2014/09/30/words-of-freedom-video-made-from-mario-savios-1964-machine-speech/.

2. Joan Valérie Bondurant, *Conquest of Violence: The Gandhian Philosophy of Conflict*, vol. 243 (Berkeley: University of California Press, 1965); Arne Naess, *Gandhi and Group Conflict*, 1974; Michael Nagler, *Is there No Other Way? The Search for a Nonviolent Future* (New World Library, 2001).

3. See Peter Ackerman and Christopher Kruegler, *Strategic Nonviolent Conflict: The Dynamics of People Power in the Twentieth Century* (Westport, CT: Praeger, 1994); Gene Sharp 1973.

4. Jane Fonda, Colin Kaepernick, and Martin Sheen stand out as relevant examples here.

5. Crowley, interview.

6. See Ched Myers. "By What Authority? The Bible and Civil Disobedience." *The Rise of Christian Conscience* (San Francisco: Harper & Row, 1987) 243.

7. Ellen Grady, interview.

8. William Broad, *The Nun Who Broke Into the Nuclear Sanctum*, 8/10/12, https://www.nytimes.com/2012/08/11/science/behind-nuclear-breach-a-nuns-bold-fervor.html.

9. Security at the scale of the body means things like health care, education, jobs—not nuclear weapons and missile silos. This links to a long feminist insistence of the same. See Hyndman and Mountz 2006; Alice Cook, and Gwyn Kirk. *Greenham Women Everywhere: Dreams, Ideas, and Actions from the Women's Peace Movement.* (London: South End Press, 1983); Gwyn Kirk. *Our Greenham Common: Feminism and Nonviolence.* (New York: Routledge, 2018); Jean A. Tickner, *Gender in International Relations: Feminist Perspectives on Achieving Global Security.* (New York: Columbia University Press, 1992).

10. This statement can be illustrated with an example from the movement for Civil Rights. The movement began in Montgomery, Alabama—the deep South, and the heart of Jim Crow. The choice to activate the movement from Montgomery was intentional, as Martin Luther King Jr. knew that the leaders and safety departments in that city would respond to protestors with gross acts of violence (using fire hoses, police dogs, and batons against peaceful protestors). In the process, King ensured that it would be impossible for Northern whites to continue to deny the injustices highlighted by the civil rights cause. In other words, through voluntarily assuming violence in an organized way, actors in the civil rights movement were forcing people to see (and specifically, people who could otherwise be protected from seeing) the violence already present in the system. Protestors voluntarily but literally "embodied" the violence of Jim Crow, as they simultaneously articulated an alternative route toward justice. This strategy "worked," in a classical nonviolent sense—through the

anonymous "suffering" of (clearly innocent) others, and the forceful state response that made the violence impossible to justify or further ignore.

11. Lisa Isherwood, "The Embodiment of Feminist Liberation Theology: The Spiraling of Incarnation," *Feminist Theology* 12, no. 2 (2004): 140–156.

12. Selina Gallo-Cruz. *Political Invisibility and Mobilization: Women Against State Violence in Argentina, Yugoslavia, and Liberia.* (New York: Routledge, 2020). See also Lorraine De Volo. "Drafting Motherhood: Maternal Imagery and Organizations in the United States and Nicaragua." In *The Women and War Reader,* edited by Ann Lorentzen and Jennifer Turpin, 240–254. New York: NYU Press, 1998.

13. All of the following comes from my interview with Kathleen Rumpf.

14. Riegle 2012a.

15. Ellen Grady, interview.

16. Linda Martin Alcoff. *Visible Identities: Race, Gender, and the Self* (Oxford: Oxford University Press, 2005).

17. McAdam, *Freedom Summer*, 1988, 104.

18. Boothe and Smithey, "Privilege," 2007. In an article in the same collection, Kelly Rae Kraemer writes that the politics of being a "privileged ally" entail needing to understand one's privilege, the "inter-relationship between privilege and oppression," and the effects of this relationship on movement dynamics [Kelly Rae Kraemer, "Solidarity in Action: Exploring the Work of Allies in Social Movements," *Peace and Change* 32, no. 1 (2007): 20.]

19. Kramer, interview.

20. Various interviews.

21. William Houston Jr. interview by author, Yellow Springs, OH, March 15th, 2012.

22. Deligio, interview.

23. Gwin, interview.

24. Tiffany, interview.

25. Judith Butler, *Gender Trouble: Feminism and the Subversion of Identity* (London: Routledge, 2011).

26. For a quick primer, see Akiko Busch, "The Invisibility of Older Women," *The Atlantic*, 02/27/2019, https://www.theatlantic.com/entertainment/archive/2019/02/akiko-busch-mrs-dalloway-shows-aging-has-benefits/583480/, accessed January 2021.

27. Terrell, interview.

28. Fr. Barrios, interview.

29. Fr. Kelly, interview.

30. Sr. Pagosa, interview.

31. Sr. Platte, interview.

32. This was visible in relying on their financial status, for example, to more smoothly navigate relationships within the prison, or by imploring the movement to recruit people of color to engage in prison witness without understanding how being part of the legal system may be a different experience for members of other groups (various interviews).

33. These examples generally go well beyond the more common demands for privileged allies from movement leaders. For instance, Black Lives Matter co-founder Alicia Garza explains that the movement needs "people who are ready to act, who are ready to conspire" and not to be overwhelmed by "grief or shame" for their privileged identities. Further, privileged allies need to be ready to take risks, and to be uncomfortable. (2016). In my findings, justice action prisoners are on board with such prescriptions.

34. Michael Nagler 2001; Mathew Kearney, *The Social Order of Collective Action: The Wisconsin Uprising of 2011.* (Lanham, MD: Lexington Books, 2018); Jeffrey Juris, "Performing Politics: Image, Embodiment, and Affective Solidarity During Anti-Corporate Globalization Protests," *Ethnography* 9, no. 1 (2008): 61–97, 66. See also Gavin Brown and Jenny Pickerell, "Space for Emotion in the Spaces of Activism," *Emotion, Space, and Society* 2 (2009); Craig Calhoun "Putting Emotions in Their Place" in *Passionate Politics*, ed. Jeff Goodwin, et al. (Chicago, IL: University of Chicago Press, 2001); Jeff Goodwin, James Jasper, and Francesca Polletta, eds., *Passionate Politics: Emotions and Social Movements* (Chicago, IL: University of Chicago Press, 2009).

35. These stories come from my interview with Ann Tiffany.

36. These stories come from my interview with Julienne Oldfield.

37. Tiffany, interview.

38. Heid, interview.

39. Serraglio, interview.

40. Meyer, interview.

41. Sr. Platte, interview.

42. For example, Ann Tiffany's story was about how she stood up to her ex-husband through her line crossing—not how the movement didn't recognize her contributions.

43. See Bertram H. Raven. "A Power/Interaction Model of Interpersonal Influence: French and Raven Thirty Years Later." *Journal of Social Behavior & Personality* (1992); Johnson, Paula. "Women and Power," 1976.

44. With thanks to Dr. Terry Reeder for this insight.

45. Desautels, interview.

46. See Mary Hunt and Diann Neu, eds., *New Feminist Christianity: Many Voices, Many Views* (Nashville: Skylight Paths Publishing, 2010) for a discussion of the community of sisters in the United States.

47. Marian Mollin, *Radical Pacifism* 2013.

48. Marian Mollin, "The Limits of Egalitarianism: Radical Pacifism, Civil Rights, and the Journey of Reconciliation." *Radical History Review* 88, no. 1 (2004): 112–138; Women's Struggles within the American Radical Pacifist Movement." *History Compass* 7, no. 3 (2009): 1064–1090.

Chapter 5

Prison Communities

As white, middle-class Americans, it gives us a chance to see what these warehouses really are, where the poor are kept, because people are poor, most are people of color. And most people don't really know what goes on in these jails and prisons.—Sr. Gilbert (interview)

For most justice action prisoners, living in prison was a transformative part of their experience of resistance, and these experiences were very different for women and men. When men spoke of prison, they reiterated themes of militarism, imperialism, and racism—the very issues that brought them to resistant action in the first place. Women, on the other hand (and as usual), told more personal stories. What really captured my attention was the fact that most of the men spoke of prison as some sort of "break" from their activist lives, while women brought their organizing skills into the prisons. Indeed, they were often just as big of troublemakers within the prison walls as they were outside of them. This distinction was apparent in how women and men lived in the prison, what they did there, and how they were affected by it. Together, these varying but consistent stories demonstrate that gender matters as a key shaper of experience.

For both women and men, the vowed religious were the outliers in how they lived in prison. Priests were busier activists than were lay men, while the nuns were more likely to return to activism focused on the issues that brought them to jail in the first place. Upon release, lay women were more likely to shift or expand their activism to include a prison reform or abolition agenda. Hence, as is true for the moment of action, the significance of one's gender identity is mitigated by one's faith-life and connection to spiritual community.

This chapter briefly reviews the prison system in the U.S. as relevant to justice action prisoners, explicates how living in prison is an experience shaped by gender, discusses the activism that happens there (or not), and investigates some of the reasons why prison may be such a different experience for female and male justice action prisoners in the United States today.

THE U.S. PRISON SYSTEM: A PRIMER

Most of this study's participants served their time in federal prisons, though many have also lived in state and local jails. For most nonviolent crimes, such as trespass and the destruction of property, federal prison is the bureaucratically appropriate institution for sentencing.[1] The federal prison holds only a small portion of America's total incarcerated population (155,865 of around 2.3 million people in October 2021)—overall, the largest prison population in the world.[2] Still, due to changes in drug laws, the Sentencing Reform Act of 1984, and immigration policy and enforcement, the number of federal inmates has swelled in the last 30 years. Today, federal prisons also serve as detention centers for those with immigration violations, increasing their populations.

Policing and incarceration in the U.S. are historically discriminatory systems, and the poor are the most disproportionately affected. However, the discrimination is compounded for people of color, and especially for those who are urban, young, and male.[3] Indeed, these structural patterns run so deeply, and are so predictable (one in three men of color can expect to serve time in prison during their lifetime) that incarceration has been likened to an "inherited characteristic" for African American men.[4]

Law enforcement and prisons are also militarized. The U.S. police force receives military-style training for use against the citizens it is responsible to protect; police departments use military gear for civilian purposes; and prisons are paramilitary institutions in structure. Many prisons are located on military bases, operated by the military, and share military names (such as Fort Dix and Fort Leavenworth). Further, incarcerated people make up a significant part of the labor that keeps the military fully supplied. Each year, the Department of Defense purchases over $388 million worth of goods from UNICOR, the federal prison industry that serves as a prison labor program.[5] For justice action prisoners, these connections between civilian punishment and war are paramount. As Fr. Steve explained, the prison is part of the same administration that dropped the bomb, so resistance is necessary to *both*.[6]

Most justice action prisoners are incarcerated in federal prison "camps" (FPCs)—minimum-security institutions with dormitory-style housing, limited or no perimeter fencing, and a low staff-to-inmate ratio. Prison camps are work- and program-focused. Inmates spend their days in paid employment, but may also take courses, attend church services, and engage in other programming. Of course, many justice action prisoners also serve time in higher-security federal prisons, as well as in state and local jails.

In general, jails are more difficult places to live in than are federal prisons. By design, local jails are meant to house prisoners temporarily; however, the reality of incarceration in the U.S. today (overcrowding, backlogged courts) means that many people spend months and even years in these institutions. According to my participants, state and local jails are dirtier, noisier, more crowded, have fewer programs, and have more transient populations than the average federal institution. This last issue, living with changing populations, has significant effects on inmate safety, as security in prison often depends on one's connections with other prisoners. Indeed, one of the ways for an administration to deal with a "difficult" prisoner—such as an activist who likes to organize people—is to move them from one institution to another, sometimes frequently. The stresses of prison transport (what prisoners call "diesel therapy"), arriving in new places (with its routine strip search and other discomforts), and being a new person among strangers is an effective way to induce stress and minimize people's potential for coalition-building, consciousness-raising, and institutional troublemaking—of any sort.

Most of the justice action prisoners I spoke with chose to self-surrender into federal prison. To do so requires paying bond upon sentencing, with the instruction to self-report about one month later. For a number of justice action prisoners, the requirement to pay bail is an unacceptable form of complicity with "the system" and is regarded as an exercise of privilege. (Over 555,000 people incarcerated today have not been convicted or sentenced, but are in prison because they cannot afford to pay bail, the median cost of which is $10,000 for felonies—equivalent to eight months' salary for the average defendant).[7] Hence, as Kathleen Rumpf tells her sentencing judges, "I want to be treated like the poor in this country," which means immediate detention in a local or county jail before assignment to a federal prison.[8] Refusing to pay bail and awaiting sentencing while incarcerated is the most common reason that some justice action prisoners spend at least some portion of their sentence in state and local jails, for as soon as they are sentenced (a process that can last days or years), they are most often sent to federal camps.

Once sentenced, 100% of those who are able are required to work. The prison labor force is made possible by a loophole in the 13th Amendment that forbids slavery except as punishment for a crime. Most inmates in the federal system—about 75%—work for the prison itself, cooking, cleaning, teaching, and performing administrative tasks. The other 25% work for the Federal Prison Industries (UNICOR), which currently pays between $0.12 and $1.12 per hour.[9] UNICOR employs people in farming, forestry, highway construction, and other public services, and has contracts with the U.S. postal service, clothing and textiles companies, communications services, furniture-production companies, and the Department of Defense.[10] Almost always, justice action prisoners refuse any work that supports the military or the prison itself (though these are often the best-paying jobs), but willingly take on jobs that help other inmates, such as cooking, cleaning, landscaping, and teaching. About 80% of the average inmate's income is withheld to pay for such things as restitution, court fees, and family obligations, while the rest of the money earned is usually spent on needed goods, often sold at inflated prices, at the prison commissary (such as sanitary supplies, supplemental food, and postal stamps).[11]

DANBURY VS. ALLENWOOD: GENDERED INSTITUTIONS

That there were significant differences in men's and women's prison experiences was evident early in my research. My fourth interview was with Doris and Dan Sage, a married couple who I interviewed together in 2012, when they were both in their 80s.[12] Doris and Dan explained that the differences in their experiences were "institutional" more than anything else. Women and men serve time in very different types of prisons, they explained, and alongside different demographics. Women's and men's prisons are dissimilar in funding, culture, and population. These differences, Doris and Dan insisted, affect the public gaze of the place and, hence, what it is like to live there.

The Sages served simultaneous six-month sentences for protesting the SOA. Doris, a professional storyteller and educator, was sent to Federal Correctional Institution (FCI) Danbury in Connecticut, while Dan, an emeritus professor at Syracuse University who has since passed away, went to Allenwood FCI in Pennsylvania. Their joint sentences in what are designed to be similar institutions (minimum security camps with populations largely from the greater New York City area) gave the couple the opportunity to directly compare what happened to them.

Dan explained that men's camps house a goodly number of higher-status men, convicted mostly of financial and legal crimes. Hence, not only are the institutions gendered, they are critically affected by class. Doris described Dan's prison: "The population at Allenwood included people who were there for legal reasons . . . lawyers, doctors . . . men of power, there were more of those." Frequent recidivist Fr. Bill Frankel-Streit reiterated this observation of class difference when he told me that he never sees as many "yachting magazines and *Wall St. Journals*" as he does at Lewisberg Penitentiary, a minimum-security men's prison in Pennsylvania.[13]

Allenwood, Doris continued, had "carpeting, a library, the *New York Times*." The inmates knew that Dan was coming because they had read about his case in the newspaper. In many ways, male justice action prisoners fit well within this segment of the prison population at a place like Allenwood: white and well educated, they are readers of the *Times* themselves. A television reporter interviewed Dan during his stay, but once the telephone interview was underway, both realized that he did not have enough of a "story" to be very interesting. "The place is dull," he recalled telling the reporter, "there's nothing I can put my finger on that's really objectionable." There were "good programs, study carrels, comfortable chairs." Dan advised the reporter to speak to Doris if he wanted "something more controversial" because "she was having a hell of a time" at Danbury (the reporter declined).

In contrast to Allenwood, Doris remembered that Danbury FCI was a "snake pit . . . totally out of compliance with international standards . . . the sewers backed into the dining room. . . . The library was three footlockers, opened on Tuesday and Thursday evenings from 7:00 till 7:30." The women were "African American, Hispanic, and poor. Uneducated, mostly. And powerless. At the mercy of the system." The women had few visitors, and were shielded from observation by the outside world. Because they were marginalized people lacking connection to others in positions of power, Doris implied, Danbury's prisoners were kept invisible. As a result, they were more susceptible to abuse.

Doris and Dan spent time in institutions designated to be similar, but their experiences were shaped by the different populations they lived among— Doris with poor women of color, Dan alongside some "men with power." In terms of the impact of the institution on their experience, Doris and Dan were certain that it was class—and not gender—that mattered most. More precisely, it was access to power that made the crucial difference, and in this, women were especially lacking.

THE MEN'S PRISON: "A MONK'S CELL"

When discussing their experience of prison, most of the men included in this book explained that their incarceration was a stressful but solitary time that taught them about the prison industrial complex, as it also strengthened their resolve to fight imperialist, racist, militaristic domestic and foreign U.S. policies.[14] The men generally did not recall the time in personal ways, or feel a need to shift their politics or sense of self upon release. Instead, most often the oppression and violence they witnessed (or less frequently, directly experienced) served as further evidence supporting their already-existing analysis of a racist and violent status quo. Concurrent with this, and in alignment with Phil Berrigan's insistence that "the bomb makes every other issue redundant" so one must stay focused on the bomb, almost all of the men maintained their original activist commitments upon release.[15] The injustice of the justice system was not seen as an aberration, but as symptomatic of what they were resisting in the first place.

Men's prisons were described in ways that reflect media stereotypes: the environment is loud, crowded, and uncomfortable; there is an ever-present threat of physical violence; groups of men fall into cliques organized by race; and there is an overriding ethos of "each man for himself." The guards are remembered as not particularly helpful (and sometimes as deliberately harmful), and are often corrupted by their positions of power over the inmates. Guards can intentionally turn a blind eye to abuses. Rules are arbitrary, and sometimes act as their own form of harassment. Recalling his time in the Muscogee County Jail, Jack Gilroy explained that mail call was at midnight, breakfast at 2:30am, lunchtime was 10:30, and supper was served at 4:00. The schedule alone is a form of punishment for the inmates, it was "awful, awful stuff."[16] There is also a prevalence of prison "rats," or prisoners who snitch on others to curry favor, and this makes organizing difficult. Randy Serraglio described Arizona State Prison Complex (ASPC) Safford, the medium security prison where he was housed for six months, as being like a "high school locker room . . . with all of the bizarre, psycho, sexual, homophobic brutality" of that space.[17] Administrative failures leading to real harm (for example, rooming members of opposing gangs together) are a continual danger for inmates. Televisions are set to "the worst shows," and yelling is the primary means of communication.[18] The ethos of the men is chauvinistic, something frequently noted as problematic by the men I talked with. Randy told me that he "needed" his nonviolence training in prison; it was the only way he was able to avoid fighting with the other inmates.

Men recalled prison as an oppressive place, a difficult place, a sad place, but also as a space for the development of faith. For former priest Bill Frankel-Streit, prison is the most appropriate place to study "the scripture in context." Most of the scripture, he told me, was written under some sort of prosecution—"Paul was usually in custody"—so a prison stint can do wonders to deepen one's faith life.[19] Other men echoed this; both Fr. Louis Vitale and Fr. Steve Kelly explained that they live in a "monk's cell" while in prison (echoing Plowshares philosophy more widely, which recognizes prisons as the "monasteries of the future": they give one the opportunity to depend "entirely" on God).[20] Brian DeRouen recalled that his "prayer life" was "amazing" at Taft Correctional Institution, the private prison where he served his sentence for protesting the SOA. It felt "like a monastery," he said, and he "learned more about theology" during his six months there than in his graduate theology program.[21]

Three men spoke of making friends in prison. For most, it was a solitary time. Seven lay-men, all of whom lived in a variety of prison types, told me that living in prison induced feelings of loneliness and stress, and two discussed more severe depression resulting from their incarceration. In contrast, 13 of the men I spoke with did not discuss personal hardships at all. Nine of these were lay men sentenced to low-security institutions or camps, while the four priests in this group lived in higher-security institutions but still had no personal complaints. As such, among the men, religious identity trumped security levels as the most significant factor in determining the emotional quality of one's experience, and those with the "easiest time" were those with deep faith lives, regardless of setting.

Interestingly, several men recalled their experiences of prison in a disembodied fashion, almost as if they were telling the story of another person's experience rather than their own. Jerry Berrigan was the most abstract. He spoke of prison as "Satan's terrain," as Satan loves any place in which one human can "overmaster another."[22] How it felt to actually live in that space, however, Jerry did not say. Other men described prison as easy, dull, or a "walk in the park"—but not as *personally* challenging, difficult, or illuminating.[23]

Both Karl Meyer and Ed Kinane described prison as a "sabbatical" from their activist lives. Ed explained, "I spent a year reading. . . . It was fat city. Having been an activist I didn't get much time to read, and I love reading."[24] For Karl, prison was a "country club" compared to his daily efforts in activist life. He said:

> You don't hear me complaining about prison. There are some awful things that have been done and I hate the prison industrial complex. . . . But it wasn't risk for me. . . . Being in jail was almost a sabbatical from the stresses of working full time, and putting my income into running a house of hospitality and managing a dozen alcoholic and mentally ill men in a very crowded house of hospitality. So being in jail was like being on vacation, for me. In terms of difficulty. . . . I got knocked down by a guard but it didn't bother me much. My first time in prison, when I was 19 at Riker's Island, I got threatened with rape, didn't bother me. Young guys got around me while I'm sitting on the toilet in these open toilets, a gang of young thugs from New York. . . . They said, "If you were up in Greenhaven, it would be shit on my dick or blood on my razor." I just smiled and said, "Well, it's a good thing I'm not up in Greenhaven, then." So I wasn't frightened, it wasn't a dehumanizing experience of pain or violence. . . . I always said, Stalin would have broken me easily. You think I'm going to be broken by some country club federal correctional institution? Or even by a county jail in the U.S.? You never miss a meal. I put on weight. I got edema during my six months in jail. These are country clubs. I mean, I've spent time in very crowded conditions and so on, but it's not like being in Siberia. Have you read Solzhenitsyn? . . . I'm honest about it. Stalin would have broken me in Siberia in a minute.[25]

Karl's easy dismissal of prison as a "country club" that is not traumatizing is puzzling, given the content of his story. However, he is also not arguing that

U.S. prisons are fine or fair. Rather, the point of Karl's story is that "what happens" to him should not be the subject of anyone's attention—including his own. In truth, being harassed by a group of thugs at Riker's Island as a teenage boy may have been difficult, but to focus on this is to miss the point of his action. In 1955, Karl was incarcerated at Riker's Island for disobeying an air raid drill simulating a nuclear attack in New York City. In protest, he stayed outdoors that day and handed out pamphlets reading:

> We will not obey this order to pretend, to evacuate, to hide. In view of the certain knowledge the administration of this country has that there is no defense in atomic warfare, we know this drill to be a military act in a cold war to instill fear, to prepare the collective mind for war. We refuse to cooperate.[26]

Alongside those he admired and in concert with his own beliefs, Karl was protesting something that could end life on the planet as we know it. Compared against this, the conditions of the prison are truly *not significant.* He was not just being cocky when he told me that he was fine, because *in comparison to* nuclear annihilation, he was. Viewed in this way, it is reasonable to believe that the cruelties of the prison are nothing to be concerned about.

The Plowshares movement encourages this separation between the experience of prison and the subject of action. Before he died, Phil Berrigan was insistent that the cruelties of prison and the horrors of nuclear war remain distinct for Plowshares activists, and that Plowshares attention remain on the bomb. So, when Plowshares activists did not speak of the hardships of prison during interviews, this "absence" must be contextualized within the movement's principles; there may be a philosophical reason for their personal silences.[27]

All this said, not everyone is Karl Meyer or Phil Berrigan, and prison can be harmful to those who experience it. In particular, an articulation of prison as "nothing to complain about" reveals a larger problem; an under-acknowledgment that having race, class, education, and other high-status privileges allows a person to experience prison as a spiritual, solitary, and dull but not especially traumatic time. Specifically, one must wonder, for whom is prison "dull"? Discounting the potential for real personal harm during incarceration as a "distraction" from movement goals exposes a dangerous ignorance—specifically, ignorance that only a white, well-educated, well-supported person could reasonably count on an easy or "soft" prison experience. For those with fewer privileges, prison is experienced differently.

Going Deeper: Privilege Matters in Prison

Upon reporting to prison for their first-time offense of illegal trespass onto Fort Benning, this study's two participants of color, Fr. Luis Barrios and Derrlyn Tom, were both sent immediately to the SHU (solitary confinement), rather than released into the general population as is usual for defendants convicted of trespass. Derrlyn spent one week alone, while Fr. Luis spent three. Both were then transferred into the maximum-security-level prison at their respective institutions. After two months, Fr. Luis was then released, while Derrlyn was transferred to the prison camp for another four months.[28] There, she joined her four white co-defendants, who could not understand what had taken her so long to arrive.

While several other participants endured difficult prison sentences, there were always other explanatory rationales (Kathleen Rumpf and Clare Grady's status as alleged members of a terrorist organization, for example) that could—at least ostensibly—"justify" their treatment. As first-time SOA offenders, Derrlyn and Luis's severe treatment stands out as truly bizarre.

In her interview, Derrlyn explained that other SOA Watch activists were baffled by her different experience. "Because you are not of color," Derrlyn explained to them. She said that it would be harder for the prison administration to justify its treatment if she were "a nun, or an old white lady"—the kinds of people who *usually* get arrested for nonviolent actions. She had a traumatic experience that she correlates with not being white. Not understanding the importance and real effects of her racialized experience made Derrlyn feel "resentful" toward the movement's (former) reliance on prison witness, and the unexamined white privilege that the strategy relies upon.[29]

For many of the justice action prisoners who endured more challenging or abusive treatments during incarceration, brushing off the violence of prison is misleading at best, and the effects of movements not-knowing or not-disclosing its harmful potentials can hurt both the movements and their activists.[30] In contrast to Plowshares, which still relies heavily on prison witness, SOA Watch seems to acknowledge this danger and its complexity. In any case, since 2011 (and the horrific prison experience of Theresa Cusimano), SOA Watch has not encouraged prison witness as a way to protest the school, or recommended it for issues of migrant justice.

Quite simply, an identity of compound privilege may be essential for the perpetuation of prison witness as a strategy of nonviolence. The contemporary United States is a "prison state." In this context, prison as an "easy time" must be understood as a possibility-for and product-of privilege: not simply the privilege of short and fixed sentences, but also of the visible and subjective identities (including the inner resources) that enable months and years behind bars to be something that can move ideas and movements forward without grossly harming its participants in the process. To be safe, and replicable, one's time in prison must be at least a little bit "soft." Better yet, one should have internal resources—one should be "unusually fearless," as Brian Terrell describes Karl Meyer, superbly intelligent, robustly healthy, or so religious that one's earthly experiences are not one's primary reference points for meaning or well-being.

Not everyone has access to these possibilities, of course, and both justice action prisoners and the movements to which they are attached should be more forthcoming about the personal complexity, and costs, of enduring prison in the U.S. today. (Though for adherents to the Prophetic Tradition, "what happens" to a person in prison is not necessarily relevant in either their discernment process or to the experience itself, as they are interacting with a religious rather than legal moral code and authority.)

All this said, while compound privilege may be necessary, it is not sufficient to guarantee humane treatment in prison. U.S. prisons today are violent and brutal places. In our interview, Brian Terrell explained that the Honduran jail where he served a brief sentence was "not worse than the DC jail."[31] Given this, it is remarkable that almost all of the men included in this book were able to keep their prison experiences from impacting their lives in more serious or personal ways. By and large, prison was something that happened to them, and sometimes it was rough. It confirmed their analysis of systemic violence, and gave them new experiences from which to think through what they know and believe to be true. But it did not change their lives.

Men's Activism in Prison

With few but important exceptions, the men I talked with did not maintain their identities as activists during their periods of incarceration. Several used the time to read and deepen their faith lives, a form of enriching their spiritual and political understandings that must count as activism, but that are fundamentally personal. Of the 19 men included in this research, five (four priests and Brian DeRouen) spoke clearly of maintaining their activist lives throughout incarceration. A few others maintained "activist identities" that were disconnected from prison life itself; this includes Randy Serraglio, who replied to every letter sent to him (about 45 per day) and recorded every address to add to the SOAW mailing list.[32] In this way, Randy continued doing organizing work while in prison, but it was of a type that kept him isolated from other prisoners rather than engaged with them. Each of the five men who discussed "prison activism"—activism within the prison walls—described different versions of what this meant to them.

When I probed some of the men about their lack of activism in prison—an important part of the historical legacy of prison witness that I was surprised to see absent in their stories—I was told that the structure of the institution today stymies organization.[33] The overcrowding, restrictions on group interactions, and frequent moves make organizing difficult. For those who were active alongside other men while in prison, religious identity was the determining factor, and not the security level of the institution, movement affiliation, or recidivist status. Despite claims that the structure of the prison system disabled potential organizing, "prison activism" did occur, and it occurred in camps, as well as in low, medium, and high security institutions. It was almost exclusively performed by priests.

The exception was Brian DeRouen.[34] Brian is not a priest, but he is a man of deep faith. Born into a devoutly Baptist family, he studied theology as a graduate student and now runs a Catholic Worker house in Virginia. He remembered being told that going to prison was a "waste of time," a view that frustrated him. He explained matter-of-factly, "in what few months of your life did you do such great work that if you would've missed it, it would've been a loss to society? Secondly, what do you mean? Those are people, too!" For Brian, prison was not a place of rest, but a place to continue struggling for justice alongside people who surely needed some. He manifested this commitment through his use of "jail solidarity," or using his privilege to protect others within the prison. He explained the technique:

> Jail only works with the cooperation of those incarcerated. So, if I can say, I will not cooperate in any way until my attorney tells me that you are being released with the same charges as me, at the same time as I am, then we'll do it. . . . So not only does my privilege protect me, I can use my privilege to protect others, and I can use that to completely . . . turn the system on its head.

For Brian, prison is an essential place from which to conduct activism. It is a hierarchical and violent place, in which there is much to be done if one is willing to take on a bit of personal risk for the sake of others, and particularly for those who are less privileged.

For his part in a 2004 SOA action, Fr. Luis Barrios was incarcerated at the Metropolitan Correction Center (MCC) in Manhattan, a maximum-security administrative prison.[35] He spent the first three weeks in the "hole" (Segregated Housing Unit or SHU—popularly known as solitary confinement) with a hallucinating man who had killed his last cellmate while he slept. "They gave me hell," Fr. Luis said, "so I gave them hell also, 'cause I started organizing!" A priest-professor-activist originally from Puerto Rico, Fr. Luis found himself "useful in the middle of that colonial environment. I say okay, I have these skills, I can build their strengths. . . . I went to prison, it's not like I stop there and take a break. No! You take advantage of where you are, there is always an opportunity." Agitating from within the walls of

MCC led to an accusation of gang affiliation by prison officials, but a guard told Fr. Luis to protect himself by telling everybody "to open a Bible, then nobody will give you a hard time." I asked him what he did when he "organized" within the prison. He explained:

> They have these churches . . . saying there is a strong possibility that God brought you here so you can have an experience of God. I say "Ha! He didn't put you here." There's something else. . . . Look around, who we are? So what is going on? (The issue of being black or Latino) . . . developing that critical thinking or knowledge . . . and not just something magic that God brought me here so that I can have an experience of God. That's bullshit! . . . Then, I started becoming part of the literacy program. A lot of these young men, they don't know how to read. . . . And, talking to people. I like talking to people. . . . Also, we often read biblical reflection from a liberating perspective. . . . And then, the issue of positive thinking. I spent a long time on that, because it was incredible, these male chauvinist mentalities and reducing a relationship with a woman to sex . . . and because I reduce my relationship to sex, I am thinking that she is fucking someplace, someone. I said "my friend, why the hell do you need to waste your time with that stupid thought?"

Fr. Luis describes days spent as an activist-priest while incarcerated. He used the time to minister, to teach—about Liberation Theology, but also literacy, relationships, "positive thinking," and racialized structures of oppression. Because of this, and despite the risks, in a short period of time and in an overcrowded high-rise prison under maximum security conditions, he managed to do consciousness-raising and organizing work. He was engaged, from the beginning, in activities that challenged the institution as he supported its incarcerated population.

Other priests told very different kinds of "prison activism" stories. Fr. Bill Frankel-Streit talked about being caught up in a prison fight, in which he was badly beaten by a guard but "stayed nonviolent" in response (he did not strike back).[36] For him, activism in prison entails nonviolently but forcefully challenging the institution from the inside out. Fr. Louis Vitale spoke of trying to bridge racial differences within the jail (which remain its central organizing principle) even though he is a "really really white person, middle aged . . . and to top it off, a priest!" (Father Louis was 82 when interviewed but wonderfully described himself as "middle aged").[37] One of the ways he attempts to bridge divides is to celebrate Ramadan ("it's a bonding"), which he has done each year since September 11, 2001. For Fr. Vitale, prison is an opportunity to forge connections between people, regardless of religion, race, or creed.

Fr. Steve Kelly's prison activism is unique within the world of justice action, although in line with Plowshares ideals. In total opposition to the prison system ("it is the same system that dropped the bomb"), he refuses to cooperate on any level with its "dehumanizing" demands. For example, he refuses to pay bond or do a drug test upon entry.[38] For this refusal, he is sent directly to the SHU, where he spends his confinement alone. He was released from 54 weeks in solitary confinement, for the 2009 "Transform Now" Plowshares action, one month before our interview. He had given each cell he lived in a deep clean, and spent the bulk of his time in spiritual practice. For his participation in the 2018 Kings Bay Plowshares action, Fr. Steve was released in April 2021 after over 3 years in solitary confinement, including four months in transit between Georgia and Washington State for a probation violation from an earlier conviction. This extra four months—endured in principled resistance to a small fine—meant stressful travel to a variety of jails and prison (shackled, during a surge in the Covid-19 pandemic in the United States). "I will in conscience refuse any fines and restitution," he told his sentencing judge in Brunswick, Georgia, and he meant it.[39]

Through absolute noncooperation with the system—and though almost always alone while incarcerated—Fr. Steve is committed to his identity as a nonviolent resister every day that he is in jail. Though he rarely comes into contact with other prisoners, his activism threatens the "whole institution," according to his friend Fr. Bill Frankel-Streit, demonstrating what "could be" if prisoners routinely failed to comply with the arbitrary and stringent rules imposed upon them. Fr. Steve's behavior "terrifies" prison administrators, according to Fr. Bill.[40] Thus, though Fr. Steve's resistance may not look like "activism" in the traditional sense, in his isolation he is both allegiant to his beliefs and vigorously active against the war state.

Fr. Steve's non-compliance with the carceral system is well-known throughout the disarmament movement, and he inhabits a sort of sacred or ideal position as one who is fully and truly "committed" to the work. Interestingly, in today's overcrowded prisons, Fr. Steve explained that his strategy is effective at furthering disarmament messaging within the prison walls, where he is "better known" in his absence than he ever could be in his presence. The guards talk about the "crazy anti-nuclear guy," the prisoners overhear them talking, and soon the whole compound knows about his "private witness" in a way that being a part of the general population could never similarly accomplish.[41] This witness is about disarmament, and does not include organizing around prison conditions or the lives of fellow inmates. But other prisoners relate to it and, according to Fr. Steve, they understand his resistant action. It is anti-state action; he is refusing to comply with a system they also know to be evil.

Release from Prison

Upon release, Brian DeRouen and Michael Pasquale shifted their activist work away from the SOA and toward a prison agenda. Brian now runs a Hospitality House near Alderson prison, where he houses women on the eve of their surrender, as well as their visiting families. Michael works to help the formerly incarcerated integrate back into society, specifically helping them to find employment. Ed Kinane and Brian Terrell told me that they are prison abolitionists. These men believe that the system cannot be reformed incrementally, it must be re-imagined and constructed anew.[42] Fr. Bill Frankel-Streit shared his personal commitment to include the topic of prison when he gives public talks about nuclear weapons and foreign policy, understanding that his experiences provide unique opportunities for people unfamiliar with the carceral system to learn more. He also serves as an expert witness, during other people's trials, on prison conditions generally, having lived in so many of them. His own activist work, however, remains firmly centered on disarmament.

Otherwise, upon release from prison, most men described feeling increased resolve to work against militaristic foreign policy and U.S. imperialism. Their experiences of the justice system serve as more evidence supporting their existing analysis of unfair, racist, classist, colonialist policies of the U.S. war state, and not as a new problem to be attended to separately. Hence, upon release, the men generally return to agitating over the same issues that got them locked up in the first place. The men's anti-imperial commitments are often deeper than they were before incarceration, and their certainty in their knowledge of structural violence more secure, but their geo-political outlooks are not fundamentally different. For Plowshares activists, this is surely connected to Philip Berrigan's insistence to stay focused on the bomb; movement principles define the issues of focus. However, it also seems to be a result of the kinds of experiences that men have when they live in prison, for even women who are just as firmly committed to disarmament upon entry—as well as upon release—come out of prison telling different kinds of stories about their time in the institutions, as well as what their time "means."

THE WOMEN'S PRISON: A STRANGE, SAD COMMUNITY

The majority of the female justice action prisoners included in this book spoke of their time in prison at length, and most often in very personal ways. They spoke of things like how it felt to live in prison, what got them through their days, what was most difficult, how their families responded to their incarcerations, and about the other women. A minority of the women—including all of the nuns—did not include talk about personal experiences that were challenging, and this was true regardless of the security levels these women lived within. Thus, as with the men, religious identity proved more telling of the emotional quality of one's experience than did the security level of the prison. For all but one woman, friendships with other women—a sense of solidarity, allegiance, and connection, were described as central to their lives while incarcerated.[43]

Again and again among the women, I heard the word "community" when describing the prison. Ann Tiffany told me that she entered a "community of women" when she entered Danbury FCI for an SOA violation. Kathy Kelly remembered the "strange community" that exists in women's prisons. Rae Kramer said, "The community was experienced on a very personal, almost a family kind of level."[44] Like the men's prison, women's prisons are organized by the prisoners along racial lines (in which the people who look out for you are people of your racial group), but the feelings and tangible benefits of community—a loan of shower slippers, relationship and parenting advice, someone to celebrate your birthday with a "homemade" microwaved Jello cheesecake—are distinct among the women. I heard many variations of Kathleen Rumpf's observation that "these people are me!"[45] The women I talked with recognized themselves in the women they lived with, and they made friends. No men told stories that mirrored this part of women's experiences in prison.

Certainly, women's prisons are institutionally distinct, but this does not make them less violent or painful places than men's prisons. Kathleen Rumpf, Clare Grady, and Derrlyn Tom told hair-raising stories of institutional violence, and several female justice action prisoners across time have endured severe mistreatment.[46] More often, however, participants described women's prisons as uncomfortable spaces of oppression and pain, but also as spaces of courage and beauty. Describing why she does not like the term "prisoner of conscience," Kathy Kelly recalled her life at Pekin, a now closed women's camp in Illinois:

> When I was in Pekin in 2004, my bed was very close to a bank of phones, so I'd hear the same phone conversation going on again and again and again. It would very often be a woman, probably in for drugs, wanting to call the mom or the grandmother who was taking care of the children, and just trying to keep that connection open, but it gets harder over time. And sometimes people would send a postcard asking, "I'll call at this time, can the kids be there?" And you just hear this disappointment: "Oh, they're not there.". . . And because of the impoverishment that the system imposes on women, they have to beg, "please put your money on my commissary . . . I can't send the cards I made for the kids because

I don't have stamps, and I'm out of shampoo. Is there some chance that Uncle Bob can drive the kids to see me? It's been 2.5 years, they don't remember what I look like anymore." And then you'd hear the person at the other end kind of saying, "Well, I'm out of resources. The lawyers are costing us money still. We can't do this." And just this sense of despair and frustration. Often you'd see a woman hang up the phone and just go right into the shower and into the toilet stall, and then come out and her eyes would be red and her face would be stained with tears. I was just amazed at how people found this kind of courage to face the rest of the day and the rest of week and the rest of the month and the rest of the year. Years separated, and the punishment that's just so merciless. And yet, I didn't find bitterness and intense cynicism. Women were trying to make the best of it and looking out for each other in ways that were often very kind, even looking out for some of these guards, who, many of them were veterans of wars who were pretty traumatized themselves. It's also interesting, within these very odd communities, there's actually more of a bond between the guards and the prisoners who've been there a long time. They start to know each other's kids' names. . . . So it's a very strange community that develops. And that's why I never want to be, it's not even honest to say, "Well, we were the prisoners of conscience living with these other people."[47]

Kathy says many things here, but what holds her story together is her connection to the women she lived with. These women are not anonymous for Kathy, and caring about them makes specific and alive some of the tragic consequences of poverty, violence, and injustice—the very issues that Kathy is resisting on the outside. Kathy is in prison because of, but also *with,* the fallout of the issues she most cares about.

In general, female justice action prisoners told stories about how they made friends, organized other women, resisted prison conditions, learned about themselves as well as structures of oppression, and taught classes (GRE, art, storytelling, and nonviolence) during their time behind bars. Prison was not an easy time, but it was a fundamentally important and communal time. Overall, women deemed their time in prison to be "worth it." Social worker Meagan Doty explained:

The women's prison was very much focused on, "We're all in a really shitty position, let's focus on getting through it.". . . I think you find out a lot about yourself when you go to prison. It's a trying place . . . but it's also beautiful. It's such a beautiful moment to discover both sides of humanity. And I'm willing again, to take those really terrible moments if I can also take the beautiful moments of humanity. You know? I'm willing.[48]

For Alice Gerard, going to prison was empowering. Spending a night in segregation (solitary) was better than years of therapy. She explained, "I learned that this is the worst thing that they can do to me . . . and I survived the experience. Therefore, I have no need to be afraid of anything . . . and I used to be very much afraid."[49] For Ann Tiffany, prison provided an opportunity for her to shed her external identity (as activist, mother, and professional) and "create" herself anew, the initial strip-search metaphorically catapulting her into a new self, a self who is grounded in resistance.[50] Both women explained that the impact of these experiences transcended their time in prison; upon release, it changed how they lived their lives.

Sometimes, the women's stories showed that the costs of incarceration were too high. A few women experienced significant physical and psychological harm while incarcerated, though—as it was for the men—such harm was always perpetrated by the administration and never by other inmates. Kathleen Rumpf's stay at Carswell Correctional Facility (a medical prison in Texas, the only one in the country for women) stands out as the most directly violent among my participants. Since completing her sentence there, Kathleen has suffered from PTSD, a result of the death, as well as the disregard for *life,* that she experienced at that institution. Since surviving Carswell, Kathleen has been unable to return to prison for resistance actions (a significant turn of events for this "one-woman crime wave"). Kathleen now focuses her activism entirely on prison abolition and reform.[51]

I did not interview Theresa Cusimano, but her story is well known in the SOA Watch movement. Theresa has celiac disease, which means that her body is not tolerant to gluten. The prison system's inability to accommodate this relatively straightforward food allergy made her so sick that she needed to be transferred to the medical unit at Carswell early on in her sentence. A combination of insufficient food, non-potable water, and food that worked like poison in her body almost led to Theresa's death at that prison, and she credits the pressure, momentum, and attention of the movement with her survival. Upon her release, she wrote a letter entitled "Hope: A Message to the Movement." She wrote:

My body gave out under the stress of being moved to four different facilities in two weeks' time. My kidneys shut down without water or nutrition. My legs could no longer stand. The darkness of my 44 day seclusion, a "gift" to me from the feds on my 44th birthday, broke me. I lost hope when I was disconnected from all of you and your generous solidarity. The strength of your collective prayers began to carry me out of the darkness of that rabbit hole. They shot me in the ass like a horse, to silence me. My eyes lost their ability to focus. They made me beg for my food and crawl, naked on concrete because I was unable to walk. You gave me hope that there are people who want to live a different way of life, centered on love. I wish to formally seek political asylum and live in your world.[52]

Though such dramatic institutional violence was not a common experience among my participants, the reality is that—even for those protected by multiple forms of privilege *as well as* the support, solidarity, and noise of a powerful social movement—near-death levels of harm can happen to anyone. In America's prisons, no one is ever truly "safe."

The risks inherent in incarceration have been driven home by the Covid-19 pandemic, which is disproportionately affecting the incarcerated population in the United States. In 2021, the U.S. prison population includes several elderly members of the Kings Bay Plowshares, for whom 12 months in prison may actually be a life sentence. Despite such unpredictable (and yet, absolutely predictable) challenges, for most of the women included in this book, living in prison facilitated personal growth that they are grateful for, if also scarred by.

For almost everyone, what made prison endurable were the personal relationships that the women formed, enabling them to feel a "part" of the prison community. Martha Hennessy spent three months in prison when her son was two years old, which was hugely difficult but also made her feel "a part of everyone in that prison, not just the two women I had entered it with."[53] In other words, the pain of being separated from her son was precisely what most connected her to the women, the majority of whom were also separated from their children. The focus on relationships with others is illustrated by the many stories women told about medical care in prison; they simply worried over the other women they lived with. Friendships were often centered around a relationship with a "bunkie" (cell mate), and expressed around what Nancy Gwin described as "survival's guilt"—knowing that she could return to a life very much un-changed by her relatively brief incarceration.[54] The women Nancy was living with, on the other hand, generally had much longer sentences. When they are eventually released, they will return to lives that rarely resemble those they left behind.

Such relationships, and the emotional experiences resulting from them, were central to women's stories of prison. Of course, such stories must similarly exist for men, but the men I interviewed did not tell them to me. Instead, the widespread concern for others, the integration of another's experience into one's own experience, and the decision to tell this other person's story as important to *their* story, were characteristics and intentions unique to the women.

Women's Activism in Prison

Women were almost all "busy" when they got to jail. They intentionally tried to break down barriers between themselves and other prisoners, and they worked on behalf of other women. In pivotal moments, they allied with the inmates, never the guards. As Susan Crane explained, "There is so much to do" behind the fence, and doing it "brings a certain dignity to being there."[55] Within my sample, Rae Kramer was perhaps the busiest woman while incarcerated. She interacted with women at Danbury FCI directly as a teacher and mentor, challenged institutional authority daily, worked to publicize systemic injustices, and continued organizing around prison issues after her release. Hence, this section is grounded in her story—not as the norm, but as encompassing of the range of activities women described when they told me about their lives in prison.[56]

"I preached nonviolence all the time, all the time," Rae said of her six months in 2001 at the camp of Danbury prison. "I was a real pain in the ass." Soon after arrival, she realized that she needed to "stop preaching and start doing," and so she became the self-appointed "Litter Lady" and picked up cigarette butts. She started a recycling campaign, whose proceeds went to the women (the program was stopped after she left). She advocated for better art classes and supplies, and more beauty in the women's environment. Using her undergraduate skills as a sociology major, she wrote a survey asking about the women's lives, and spent hours talking with over 70 women, listening to and taking notes about their stories. She was trusted among the women, a point she illustrated with an example: "I could nudge the snorers." She made a mug in ceramics class and etched it with the words "if you want peace, work for justice" on one side and "question authority" on the other. Rae was a constant thorn in the administration's side. For example, almost every day she wrote "cop-outs"—the complaint forms prisoners can use to tell the warden about problems in the prison. She used this form to discuss structural problems affecting the women. For Christmas, there was a sponsored project for the incarcerated women to make short videos to send home to their families. Rae brought eight pages of notes to her recording, and her video was "a litany of shit about Danbury prison." The warden confiscated the video, but Rae was eventually able to smuggle it out.[57] Altogether, Rae felt that:

> In prison, I did a number of good things for the women. I think my credibility was good . . . and I was seen relatively quickly as kind of interesting because sometimes I would get into trouble and people would be kind of intrigued by that. . . . And as my credibility got better, I think that the nonviolence conversations got a little bit better, and I stopped being quite as preachy. I didn't make my pitch in the abstract. It was the people I was getting connected to.

Connecting with "the people" is a crucial way to metaphorically break through the walls that the prison erects, as the system relies on dehumanization to run efficiently. The cruelty of prison, Rae explained, is its "casual disregard for people," a disregard that she challenged in her job as the "Dessert

Lady." Rae brought an "ethos of service" to her role, exclaiming things like
"today we have Jello!" and later serving leftovers to the incarcerated women
"like a waitress." Allowing people to make choices about which parts of the
cornbread they wanted—center or side—may seem like a small thing, Rae
explained, but in an institution that relies on an erasure of individuality (and
an absence on "choice" or self-control), insisting on "regular" human interactions can be a defiant act. Small, yes, but it works like sand in the smooth
running of the punishment machine.

Rae's activism on behalf of the women at Danbury continued after her
release, and with her colleague, the late justice action prisoner Anne Herman,
Rae was instrumental in pressuring Danbury FCI to purchase new mattresses
and upgrade the bathrooms. (When she was there, there were facilities for 40
in a prison housing over 200 women.) Despite her incredible efforts, Rae said,
"I still feel, and probably always will feel, I could have done more, I should
have done more. Both while I was there and afterwards."

After prison, Rae became a co-facilitator of a domestic violence class for
male offenders in prison. There, she explained, her message to the men was
the same as to the women in prison:

> I would say to them, there is no scenario, leaving out self-defense . . . that jus-
> tifies you being violent. . . . She belittles you, she insults you, she aggravates
> you, she annoys you, she defies you—ya, that's true. And to all of that, a violent
> response is not the right response. Never. Never. So it was very empowering, to
> be able to be so unequivocal and say . . . there are *never* only two choices. So if
> you *ever* tell me that it's this way or this way, right away your antenna should
> go up. 'Cause it's fake! It's an artificial description of reality. . . . If someone
> came along and said "I'll give you ten thousand bucks if you can come up with
> two or three other alternatives," you don't think that someone would come up
> with two or three other alternatives?

Rae was confident that her message of nonviolence could be heard, both
within the prison and in the classes she subsequently taught. She advocated
for self-empowerment, the ability to control one's own life, which Rae characterized as being distinctly feminist work. "I think that the same things that
frightened the powers that be frightened the women," she explained. One of
these was, "you mean the world could be different?" She clarified:

> The message . . . was one of empowerment. You're letting that person run your
> life. And what will happen is, you'll get sent to segregated housing. . . . And you
> won't get to see your kids this weekend. Why? Because she dissed you. Who
> gives a shit? . . . So they would start saying to me, well what would you do? I'd
> say . . . I'd walk away. . . . I'd say, MY life, I control my life. Not her, me! ME!
> It was a revelatory thought for many of these women.

Rae credited the behaviors that led to discord among the women at Danbury to an absorption of patriarchal ways of being, learned in a patriarchal culture—ways of being that were particularly maladapted to life in prison. Through providing ways of thinking about, enacting, and responding to the conditions of their lives that were different than these dominant models (not "better," Rae insisted, just "different"), her presence created a schism in inmate expectations about what was "normal." For Rae, the "gift" of her incarceration was:

> The impact of people like us on the people in prison . . . and to me that was worth it, if nothing else. Not that we're good or special . . . but that we're different. And that to offer *women* who've been raised in . . . this patriarchal violent consumer oriented (culture) . . . to offer them that there are people who see the world differently. . . . That was the gift, and it was fabulous.

Rae used her particular position, and her privilege (well-educated, feminist, and "different"), to connect with and challenge her fellow inmates. Her message was about empowerment and nonviolence, but her tools were distinctly those of her own identity.

Rae's experiences as a prison activist and a woman *connected* to those around her are echoed in the stories told by other women. Several spoke of attending prison programming (art classes, reading circles, and religious services), if only to ensure that enough people signed up to keep them running. Alice Gerard spent a night in the SHU to protest the GED teacher's sexual harassment of his students (and was only released, she believed, because the other inmates would have rioted had she been kept longer). Doris Sage organized clandestine storytelling sessions after the administration barred her (a professional storyteller) from offering workshops. These sessions gave the women a space to share some "really good, wonderful things about their lives," and provided an important source of relationship building and healing.[58] Ellen Grady was part of an action organized by the Trident *Nein* to end mandatory gynecological exams (what she called the "vaginal search") as standard procedure for inmates returning from court to York Correctional Institution in Niantic, Connecticut.[59]

The women also frequently engaged in other forms of institutional trouble-making—activities that may or may not be directly political or noble, but that clearly indicate where their allegiances lie. Alice Gerard raised pet mice and grew tomatoes with seeds smuggled out of her sandwich. Nancy Gwin broke the prison rules by perpetually trying to grow flowers in her cell window. Sr. Ardeth Platte kept a locker full of shower shoes, shampoo, stamps, and snacks to give to new inmates in need (gifts are forbidden in prison). Alice Gerard insisted that all of the things that she did in prison are "perfectly legal" in the outside world (growing plants is not indicative of "bad" behavior in free society), but were rebellious (and against the rules) within the prison.[60] Such small acts are not necessarily political, but they demonstrate a different way of interacting, a disobedient way of being, within an institution that constrains and even punishes "normal" forms of human interaction.

Release from Prison

For female justice action prisoners, the effects of living in prison are often long-lasting, and they frequently shape the women's future activism. Meagan Doty explained, "after going to prison, prisoners' rights automatically become a new focus." Sr. Mary Kay seconded, "a lot of us go into prison with the SOA Watch agenda and come out with a prison one, too." Kathleen Rumpf was unequivocal: women justice action prisoners "all come out talking about prison. Every single one. Every one."[61] Unlike the men, no women mentioned a tension between focusing on the bomb and working against the prison (though most Plowshares activists remained firmly focused on disarmament). More than half of the women included in this book have added a prison reform or abolition agenda to their activism since release, and others expressed guilt for not doing more in this area. This expansion of activism does not seem to cause the women existential anxiety; they don't worry over whether or not it's the right thing to do. They just *do* it.

WHY ARE MEN'S AND WOMEN'S EXPERIENCES SO DIFFERENT?

The variation in men's and women's prison experiences are multiple and significant, and together reveal a trend of difference that holds steady across this research. The easiest way to make sense of this is through justice action prisoners' assumption of mainstream gender roles, in which women are socialized to value connection and relationship, while men must be independent and emotionally reserved. In this binary, women are expected to talk more—and to talk about things that are important and intimate. Performing this gender role facilitates personal sharing among the women, as well as the formation of friendships. Men, on the other hand, are expected to be loners who do not rely on the support of others to get by (and thus, may leave prison without really knowing the other men whom they shared the time with). In addition to gender socialization, institutional differences matter, including the demographics of women's and men's prisons. For whatever reason, the difference between men's and women's stories of prison seems to spring from how they enter the space on that very first day: as loners who hope to get through the time alone, or as members of a community with whom they plan to build relationships and be helpful.

Training, Institutions, and Socialization

Dan Sage suggested that prison was easier for him than for Doris because of his training in the army reserves, which made him good at following rules—a helpful trait for an uneventful stint in federal prison. Doris dismissed this out of hand, however. It was not her gift of gab (socialization) or her lack of military experience (training) that made Danbury a "snake pit." Instead, the difference in their experiences was "institutional."[62] Specifically, Doris explained that Danbury and Allenwood are different because of who lives within each place—not just women versus men, but people with differing levels of power and access, both within the prison and without (who you can call on the phone matters).

The institutional differences in men's and women's prisons are certainly important—beyond the demographics. These are prisons divided by genitalia, and they are not progressive on matters of gender. Feminist research has found the U.S. prison to be an institution that not only supports the gender binary, but is also an actively "gendering institution," in which feminine behavior (sewing, cooking, cleaning) is rewarded, while transgressions of a traditional female role may be harshly penalized.[63] Men's prisons also uphold gender norms—characterized by physical toughness and violence, and in which emotional openness or caring personal relationships may create dangerous vulnerabilities.

These institutional differences create not only different cultures within each prison, but also varying expectations around who one is and what can be said within that environment. The men's prison, according to my participants, is a hostile, sexist place in which "connection" with other men may be nearly impossible. Hence, even for men who may hope for more thoughtful interactions, the chauvinistic prison culture makes doing so difficult. Fr. Vitale also reminded me that as the sex crimes of Catholic priests have been increasingly prosecuted over the last 20 years, his position as a priest in prison is no longer a safe or necessarily positive position from which to act. As a result, he often keeps his identity quiet while incarcerated, interacting with others only as a fellow inmate, but not as a priest. This reality lessens his leadership potential.

Ways of being in prison are also shaped by institutional overcrowding. It matters that today there are, proportionately, very few incarcerated justice action prisoners in the mix. Historically (and during World Wars I and II, most significantly), there have been moments when "prisoners of conscience" have been incarcerated together (sometimes in large numbers), in federal prisons that were far less crowded than are today's institutions. As a result, those incarcerated for reasons of conscience have at times made up a sizable part of the population. Being together made it easier to organize a work strike, for example, or a fast protesting racial segregation. Today's prisons, on the other hand, are overfull—while incarcerated justice action prisoners generally number in the single digits nationally at any given time, a drop in the ocean of America's prisoners. Further, in today's prisons, people are discouraged from talking with each other, forming trust, or building coalitions. Institutionally, it is absolutely harder to make an impact on policy, or maybe even to "be an activist" from inside the prison walls than it has been in the past. Clearly, it is still possible in men's prisons—but it is absolutely less common. In the women's prisons, on the other hand, female justice action prisoners still find much to do.

There are other ways to think about why women and men describe such different experiences in prison. The differences seem to start from the moment of entry. Male justice action prisoners enter the prison metaphorically alone, and they do not seem to be surprised by what they find there. They engage in resistant action as knowledgeable political actors, and their experiences of prison are generally congruent with what they already know. Living in prison, they are able to separate themselves from their daily environment—to read, pray, and rest—as the injustices they witness or experience work to reinforce their understandings of U.S. violence and imperialism. The problems of the prison—the ways that the poor and people of color are disproportionately affected, as well as the inhumane cruelties of daily life—cohere with their already-existing analyses of the world. Hence, living in prison bolsters their prevailing commitments to disarmament/anti-imperial/peace and justice work, rather than provides a new form of injustice to resist.

Female justice action prisoners, on the other hand, enter prison as individuals who are co-habitating with what they see as a community of vulnerable and violated women. They live there as women, as mothers, as activists, and as people who care about others. By and large, they are busy every day, using their organizing skills to attend to whatever issues require their attention; from calling out prison conditions to writing letters for a bunkie, from protesting mistreatment by the guards to exposing unjust (or absurd) carceral protocols and systems. The women's experiences are shaped by their relationships and interactions with the women they live with, and this affects them both while they are in prison and upon release. For the women, prison reform and/or abolition very often becomes a part of their activist agenda upon release—and much more commonly than it does for the men.

These fundamentally different ways of living (which may be bluntly abbreviated as "living among" versus "living with") cause men and women to fall into distinctive and binary gender camps, as male "knowers" and female "carers." These are stereotypical and traditional gender roles in U.S. culture, and seeing them so clearly performed among this book's participants makes some sense, given their demographics. The average age of my participant is older, and their more "traditional" life experiences (cis-gendered, heterosexual, married with children or chaste) seems to make inhabiting mainstream gender roles feel quite comfortable to them. It is a cliché that it is easy for women to talk with other women about feelings and children and local gossip, while men are socialized to be silent on these fronts. In men "knowing" what's what and women "connecting" with other women, justice action prisoners are performing gender roles in the most typical, culturally "normal" and non-transgressive of ways.

Feminist psychoanalytic theory from the 1980s also helps to illuminate the difference between men's and women's prison experiences, by showing how "being good" is deeply gendered (and justice action prisoners act as "good" people, in alignment with their best—most moral and faithful—selves). According to Dr. Carol Gilligan, "male" morality is centered around protecting autonomy and independence (respecting the rights of others, not interfering, upholding the rule of law/faith), while women's morality is geared toward integration with others, personal responsibility, and "care" (an enlargement of responsibility that is protective).[64] This explanation, while dated and somewhat troublesome in and of itself, helps to make sense of the differing experiences described by male and female justice action prisoners. The theory explains why men trying to be "good" may choose to live more solitary lives while in prison—lives they are able to leave behind upon release—while women are more likely to spend their time caring for others but still leave feeling burdened, sad, and guilty that they did not do more while there. Both are ethical and appropriate ways of responding, within the morality prescribed by what it means to be a good man or good woman.

There is another difference that seems crucial in understanding the variance in women's and men's stories of prisons, which has to do with who one is incarcerated alongside. To some extent, this matters in terms of the types of crimes committed—about ninety percent of incarcerated women are serving sentences for nonviolent property and drug crimes, while for men these numbers are closer to fifty percent.[65] Much more important from the perspective of my participants, however, is the role of parenthood, and what leaving families behind means for incarcerated families. Sixty-two percent of incarcerated women are mothers of minor children, and one in 25 is pregnant when admitted.[66] When a father is incarcerated in state prison, eighty-eight percent of the time their children live with their mothers. However, only thirty-seven percent of children live with their fathers when their mothers are in jail; many enter the foster system.[67] Thus, whole families are torn apart when a woman is incarcerated. During interviews, women repeatedly told me that the federal prisons where they served their time are warehouses for the nation's poorest and most vulnerable women, that women's incarcerations affect whole fami-lies rather than just the individuals behind bars, and that the rippling effects of a woman's imprisonment are massive and tragic for their entire family; it is never just the woman who is punished. The men shared no similar stories.

I had a memorial personal experience of what it might feel like to live among mothers separated from their children when I visited my friend Nancy Gwin in 2010, at Danbury FCI. As I sat with Nancy in the visiting room (which resembles an airport lounge with no airplanes by which to depart), she told me about the other women in the room. A young mother held her baby intensely, and Nancy explained that she had given birth while incarcerated (an ordeal that includes chaining the laboring woman to the hospital bed, and allowing her only limited contact with the child after delivery). The woman's mother and baby had traveled via an elaborate bus route from New York City to visit. Another family picnicked on vending machine goods, sitting in a cir-cle around Snickers bars and Gatorade, laughing and talking. After an hour or so, an inmate named Cadence (pseudonym) walked into the room. "She is my music teacher," Nancy explained. "She stands on the picnic tables and plays jigs on the violin." Cadence is a young white woman; she had braided her hair so that she looked like a Renaissance maiden, dignified in her neatly ironed tan uniform. "Her husband and daughter are visiting from Idaho," Nancy told me, "and things are not going well with the husband, so who knows when she will see her daughter again." Cadence and her five-year-old pixie of a daugh-ter giggled and played for three hours—without a break—while the father sat apart. Wanting so much to talk to Nancy, I could not take my eyes off of them. In this sterile place, they were a contradiction: love, smiles, silliness, play. When visiting hours were over, I watched Cadence and her daughter blow kisses to each other across the span of the room, Cadence catching each one like a ball, playfully shoving each into a pocket for safe-keeping. The little girl was delighted and blew kisses wildly as the iron doors closed in front of her, separating her from her mother. As soon as she was out of sight, the joy that had filled Cadence for the last three hours vanished, and she melted into the arms of a nearby inmate, quiet tears streaming down her face.

In that moment and in a profoundly visceral way, I experienced the hubris of the criminal justice system: the costs of monopolizing judgment about what and who are right and wrong, and the real effects of a system that is empowered to define individuals as "criminal" and hence to punish them and their families in such severe ways. The vast breadth of who is included in the punishment of women hit me hard that day, and sitting in my car in the parking lot after our visit, I sobbed until I was too tired to cry anymore. Nancy was doing fine, but in just the few hours I was there, Danbury had broken my heart.

Of course, this experience cannot be compared against men's prisons in any sort of fair way. Certainly, men's institutions are just as abusive and arrogant as women's, and the effect of fathers being separated from their children can be just as terrible. However, from the stories relayed in this chapter, these realities are not as important in the men's experiences. The relationships developed in women's prisons, on the other hand, critically shape how women experience their lives while they are there. Incarcerated men are just more solitary, and so other men's stories simply affect them less. Seemingly, they never even hear them. Further, while many male prisoners are fathers, this fact was rarely mentioned by the men included in this research. (Although Tom Mahedy was a distinctive exception, and he framed his action against the SOA very much around his fatherhood.)[68] Motherhood, on the other hand, was crucial. It was crucial, and in prison it was tragic. Women's incarceration tears families apart, and the women who are close to it do not recover. Like I did, the female justice action prisoners who observed these family separations felt their impacts deeply. These realities profoundly impact how female justice action prisoners live and what they learn during incarceration, and there is no similar equivalent in the men's stories.

CONCLUSION

The experiences of incarcerated justice action prisoners provide a novel window into the U.S. prison system, a system that relies upon the dehumanization of its subjects to run smoothly. It can be a breathlessly cruel system, and it can also be a place that is simply extraordinarily boring for those who live there. For activists engaging in prison witness, the modern prison state affects their experiences of incarceration; through over-crowding, neglect, and demographics.

Prison was experienced very differently for the men and women included in this research, with men primarily recalling incarceration as a solitary time, while women told stories of injustice, inhumanity, and persistent resistance. Thinking about the different ways that men and women live in prison, my message is absolutely not that either is "better," or more appropriate, than another. I do know that the women's stories stand out, but the prayerful forms of engagement articulated by the men are also experienced as important, meaningful, and radical. Both men and women have transformative experiences during their time in prison, they are just different from one another.

What my data makes undeniably clear is that gender does make a difference in people's experiences. Gender affects how women and men live in prison, what they do and learn when they are there, and what they believe and remember upon release. There is no simple accounting for these variations.

They seem to stem from a combination of gender socialization and performance, as well as institutional differences, that are multi-layered and complicated. However, from the stories justice action prisoners told, it does seem that who one is incarcerated alongside is crucial in how one experiences prison. In general, women formed relationships with the other women they lived with. In learning their stories, the female justice action prisoners came out changed. Living more solitary lives while incarcerated, men were protected from similar experiences, and were able to return to their activist lives without losing focus on their international concerns, and without the intensity of residual concern for those they left behind.

NOTES

1. Defendants rarely have any influence over where they are placed, and it is the policy of the Bureau of Prisons (BOP) to place inmates in the least restrictive facility for which they qualify, preferably within 500 miles of one's home. Some military bases are under joint jurisdiction, so prosecution can be either federal or state. Whether the crime is prosecuted under state or federal laws determines where a person will spend their time.

2. "Population Statistics," *Federal Bureau of Prisons*, https://www.bop.gov/mobile/about/population_statistics.jsp, last updated 07/01/2021, accessed July 1st, 2021.

3. Loic Wacquant, *Punishing the Poor: The Neoliberal Government of Social Insecurity* (Durham, NC: Duke University Press, 2009).

4. "Mass Incarceration, Visualized," *The Atlantic*, https://www.theatlantic.com/video/index/404890/prison-inherited-trait/, accessed 12/11/20.

5. "Section III: The Prison Economy, Prison Labor," *Prison Policy Initiative*, https://www.prisonpolicy.org/prisonindex/prisonlabor.html, accessed 12/11/20.

6. Fr. Kelly, interview.

7. Wendy Sawyer and Peter Wagner, "Mass Incarceration: The Whole Pie," *The Prison Policy Initiative*, 03/24/2020, https://www.prisonpolicy.org/reports/pie2020.html, accessed 07/01/21.

8. Rumpf, interview.

9. "Section III: The Prison Economy," *Prison Policy Initiative*, https://www.prisonpolicy.org/prisonindex/prisonlabor.html, accessed 12/12/20.

10. J. Roberts, "Factories with Fences: The History of Federal Prison Industries, UNICOR, https://www.unicor.gov/publications/corporate/FactoriesWithFences_FY19.pdf, accessed 12/15/2020.

11. Inmates also need money to pay for expensive telephone calls; nationally, the average cost for a 15-minute in-state call from a state jail is $5.74 (in California, it is $17.80). Peter Wagner and Alexi Jones, "State of Phone Justice: Local jails, state prisons and private phone providers," *Prison Policy Initiative*, February 2019, https://www.prisonpolicy.org/phones/state_of_phone_justice.html accessed 12/20/20.

12. The following comes from my joint interview with Doris and Dr. Daniel Sage, Syracuse, NY, April 8th, 2010.

13. Fr. Frankel-Streit, interview.

14. Fr. Vitale, interview.

15. John Dear. "An Interview with Phil Berrigan," http://www.jonahhouse.org/archive/interviewJohnPhil.htm, accessed 01/10/21.

16. Gilroy, interview.

17. Serraglio, interview.

18. Fr. Vitale, interview.

19. Fr. Frankel-Streit, interview.

20. Quoted in Anne Montgomery. "Spiritual Power Behind Bars." In *Swords into Plowshares: Nonviolent Direct Action for Disarmament,* edited by A. J. Laffin and A. Montgomery, 73–75. San Francisco: Harper and Row Publishers, 1987.

21. DeRouen, interview.

22. Berrigan, interview.

23. Mahedy, interview.

24. Kinane, interview. After reading an early draft of this chapter, Ed confirmed that his time in prison *was* "soft." Committed to "intellectual honesty," he explained, he cannot tell me otherwise. But Ed also said that he understands that not everyone has his experience, or is as well suited to prison as he is (personal email 2013).

25. Meyer, interview. When Brian Terrell read an early draft of this chapter, he took issue with Karl's dismissals of difficulty or abuse. "If somebody said that to me," Brian explained, "I would be traumatized by that. I also think Karl would be fine in a gulag." Some people, according to Brian, "just don't want to admit that they are exceptional people." Brian urged me not to think of Karl's experience as normal, or replicable—it is distinctive to who he is (Personal email, 2013).

26. "June 15, 1955: Protest of Nuclear Attack Drills," *Zinn Education Project,* https://www.zinnedproject.org/news/tdih/nuclear-attack-drill-protest. Accessed March 24th, 2021.

27. John Dear, "A Conversation."

28. Tom and Fr. Barrios, interviews.

29. Tom, interview.

30. This was discussed during interviews with Ken Crowley, Kathleen Rumpf, and Derrlyn Tom.

31. Terrell, interview.

32. Serraglio, interview.

33. For example, conscientious objectors de-segregated the cafeteria at Danbury, led successful labor strikes, and changed other harmful prison policies [see Gretchen Lempe-Santangelo, "The Radical Conscientious Objectors of World War II." *Radical History Review* 45 (1989), 5–29; Lawrence Wittner, *Rebels Against War: The American Peace Movement, 1933–1983* (Philadelphia: Temple University Press, 1984].

34. The following comes from my interview with Brian DeRouen.

35. The following comes from my interview with Fr. Barrios.

36. Fr. Frankel-Streit, interview.

37. Fr. Vitale, interview.

38. Fr. Kelly, interview.

39. "Colville Sentenced, Kelly Released," *The Nuclear Resister,* no. 197, April 21, 2021, http://www.nukeresister.org/wp-content/uploads/2021/05/NR197web.pdf. Accessed April 28th, 2021.

40. Fr. Bill remembered entering the prison at Fort Dix a few weeks after Fr. Steve was released from that institution. In a "panic," the warden asked Fr. Bill "What do you want us to do? Steve Kelly was a threat to this whole institution." Bill thought, "Steve? The Jesuit?!" His noncompliance "terrifies" the administration. Such is the power, Fr. Bill explained, of nonviolence (Fr. Bill, interview).

41. Fr. Kelly, interview.

42. Michelle Alexander, *The New Jim Crow: Mass Incarceration in the Age of Colorblindness* (New York: The New Press, 2012).

43. Derrlyn explained that she did not seek out relationships with her co-defendants, nor did she seek out friendships with the other women in prison. She said it was "easier to keep to myself" (interview).

44. Various interviews.

45. Rumpf, interview.

46. Theresa Cusimano, Kathleen Rumpf, and Sr. Jackie Hudson for instance.

47. Kathy Kelly, interview.

48. Doty, interview.

49. Gerard, interview.

50. Tiffany, interview.

51. See Betty Brink, "Hospital of Horrors: Time in Carswell's prison medical facility can be a death sentence for women prisoners," *Fort Worth Weekly,* 10/19/2005, http://www.aclutx.org/2005/10/19/hospital-of-horrors-federal-medical-center-carswell-prison/.

52. Theresa Cusimano. "A letter from Theresa Cusimano, recently released SOA Watch prisoner of conscience." *The Nuclear Resister.* July 20th, 2012. https://www.nukeresister.org/2012/07/20/a-letter-from-theresa-cusimano-soa-watch-prisoner-of-conscience/

53. Hennessy, interview.

54. Gwin, interview.

55. Crane, interview.

56. All of Rae's story comes from our interview.

57. For her filming, "I said, 'if I look a little tired, it's because I was doing my laundry at 4:30 in the morning today, because there is only one working washing machine for 225 women.' . . . She (the woman filming) like perked up a little bit . . . and then left and went to get the warden. And she came back and the warden peeked in . . . and the upshot was they let me finish filming the whole thing" (but never sent it home to her children).

58. Various interviews.

59. Ellen Grady, interview. See also Judith Beaumont, "Prison Witness: Exposing the Injustice" in *Swords into Plowshares,* 1987, 80–85.

60. Various interviews. Other research shows that it is more common for incarcerated women to look out for one another, to exercise creativity, and to push against the administration generally than it is for incarcerated men. See Bosworth, Mary, and Emma Kaufman. "Gender and Punishment." In *The Sage Handbook of Punishment and Society,* edited by Jonathan Simon and Richard Sparks, 186–204. (Fair Oaks: Sage Publications, 2012).

61. Various interviews.

62. Sage, interview.

63. See Mary Bosworth. "Gender, Race and Sexuality in Prison" in *Women in Prison: Gender and Social Control*, ed. Jim Thomas and Barbara Zaitzow. (Boulder: Lynne Rienner Publishers, 2003): 137–154; Bosworth, Mary, and Eamonn Carrabine. "Reassessing Resistance: Race, Gender, and Sexuality in Prison." *Punishment and Society* 3, no. 4 (2001): 501–515; Dana Britton, *At Work in the Iron Cage: The Prison as Gendered Organization* (New York City: NYU Press, 2003); Dana Britton, "Gendered Organizational Logic: Policy and Practice in Men's and Women's Prisons," *Gender & Society* 11, no. 6 (1997): 796–818.

64. Carol Gilligan, *In a Different Voice: Psychological Theory and Women's Development* (Cambridge, MA: Harvard University Press, 1993), 100. See also Sara Ruddick, *Maternal Thinking* (Boston, MA: Beacon Press, 1995).

65. See Lynne Haney, "Motherhood as Punishment: The Case of Parenting in Prison," *Signs* 39, no. 1 (2013). Jennifer Bronson and Ann Carson, "Prisoners in 2017," *Bureau of Justice Statistics*, 04/22/2019, https://bjs.ojp.gov/library/publications/prisoners-2017.

66. "Incarcerated Women and Girls," *The Sentencing Project*, 11/24/2020, https://www.sentencingproject.org/publications/incarcerated-women-and-girls/.

67. Bulletins for Professionals, Children's Bureau. "Child Welfare Practice With Families Affected by Parental Incarceration." January 2021. https://www.childwelfare.gov/pubPDFs/parental_incarceration.pdf.

68. Mahedy, interview. Tom's children were four and six years old when he served his sentence protesting the SOA. He told me that he "cried so hard" during his trial statement, he could not speak. The judge later sent a note to him, addressed to "the weeping father."

Chapter 6

A Visitor in Someone Else's House

The Standpoint of Justice Action Prisoners

The sun . . . I dreamed that the sun
Came alive in my brain.
I felt light pour in
To my skull, and I *knew*. . . .
And I saw
All things that are to come.
Then he said, "Now pay me.
Give yourself now. Let me own you
And I will give you time to rule
Forever." . . . I was frightened.
I said I would but I could not.
My mind was riddled, scorched
With too much seeing and brightness.
. . . all I wanted
was to hide from him, from seeing.
I hid. I shut my eyes . . .
Please, Apollo, I cannot
Give you myself. I'm frightened.
Then he said, "so be it,"
And he grew quiet and gentle.
He begged one kiss of me.
I gave my lips to him.
And he spat into my mouth
And said, "keep my gifts.
Keep my brightness in you.
See it all, the truth
About the war and all things
But since you lied to me

> When you tell that truth
> It will seem to those you tell it
> Toys, baubles, babble,
> And they will laugh at you."
> —Euripides, *Hecuba. The Actor's Book of Classical Monologues,*
> ed. Stefan Rudnicki, adapted by John Barton and Kenneth Cavander,
> translated by Kenneth Cavander (New York: Penguin Books, 1988).
> Reprinted with permission.

*"I see. I've seen, I remember. . . . I saw, I saw, I saw. . . . I've seen a lot . . .
I see the people who don't matter, I see through their eyes."*—Rumpf
(interview)

Cassandra's words from Euripides's 424 BCE play haunted me as I left my interview with Kathleen Rumpf. This chapter is the result of that haunting.

* * *

There is a long legacy in literature of portraying those who see the world differently as hysterical or crazy; women, especially, are objects of suspicion for speaking an alternate truth. In Euripides's play, Cassandra sees the future, but as per Apollo's curse, when she tells it, she goes unheard. These fictional stories, of course, reflect real-world attitudes. Justice action prisoners, like the subjects of such legends, speak what they know to be true, and are also often discounted and ignored. In a patriarchal society, this is compounded for women. As Kathleen Rumpf told me, "I was so many times called crazy. It is so hard to get any credibility when you are a woman."[1]

Even before they go to prison, justice action prisoners see differently: they engage in dramatic nonviolent action at great personal risk because they *know* and *think about* horrors like the torture of civilians and the potential omnicide caused by nuclear weapons on a *daily* basis.[2] Staying mindful of these terrifying realities mandates extraordinary acts of resistance, which—for those of us who keep such information comfortably siloed and distant—really can seem insane. This alternative way of knowing, what I term "counter-hegemonic knowledge" in Chapter 3, is strengthened and transformed by the experience of living in prison.

Prison deepens and shifts the knowledge that lands justice action prisoners there in the first place, and through incarceration the "knowing" becomes bodily. The realities of imperialism, racism, poverty, and so on are *felt* as real, and this experience changes people in ways that manifest as a broadened "vision." This vision affects how they see and understand their own subsequent life experiences, but also what they may read in a book or hear on the nightly news. Things resonate differently than they did before a person went to prison, and what stands out is not necessarily the same as what stood out before. Living in prison, then, produces and solidifies new ways of knowing.

Social movement scholars are interested in the "biographical consequences" of participation in high-risk activism, and the creation of this new way of thinking can be thought of in these terms: it is part of what changes in a person, as a result of engaging in prison witness. Similar to Doug McAdam's discussion of how participation in Freedom Summer shifted volunteers' ways of thinking about daily life, or how the travel offered by groups such as Witness for Peace or Peace Brigades International transforms participants' understandings of geopolitics and personal responsibility, living in prison alters how justice action prisoners think about and see the world.[3] The "consequences" of engagement are generally aligned with the knowledge that preceded participation (people who travel on peace delegations, for example, are already critical-of and engaged-with U.S. foreign policy). However, there is a distinctive "after" that is created through the immersive experience. This chapter shows that the results of living in prison can cause a broadening of activists' political *standpoint*—the vantage point from which they see and make sense of the world.[4]

This "standpoint" is unique because of who justice action prisoners are (privileged, unashamed), and where exactly they find themselves (in prison). It may be thought of as a continuation of the identity-work that gets them locked up in the first place, the next step in "how" they know. The new sight achieved in prison facilitates a visceral knowledge of such things as the gospel, structural violence, one's own privilege and identity, and the U.S. justice system. Unlike the more direct experiences of prison witness (the moment of action and living in prison), the new standpoint does not seem to be significantly affected by public identities; of the 43 activists included here, gender and religious identity made little difference in the kinds of knowledge gained. Rather, what critically facilitated this "new way of seeing" was justice action prisoners' unique positions within the carceral system. As well-educated, white, high-status, and otherwise privileged people, people who are widely considered to be "good" and who feel empowered by their disobedient actions (rather than ashamed, guilty, or enraged—more common feelings for incarcerated people), justice action prisoners experience prison differently than do other incarcerated people. The knowledge that is gained is personalized, bodily, critical, intellectual, and crucially, *different*.

This chapter is about what justice action prisoners learn through their travels across the U.S. justice system, journeys that challenge deeply engrained epistemic ignorances, as they also provide a source of understanding that is, in and of itself, unique and valuable. I call this perspective a "prison standpoint." The prison standpoint springs from the experience of "good" and privileged people who—as its former wards—identify the U.S. prison system as violent, unjust, and inhumane. It is a form of knowledge that relies upon privilege at every step: in how it is achieved, how it is communicated, and to whom the perspective is strategically "for." Among my participants, there was some disagreement about whether or not time in prison was necessary for the achievement of certain knowledge, but no matter what, as Kathy Kelly argued, "there's nothing like being locked up . . . to get a quick education."[5]

For almost everyone represented in this book, living in prison fundamentally affirmed their political analysis and commitments to social justice and resistance. It opened their eyes (or widened their view) to the ongoing realities of racism, imperial power, capitalist goals, militarism, and their own privilege. As Sr. Mary Kay Flanigan explained, despite its many difficulties, she is glad that she went to prison because "I understand so much more about the whole prison system from the inside out."[6] This understanding, from their perspective as empowered prisoners, is distinctive and valuable—both for the activists themselves and for what it reveals about the (in)justice system in the U.S. today.

FEMINIST STANDPOINT THEORY AND THE U.S. PRISON SYSTEM

The next part of the chapter explains what a political "standpoint" is, according to feminist philosophy, as well as reviews the deeper cultural work of the U.S. prison.

Feminist Standpoint Theory

The basic idea of feminist standpoint theory (also known as "situated knowledge") is that "where you stand determines what you see." We all have a particular perspective that is based on our identity categories, and "who we are" lies at the intersection of where we fall along lines of gender, race, class, and so on. These identities facilitate understandings of the world that may be "true," but that are also always, in Sandra Harding's words, "partial and perverse."[7] In this framework, everyone's knowledge is incomplete and there is no such thing as a "God's eye view," no ultimate or universal truth that any one person may obtain through their own individual experience. Instead, our social identity categories at once enable and eclipse various forms of knowledge, and so *what we know* is always and already shaped by *who we are.* In this way, our identities work as both lenses and blinders: they make possible understandings of what is in our view, but they also preclude understanding (or even awareness of) that which lies outside of it. We may be able to enlarge our field of vision (standpoint) through intentionally seeking out different forms of experience, in these ways gaining "better"—truer and more complete—understandings. However, there is always a limit to what we can know.

Like W.E.B. Du Bois's "double consciousness," standpoint theory proposes that members of oppressed groups have a wider (clearer, more accurate) perspective through which to make sense of the world than do those belonging to dominant groups. This is because the oppressed must develop understandings of at least two worlds: the one in which they actually live and that of the dominant. As a result, the oppressed see "better" than do those with more privileges.[8] Further, privilege can restrict the development of accurate knowledge, for it works to limit one's perspective and thus, one's potential for comprehension. For example, a person who can easily walk may not know whether or not the elevator at their office is working properly today—an "ignorance" that is not malicious or intentional, just something that the able-bodied person does not need to know. In this way, privilege manifests as a form of ease, but also, significantly, as a form of ignorance.

Changing their standpoint, for a privileged people, is a political project, and the impacts can be both personal and public. The development of a "prison standpoint" pushes against justice action prisoners' own privileges and the easy ignorance those privileges facilitate, as it provides new ways of making sense of the world. The gaining of a standpoint is not a passive process, as it is not just "standing elsewhere" that produces new lines of vision. Instead, one must *critically think* about oneself and the meanings of one's location: a standpoint is "political."[9]

A prison standpoint is distinct for *where* it is achieved. As Randy Serraglio explained, "prison breaks you" into two parts.[10] You may recover from the trauma of this cleavage, but you will always afterward exist as both the person you were before you went to prison and the person who came out. Critically thinking about the experience of prison and how it fits into larger, systemic patterns may constitute the work of identity explored in Chapter 3, but it also facilitates a new perspective for knowing about oneself and the greater world.

Application: How Other Inmates See Justice Action Prisoners

To understand the idea of standpoint, it is helpful to provide an example of how it works in practice. How the other inmates understood (or not) what justice action prisoners were doing in their resistance actions demonstrates the concept of situated knowledge in action.

During interviews, I was told again and again that the incarcerated men in maximum-security institutions "get it"; they accurately understood justice action prisoners' reasons for being there, and they supported the activists' rationales. As participant Ken Hayes explained, there is a lot of "sympa-thy" among the inmates for what they see as "anti-government" sentiments and action.[11] Conversely, at the men's camps (which house a segment of well-connected and more privileged men), other inmates were more likely to be confused or even angry with the justice action prisoners. Fr. Bill Frankel-Streit explained that the men in maximum saw his action "as con-fronting the whole system, a system they were victimized by as people of color . . . (they were) very sympathetic . . . whereas the whites, or even some of the blacks or Hispanics in the camps, they were just a little confused about it because they were just more tied into the system."[12] In other words, the fur-ther one stands from the mainstream (hegemonic center), the more likely one is to value and understand the need for profound (anti-state) resistance. One's "standpoint" (as formed by identity) shapes one's understanding.

In maximum-security prison, justice action prisoners explained, there is widespread appreciation for why one would be anti-government. Professor Bill Houston told me that "the prisoners could all understand why you'd be against the government. They might not understand why you'd commit civil disobedience and go to jail . . . (but) they had been screwed by the govern-ment" and so they properly understood his action.[13] Similarly, female justice action prisoners explained that, regardless of security levels, *all* incarcerated women understand anti-imperial resistance, and the women agree with what they see as justice action prisoners' anti-state critique. Meagan Doty told me that the women in FPC Pekin, where she was housed in Illinois, were not gen-erally well-versed in U.S. foreign policy, but they all understood her action quickly, completely, and correctly—in contrast to the more privileged (and often formally educated) audiences Meagan speaks with outside the prison walls. The incarcerated women told Meagan, "hell yes I believe the U.S. runs schools of torture. They run *this* place!"[14] For those who are not incarcerated, accepting such information as "possibly true" can be much harder.

Depending on where we stand, then, we understand the systemic critique of nonviolent resisters differently. Our standpoints determine what we see, what we know, what we value, and what we believe to be real. A standpoint is a fundamental lens through which we filter and process information; hence, its transformation can be radical indeed.

Inequality Locked Down: Critical Scholarship on the U.S. Prison

The perspective that justice action prisoners gain about the prison industrial complex, and particularly how the system supports a broader and more pro-found unjust status quo, mirrors critical, feminist, and abolitionist scholar-ship. Within the social sciences, the prison has long been theorized as an institution that demonstrates how power operates, as well as illuminates how imprisonment plays a crucial (if often unrecognized) part in maintaining hierarchical (and discriminatory) social structures in the U.S. today.[15]

The prison is a discriminatory institution. Seventy percent of those incarcerated today are people of color, and those calling for its abolition make explicit connections to its roots in American slavery.[16] Prison abolitionists show that the carceral system perpetuates racial discrimination, as well as ensures that people of color are continually denied full access to the life, liberty, and pursuit of happiness they were so long ago—officially at least—legally guaranteed (for example, through denying released felons the right to vote). It is not simply race, however, that predictably lands people in prison. Sociologist Loic Wacquant documents how the penal system engages in what he calls a "triple selectivity" by: (1) class, (2) race, and (3) space.[17] Only by recognizing this triad can we begin to understand the hyper-incarceration of poor, black, urban males (the fourth selectivity), a pattern that is not neutral or natural, but the result of specific surveillance patterns and policies (differently punishing crack vs. powder cocaine, for example). Together, these patterns and policies push certain types of people into prison, as others are protected, over and over again.

Scholars also remind us that the prison plays a key role in the continued dominance of capitalism and neoliberal policies. Jackie Wang writes about what she calls "carceral capitalism," the process by which incarceration *targets* the poor, but also *keeps* people, and whole communities, poor.[18] The prison also helps make capitalism appear a fair and functional system, and is a necessary support for the myth of meritocracy—the belief that those who play by the rules will be rewarded, an idea that must be protected for the smooth running of a punishing capitalist system of haves and have-nots.[19]

One remarkable outcome of incarcerating the poor is that it hides more than two million of the people who have been rendered obsolete by neoliberal policies—obscuring their troubles (and the root causes of their troubles) from the view of social policy. For example, many inmates were unemployed at the time of their arrest, but their imprisonment keeps them from being counted among its rolls. Prisons are also a holding place for the ill, unruly, addicted, and the unlucky—protecting social services (healthcare, welfare) from revealing their inadequate abilities to care for these high-needs populations.[20] Prisons contain, quiet, and disenfranchise a population of this country's most vulnerable citizens, the very people who benefit least from a neoliberal economic system.

More insidiously, capitalism identifies the factors that most often get people locked up (poverty, mental illness, addiction, discrimination, toxic masculinity) as exclusively personal shortcomings, resulting in punishment that can be interpreted as a reasonable consequence for individual people's failures, rather than also the result of structural failures or entrenched inequalities. In this view, the state's inability to protect people, to care for them when they are unwell, or to ensure access to decent livelihoods, is concealed—clouded and made obsolete. In these ways, the prison is part of the smoke and mirrors that provides cover to the neoliberal state. Prisons help the state to appear fair in what it provides and to whom, as well as adequate in how it cares for its citizens.

THE PRISON STANDPOINT

Through their acts of resistance against the state, justice action prisoners become its wards. As such, they occupy "new ground" from which they can develop a new political standpoint. By saying "no" to U.S. imperialism, they are privy to its underside. "Naturally" empire's greatest beneficiaries (white, Christian, well educated), they live among its most ignored and hated populations. Unashamed of their reasons for being incarcerated; politically aware of the imperial and militarized connections between where they are and racism, labor, and the military state; and more impervious to some of the common violences perpetrated by the prison system than are other prisoners, their incarceration provides an uncommon window into the injustices caused by the prison industrial complex, as well as into their own positionalities and identities. This is not to say that prisoners who are not incarcerated "on purpose" lack such analysis, nor that activists who do not go to jail are inherently unable to similarly produce it. Instead, it tells us that the circumstances around justice action prisoners spending time in jail provides a strange mix of factors that can lead to novel learnings, experiences, and conclusions that together comprise their own "prison standpoint."

What Makes the Prison Standpoint Distinctive?

Justice action prisoners are unique prisoners. They are not just "privileged," in structural terms, they are also often empowered—in terms of feeling at least somewhat in control of their lives no matter where they live. Importantly, resistance stands out as among the best things most justice action prisoners feel that they have ever done. Crossing a line or pouring blood on a warhead is felt as a capstone experience that solidifies their alignment between faith and action, ideal self and actualized self, word and deed. Hence, they generally lack any sense of repentance for whatever "crime" has landed them in prison, and so justice action prisoners rarely embody the expected feelings of regret, guilt, personal responsibility for wrongdoing, or sorrow that is expected of prisoners with guilty verdicts. Instead, they tend to feel sure and righteous; about both what they did and who they are. Deeply engrained feelings such as pride rather than shame make the systems by which the prison works (processes of dehumanization, guilt, shaming) differently visible to justice action prisoners: they clearly see these practices for what they are and what they do to people, without necessarily being their target (ways to put people down, to make them feel ashamed and deserving of their punishments). Further, through their relative immunity to the effects of such practices, justice action prisoners have yet another level of "privilege" within their prison experiences overall.

Indeed, how justice action prisoners feel about themselves and their actions exist in contrast to the lives of most prisoners in this country, where criminalization is generally considered the appropriate consequence for individual shortcomings—fair punishment for one's bad behavior. In this, responsibility for criminal acts—which are most often crimes of daily survival in the U.S. (drug couriering, prostitution, fraud)—lies solely with the individual; the playing field is assumed to be equal and just. The proper attitude for the prisoner, then, is of guilt and repentance. Anger, rage, and fear are also common emotions. Common feelings are certainly *not* those of pride, empowerment, justice, or a sense of biblical obedience.

The standpoint of justice action prisoners is also unusual because it is neither that of the oppressed nor that of the privileged. Though they live among the oppressed, their privilege is ever-present in the prison, and invariably affects what happens to them. That said, the standpoint also differs from what could be achieved by privileged people elsewhere—what is gained is a privileged perspective, obtained in the bowels of the imperial beast and alongside some of those who bear its greatest harms.

My research shows that for people of compound privilege, the experience of incarceration produces knowledge that is not otherwise easily replicated elsewhere. Specifically, *how* the knowledge becomes known is different, for it is based on personal, bodily experience, as shaped by individual privilege. Certainly, not everyone who goes to jail for justice gains a political standpoint, but it is generally true that prison enables the formation of different perspectives and knowledges than could be predictably or reliably produced elsewhere.

A Visitor in Someone Else's House

As with any standpoint, there is always a limit to what one can know. Fr. Bill Frankel-Streit explained:

> Going to jail means going to the house of the poor. We have Catholic Worker houses . . . where the poor come to us, and no matter how much we try to break down those walls, they still feel like they're going to somebody else's house.

And . . . that's the way it feels going to jail. It's still not my house. It's the house for the poor.[21]

For Fr. Bill, privileged people serving time for nonviolent crimes of resistance are visitors in someone else's house. The house was not built for them and they may not belong there, but for Fr. Bill, it is important to go to that house, and to think deeply about what one finds there. One may work on one's own internalized dominations within that space, but one must never think one "knows" what it means for *that* house to be *your* house. For privileged activists incarcerated in the U.S., there is no way to reach some goal of "belonging" within the marginalized and disempowered groups one lives among and speaks-for, there is just continued effort towards better understanding.

Kathy Kelly also expressed feelings of limited knowledge as a privileged woman incarcerated. She said:

I'm very much a subscriber to the idea that where you stand determines what you see and that it's important to try and stand alongside people bearing the brunt of various kinds of warfare, including the war against the poor. Because of, in my case, education, sort of middle-class experience, white skin . . . to some extent verbal abilities, but mostly because I felt no shame, zero shame for what I did, there is always a limit to how much I could really be standing with people. And of course as they used to say in 1988, "You ain't nothing but a minute."[22]

Structurally, it is impossible for Kathy to say that she "knows" what it is like to be an ordinary woman in prison, and she will never make that claim. Privilege is an obstacle to her understanding. Similarly, Sr. Dorothy Pagosa explained that, as a white nun and justice action prisoner, even when strip-searched "you don't have nothing"—i.e., her privilege (including her sense of righteousness, confidence, and divine obedience) is always still "something."[23] Hence, understanding (in the sense of knowing what other prisoners are going through) is always limited. Fr. Louis Vitale explained that despite his many long stints in prison, he still does not know what it feels like to be a prisoner. "You can say you surf," he explained, "but are you a surfer?" Clearly not. Fr. Louis is simply a visitor in another person's house.[24]

These specific limitations are crucial in making the standpoint distinct: it is because justice action prisoners are people of compound privilege, living in Empire's underbelly, that they are able to "see" so specifically—and differently than either their similarly-privileged peace activist peers *outside* of the prison, or those more oppressed within it. In addition to comprehending how their action is impacted by their privilege, by living in America's prisons, justice action prisoners have front row tickets to the impacts of racism, militarism, and poverty in this country. And crucially, they see these oppressive forces as *real*—despite the fact that they themselves are rarely their target. Still, without the standpoint gained in prison, their privilege could easily continue to insulate them from actually absorbing the knowledge incarceration makes available. Such experiences are felt strongly: visceral and intimate. They often effectively (and significantly) change people.

Living in prison also affords justice action prisoners an opportunity to experience a *lack* of privilege—limited, surely, but nonetheless an experience of being under someone else's control. For people of compound privilege, the experience of not being in charge of one's life is illuminating, and it is experienced as difficult. Explaining this dynamic, Rae Kramer told me that she loves teaching domestic violence–prevention classes to men in prison because the incarcerated men so clearly "get . . . what it means to be under someone else's control." She continued, "there was such a visceral understanding of what it meant to be an adult and have some other adult deciding things that impacted your every movement."[25] In prison, justice action prisoners are able to experience this themselves. Then, and crucially, they *think* about these experiences: what they mean, why they occur, and how their own identities affect the process. This thinking work is what transforms a set of unusual life events into a "prison standpoint."

What Does the Prison Standpoint See?

The knowledge that is solidified through living in prison does not follow the gendered patterns found elsewhere in this research, despite the sometimes profound differences in women's and men's experiences of imprisonment itself. In terms of content, the prison standpoint is centered around three areas. It provides ways for justice action prisoners to understand the prison system as a system of violence and discrimination, and it increases their understandings of their own privileged identities. The prison standpoint also provides "felt experiences" around issues of oppression and violence, as well as the "gospel in context" for those of religious faith.

What most stands out about the prison standpoint is not intellectual, however (indeed, the specific content expressed largely maps onto existing scholarship). What is unique is the way in which what is learned is felt as bodily, and hence—unshakably real—among a population for whom such experiences are unusual and unlikely. Prison gives justice action prisoners an opportunity to witness and be a part of things they care deeply about—to see and feel oppression, violence, torture, control, power, discrimination, pain, fear, punishment—and also transcendence. In the worst conditions, I heard stories of courage, persistence, and joy. As a result, *how* justice action prisoners know what they come to know is profound. They are *certain*. What is specifically learned in the prison may be different for different justice action prisoners, but for all of them, the force of what is known becomes determining: whether to reinforce one's existing political analysis or to re-direct one's activism, one can never "go back" to the person one was before becoming a prisoner.

The System: Punitive, Capitalist, Racist, and Dehumanizing

The prison is a punitive institution. Participants told me that if restorative justice (justice towards wholeness and healing, of individuals and communities) were truly a goal, it could be achieved easily. The methods are no mystery: better education, real healthcare, jobs and job training, addiction counseling, and so on. Though like Susan Crane, we commonly "know that education is a route" out of crime, the educational programming that is offered in America's prisons is "measly and insufficient."[26] Further, to prevent recidivism, the possibility of a decent job and integration into community prove essential, but we burden former felons with lifetime punishments around employment, basic rights of citizenship, and eligibility for social services. If we truly wanted to help inmates better their lives, Susan argued, solutions we know to be effective would be much more broadly implemented. However, as John Heid explained, prison is not about healing or forgiveness, but its opposite: "there's nothing . . . to help individuals forgive themselves." Instead, the logic of incarceration is to make one's worst mistake "the hallmark of your life by which everything else is defined."[27] This nation's high recidivism rates (about 43%) prove that our current form of punishment is a waste of "time, energy, and resources" for the taxpayer, according to Rae Kramer. Instead of restoring people to wholeness or health, in Susan's words, the prison is "just warehousing throw-away people."[28] There is no real interest in transforming the conditions—or the people—that create the troubled prison industrial complex in the first place. Rather, the goal is to deter, and to punish.

Ken Crowley's two six-month sentences at a medium security prison in Texas gave him opportunities to think about the structural violence that is exacerbated by the prison system. He explained that by going to prison, those he was housed with had lost whatever it was they had before. They

had no prospect for anything better when they got out. Basically, it's what we all know: Economic inequality is the ultimate cause of violence. Because even if you just have something, it deters people. . . . The pitiful thing is that it doesn't take a whole lot to undo a lot of this damage . . . it doesn't take a lot of money, it doesn't take a lot of critical thinking, it doesn't take a lot of resources to undo what's happened.

Here, Ken neatly links his visceral education in the consequences of a system that leaves some people with "nothing" to his activist commitment that this is changeable: the modern prison is not an inevitable consequence of bad behavior, but a legislative and ongoing human choice, and an unsurprising result of racialized and class-based impoverishment. In our interview, Ken cited the Marshall Plan as an example of what a little commitment towards education and job creation could do. However, despite the fact that "it doesn't take a lot" to change things, it is hard. "And I've been trying," Ken quipped.[29]

Justice action prisoners often weave their understandings of race and capital into their descriptions of prison. Such insights are facilitated by justice action prisoners' various privileges but are based in the most basic of bodily experiences. These are accounts of personal experiences that demonstrate some of what critical scholars write about, but in ways—and for audiences—who may otherwise be guarded from understanding them. Clare Grady told me a simple but haunting story that dramatizes her bodily learning of *how* the prison system works as the continuation of slavery (the argument of the abolitionists), and how this learning permanently changed her.[30]

In 2004, Clare spent six months in FDC Philadelphia for a disarmament action. It is an administrative men's prison, located in a converted parking garage in Philadelphia's historic district. It houses about 1,200 men and 200 women. The women's section was added because the men carried out a "go slow, refuse to work" action some years before Clare was incarcerated there. Rather than respond to the men's complaints, the administration built a women's section, and assigned them the care-work for the incarcerated men. Of the roughly 200 women prisoners, about half are pre-trial (and hence cannot work), leaving about 100 women to do the cleaning, cooking, laundry, and so on for a facility of about 1,400 people. During Clare's stay, guards found a cell phone in one of the two women's units, resulting in a lockdown of the unit. The lockdown meant that for part of Clare's sentence, the women's workforce was divided in half once more. It was "a slave labor camp," she remembered. "It was terror and tyranny and domination to the worst extent."

Clare worked in the kitchen, as she had at a community kitchen for 17 years in her hometown of Ithaca, New York. She thought, "what could be bad about a kitchen?"

> They just kept saying, "the way they treat you." Well when I got down there I was just all smiles, in my determination. After a week I was chilled to the bone. . . . In that kitchen I experienced . . . a sweatshop. There are no windows, you could be in hell. . . . (In the community kitchen), you greet people like "Here, here's Christ." . . . And there it's the opposite . . . it's "here's a new batch of workers" . . . and I saw the batches of women become more bedraggled. It looked like they'd come from some serious street scene, abuse, and needed

more TLC than anything, but they were the fodder. (Three meals a day for 1400 people could be smooth), but if you're coming in with a fresh batch of women who've just come from their addictions and abuse, and nonviolent communication skills are not at an all-time high, then all the guard has to do is pass the invisible whip. I saw it one day—classic—"Ladies, if you don't do this by 11 o'clock nobody's going up for lunch" and walk away. And the biggest bully would take that whip and start doing the appropriate whipping. It didn't even have to be physical, it was "whack." It was "whack" and it was wicked. . . . When I got out I read some narratives of how that worked (slavery), with the whip . . . all of this stuff is so real to me. So real to me. There was a time when George Bush went to a vegetable plant in Guatemala. . . . And I was like (makes the sound of a whip cracking), I was in tears . . . knowing the terror piece. Like if you stop for a second, or complain, or ask for your humanity, you're gone. You're gone. And in those cases, you know, it feels like life or death. When I heard the "Lucifer Effect" interview on Amy Goodman when I got out of jail, I literally fell to the ground and I went "That is fucking what they are doing!" So intentional. There's no randomness about this.[31]

Clare's first assignment was to wash the pots and pans. The chicken was baked with no pan liners, and the women were given no scouring tools. Seemingly, they were to scrape the pans clean with their fingernails. The absurdity of the carceral system and its many cruelties are evident in this simple image; a small group of vulnerable women, hurriedly scrubbing sticky, gluey chicken grease off stacks and stacks of pans with their bare hands. Women cleaning up men's messes is so common as to be invisible, so acceptable as to be unremarkable, and to this day women do the work of FDC Philly.

Clare's story shows the ways in which justice action prisoners gain a bodily experience of how the prison industrial complex is designed to support the status quo, on the bodies of those incarcerated. The prison is a construction of justice, but it is built on legacies of violence that are both personal and systemic. Justice action prisoners don't just know this, some can *feel* it, for they have experienced it as real.

It was often through the simplest stories that the damaging practices of the U.S. prison system came into clearer relief. Pairing Ellen Grady and Theresa Cusimano's accounts provides a telling example. In her interview, Ellen talked about how the inmates grew and ate from a bountiful garden in Niantic, Connecticut (York Correctional) during her sentence there in 1981. At that time, sufficient and "home grown" fresh food was served in the cafeteria, where the women ate together. Ellen never remembered feeling hungry, and she stayed healthy and strong throughout her one-year Plowshares sentence.[32] In contrast, industrial food (processed, commercial food that is pre-packaged for ease of consumption) is what is most often served to inmates in prisons today, often in their cells, on prepared trays. This change in meal procedures may seem insignificant and certainly doesn't sound newsworthy as a sound-bite of harm—who is going to get outraged about serving inmates dinner on trays? However, doing so may actually result in malnourishment, especially for those with dietary restrictions. In 2012, Theresa Cusimano nearly died as a result of being intolerant to gluten. Without "choice," she became malnourished, and then deathly ill.

Less dramatically but also importantly, serving prepared food to inmates in their cells contributes to a lack of community among inmates, *as it also* solidifies the commercialization and profit-making possibilities of the prison system. Providing nourishing food that people can eat is not a priority for an industry built around profit. In prison, food is a commodity to buy and consume rather than a community project to grow, harvest, prepare, cook, and eat together. And this changes the institution—what it does to people, how it feels to live there, the possibilities for personal healing and change, and how it may feel to leave. It is simply more punitive, isolating, unhealthy, and even dangerous to eat alone in one's cell than to be part of a community growing and preparing their own food. For those working to change the U.S. prison system, justice action prisoners' stories show that these "little things" can actually greatly impact people's lives, and that they add up. Serving industrial food to prisoners is not cruel, but it does remove a layer of self-control and healthy interaction from their lives. It can be dehumanizing, but it is hard to build a movement around.

This book's participants highlight how such "little" things can deeply matter. In their interviews, justice action prisoners relay that in prison, the quality of a prison library can be the difference between a dull experience and an experience that feels inhumane. Good vocational programs and addiction counseling can be the difference between recidivism and the chance for positive personal transformation and lasting change. A cruel or helpful counselor is the difference between communicating with and staying connected to one's support community or being cut off from everyone one knows. And staying connected with one's community of support can be the difference between freedom and recidivism, or even life and death. Seeing the small stuff (as well as, of course, the "big stuff") and showing people who are not incarcerated (and may not necessarily be interested in these issues) how much they can affect prisoners' lives thus becomes a significant way in which justice action prisoners can use their privilege, their knowledge, and their distinctive standpoints to further justice causes. Their prison standpoint, in other words, can become another force of privilege that can be used "for good."

The Self in Prison

In the challenging, dehumanizing, and structurally unjust environment of the U.S. prison, justice action prisoners learned much about themselves. Most often, they came to better understand their own values and limits around what they stand for and how much they can stand. This is an embodied knowledge, born of what it feels like to lack control over their own lives. Such deeply personal learning is exhausting. In prison, Clare Grady said, "every day you have to make a thousand little decisions about where to draw your lines."[33] For justice action prisoners, facing continual dilemmas that challenge one's sense of self helps to develop an alternative political standpoint. Cumulatively, these little "learnings" can alter people's lives. Personal learning includes coming to know oneself in an environment of dehumanization, as well as more specific lessons around deepening faith life, attachment, and social privilege.

At its core, the prison is a machine of dehumanization. Dehumanization, according to peace scholars, is at the core of violence—it is essential for the perpetration of any violent act to first put distance between self and other.[34] It is thus consequential that the prison is a profoundly inhuman institution; it turns people into *things* (numbers, cases, crimes committed) rather than recognizing them as individual, sentient, and worthwhile human beings. Jerry Berrigan described prison as "a living death . . . it's where you are forced to live as a thing, rather than a human being."[35] Quite literally, upon entry, the prison strips a person of their identity and replaces it with a new one (a number). The challenge for justice action prisoners is to accept the stripping away but to reject the new identifiers imposed (criminal, wrong, guilty, bad), instead committing oneself to finding out who one *really* is in this most oppressive and difficult space. For justice action prisoners, the self-awareness that results from living in prison is often about who they are structurally, in this place that enables seeing things as they have never seen them before. In important ways, seeing how dehumanization works—given their relative protection from the widespread shaming foisted on inmates—is a key enabler in the development of their prison standpoint.

In different ways, several participants spoke about the "stripping away" of their identity that their incarceration enabled. Often, this was a negative experience of dehumanization, fear, or violation. As Derrlyn Tom explained, "our penal system . . . is about breaking you. It is about . . . stripping you of everything that you hold dear."[36] In prison, the most basic human interactions and needs are affected by dehumanizing practices; one cannot shower, go to the bathroom, or write a personal letter without others in attendance. In a letter to me from FPC Yankton, Brian Terrell described how touch and intimacy are made "dirty" in prison, quoting Alexander Solzhenitsyn to describe the strip search as "dirty fingers on a lacerated heart."[37] The strip-search is the "most intimate touch" in a prisoner's life, Brian explained, and is "all the more demeaning" for this. In interviews, justice action prisoners told me that dehumanization is accomplished through assigning and referring to each inmate by a number rather than a name; by denying outside lives or relationships; by mandating uniforms; by discouraging the development of friendships, helpfulness, sharing, or community; and by rigidly imposing "us" and "them" lines between guards and inmates. Individually, each act is a small violation of one's complex humanity; together, they grind people down and erode their self-esteem.

What it means to be a prisoner in this country, fundamentally, is that somebody else controls your life. In practice, this means, for example, that mail sent to "Reverend Kenneth Kennon" is returned to sender because in prison, Ken is an *inmate*, not a Reverend.[38] If a loved one dies, someone else decides whether or not you can attend the funeral. If you are not feeling well, it is another person who determines if you are *really* sick or if you are just "faking it." You don't decide what to wear, watch on television, or eat for dinner. Prison is, in Randy Serraglio's words, "the center of the universe of arbitrary authority." If you are a prisoner, the only rule that is certain is that you are not in charge.[39]

Taken singly, these discomforts are not particularly harmful. In many U.S. prisons, there is nothing directly "objectionable" about the day-to-day treatment, in the words of Dan Sage. But according to my respondents, the mild ongoing trauma of living there can wreck you. "For six months," Bill Houston said, "it was fine. It would have been hell for longer."[40]

One of the ways that prison works on the body is to transform you into a *prisoner.* Kathleen Rumpf described this process when she spoke of her total surprise at being released on her own recognizance during the 1984 Griffiss Plowshares trial. She recalled her initial inability to embody "freedom." She explained, "there's a picture of me coming out of the courthouse, off the elevator, I'm the first one out, and I'm like (mouth open, awe-faced). I'm still being told what to do. I-I can't function. I've been in jail, and I've been told what to do, and all of a sudden you're free and it doesn't compute. . . . I never thought I'd get out, I mean, never!"[41] Kathleen's is a visceral description of how the dehumanization of the prison works on the body, transforming it from an agential subject (and in Kathleen's case, a committed, empowered, intentional subject) into an incarcerated object that is literally unable to function (move, talk) without being told what to do. For Derrlyn Tom, after months of insult at the hands of her jailors, "I just thought, do whatever you want. . . . I remember saying that to the warden. . . . And that's what gets created. I mean, you're going to treat me like this? I am going to act like this!"[42] The environment's relentless insensitivity and absurd cruelty can bring out these same qualities in its inhabitants.

Randy Serraglio spoke of the lasting impacts of incarceration on the body and spirit. He said:

> After six months, you become a prisoner. And if you're in for long enough, it definitely breaks you. It doesn't necessarily ruin you. You end up coming out of it as sort of two people—the person you were before you went to prison and the person you are after prison. So it doesn't necessarily break you in a destructive way. You could grow from it . . . but it definitely breaks you. . . . I thoroughly believe that.[43]

Randy explained that even as a healthy, young, well-supported person who was unafraid of his incarceration and whose prison term was "tense" but uneventful, he was hugely impacted by prison in negative ways. It changed him, "broke" him, elicited feelings of rage, and ultimately resulted in his leaving the movement and ending his relationship with a long-term partner. After Randy's release, it took a lengthy process of self-healing to adapt to his "new" self.

These impacts are all the more remarkable because the illegal act that sent Randy to prison was one he was supremely proud of. In crossing the line at Fort Benning, he acted in alignment with his conscience and with tremendous support from the movement. Even with this initial strength, however, the dehumanization ASPC Safford exacted disoriented Randy. It hurt him and it changed him, and he had to recover from his incarceration slowly and over time, finally emerging with a "new"—broken and repaired, "double" self.

Kathleen Rumpf described another consequence of the prison's dehumanizing practices. She explained that "the legal system, it's a theft of stories. They steal our stories. *And then they tell you who you are.*" Stripped of their individuality, backgrounds, and communities, people become lost in a system that is responsible for them, but fundamentally does not care about them. The complete severance of prisoners from their lives is possible because prisoners are "the most hated population" in this country.[44] For Kathleen, denying people their stories—the threads that keep them tethered to their lives as free—demonstrates that the intention of the prison is not healing, personal transformation, or reform, but punishment. Denying people their stories is consequential. One of the strongest indicators for positive post-release outcomes is consistent communication with family and friends while incarcerated.[45] As a result, if we truly want to keep people from returning to prison, we must facilitate and celebrate the connections they are able to keep with their world outside—we have to let them keep their stories.

From within the dehumanizing space of the prison, justice action prisoners often expand their understandings of what it means to be an activist, a person of faith, and a person of privilege. For example, working in that dreadful prison kitchen, Clare Grady felt a loyalty to her fellow inmates that helped her know what it means to do resistance without supportive community. She explained:

> I went in on my day off to help the women in the kitchen . . . because I wasn't gonna let them be alone. And in that moment I realized that this is exactly what you hear young people say that go to Iraq or Afghanistan, "I don't support this war, but I'm not gonna let my buddies down." Right? . . . I got a deeeeeeper appreciation of what it's like to non-cooperate from within the beast, without your community. To be a whistleblower of any kind, to step out in any way, what that meant. It wasn't even because the guard is gonna cut your head off . . . it's psychology 101. It's the relationship of the community of women who are just barely surviving.[46]

So, even though the administration she was supporting through her kitchen work was wicked and tyrannical, Clare's allegiance to her companions over-rode these concerns. Clare said that this experience put her in better solidarity with soldiers and whistleblowers, as it gave her a taste of the courage required to speak against institutions, cultures, and systems—and especially, what it takes to do so without a network of support.

The Gospel in Context and Privilege

Several participants recalled imprisonment as an opportunity to learn about the Gospel in context (as Fr. Bill said, "Paul was usually in custody"). These participants felt that being in prison illuminates Christian teachings, as it gave them an opportunity to experience them. For example, Clare told me that she had always been curious about the detail, in the Resurrection Story, of how Jesus's garments are stacked in a particular way. In prison, she realized that:

> Oh! It's really important to the author of this Gospel to have us see that Jesus took this off, *by hand.* That he didn't just disappear into the sky . . . this BIG effort put into making you get that he resurrected, in the body, that he went like this [she demonstrates unwrapping a garment from around her head]. . . . And why is that important? Because if you live with tyranny and terror and death and torture, it is good news to know that the ultimate weapons of empire still have no hold on you. THAT is good news. Like, for somebody sitting in a pew, who's raised in a pious way looking at the Bible, it's sort of like "How nice." . . . But it doesn't get the full whammo of WHY THAT'S SUCH GOOD NEWS!

For a Christian person living under tyranny, knowing that there is an after-life, that Christ resurrected, and that there is an authority greater and more just than the one currently strangling you, is *liberating* but also *life altering* information. The carefully described pile of clothing is the author of the Gospel's way of letting you know that this was *real*. Clare explained that "Jesus didn't just *poof*" magically disappear—he took his garments off carefully, intentionally, piece by piece, by *hand*. This information, the concrete reality of it, is included in the text specifically for those who are living under oppression. So other Christian prisoners "got" what Clare would say in ways that were not very interesting for those living free lives (again, our standpoints shaping what we know). Gesturing broadly as she spoke, Clare explained that when she was in prison she "started writing these Easter greetings to everybody, and I would . . . make a Sun and these radiant things and I would write things like 'Resurrection! Freedom from tyranny, terror, death!' One of her cards was reprinted in a Catholic newspaper, which was read by a man in Elmira prison in upstate New York. "A woman I know from church . . . has this guy tell her, 'did you see this? Did you get this?'" Her friend seemed ambivalent about Clare's vivid greeting in the paper, but the man living behind bars "got it," and he was excited. The message was "for" him—as the Gospel was written by and for those who are oppressed. A devout Catholic her whole life, Clare explained that she never truly understood the significance of this until she was in prison.[47]

Freedom from tyranny means something fundamentally different to those living under oppression than it does to the fortunate devout. Clare's story reveals how her own experience of "oppression"—mild and temporary as it was by global and historical standards—changed her understanding of religious texts and teachings. However, it also changed how she understood slavery and labor abuses internationally: the horrors of contemporary imperialism illuminated by those of the past, something she was able to briefly experience—but for real—in this life. Though she has spent a lifetime concerned about them, Clare now understands oppression and domination differently than she did before she lived in prison, and she sees their fingerprints in places where she previously did not. This new vision shifts the way she understands the world generally, as it also re-affirms her commitment to disarmament action.

Another theme that justice action prisoners discussed was their own privilege, and specifically their whiteness, as both a structural force and a personal possession that impacted (and generally eased) their experience of prison—another form of "privilege power." As considered in previous chapters, privilege is a common motivator for justice action prisoners' resistance to state violence; it is often part of what compels them to act. But no matter what they knew before, the participants in this research understood their own privilege differently *after* they lived in prison. As Julienne Oldfield said of the impact that white skin confers to a person in prison, "if we didn't know it before, we certainly knew afterwards."[48]

In their interviews, participants frequently noted the "difference" privilege made—how their whiteness, age, and education made their prison experiences easier than those of more marginalized groups. Ken Hayes told me that in comparison to himself, David Omandi, an African American Catholic Worker who went to prison for an SOA violation, "had it rough," whereas "the guards knew better than to mess with someone who probably had more money than they did."[49] Here, Ken does not disrupt the privilege that his social class gives him, but he is aware that it is working in his favor.

John Heid is mindful of his privilege in advance of participating in resistance. When he is arrested alongside someone of non-dominant status, John knows that their experience will likely be more difficult than his own. This means that he needs to be vigilant about what is happening to them, and as active as he can be in their process. He may need to be arrested first, for example, or to engage in some sort of jail solidarity action (to refuse to be released until everyone who is part of the action is released).[50] In other words, he must use the protective shield of his own privilege to encompass those he acts alongside. As a movement, SOA Watch is careful to educate in this direction. At one of the workshops I attended at the 2011 vigil, attendees were instructed to be vigilant about how their actions could affect those nearby. If they wanted to participate in an arrestable action, the trainers insisted, people needed to "check their privilege," and in particular—to be sure that non-citizens were informed of their plans in advance, so they could keep themselves safe from potential police scrutiny.

When they told stories of how their privilege mattered from the moment of arrest onwards, justice action prisoners most frequently spoke about how their privilege assured them better treatment or some degree of safety. John Heid remembered an officer who was hesitant to arrest him during an action to support migrants in Tucson. The officer warned him a few times of his impending arrest, and waited several hours for him to cease and desist before finally following through. When at last he handcuffed John, the officer told him gently, "next time, get a permit," meaning, John explained, "we have permits for people like you—*you* are not supposed to get arrested."[51] Sr. Kathleen Desautels told me about trespassing at Fort Benning, and an officer drove her off the base ("you could get arrested in here!" he scolded her as he drove). He dropped her off at a nearby gas station, but on the way there, asked her how she planned to get back to her hotel. "Oh, I thought maybe you'd come back and take us," she teased. A little while later, he returned in a civilian car and offered Kathleen a ride. "If I were black and had tattoos and earrings on, I wouldn't have been treated that way. I know my privilege and I'm reminded of my privilege by my friends. . . . I'm a gray-haired woman, and a nun. So I've used it, but tried not to abuse it."[52] Brian Terrell recalled a time when his privilege served as a proxy for "goodness" when he was serving a short sentence at the city jail in Davenport, Iowa. While he was there, a man he knew from the community was arrested. The social worker assigned to the man's case needed someone to sign for his release. Though he was in jail himself, the social worker accepted Brian as a reference—an upstanding member of the community. So Brian signed, and the man walked free.[53]

In prison, the effects of a person's privilege can become stark. It is one thing to know, intellectually, that one has privilege, and to feel guilt or responsibility to "use it but not abuse it." It is another thing entirely to become a prisoner—effectively handing over a good portion of control over one's daily life choices—and to experience firsthand how this privilege continues to show up and matter. By no means do people of privilege always have "easy" times in prison, but the people included in this research were, to varying degrees, all able to see how their privilege offered them a layer of protection from institutional violence. Concurrent with this awareness was the knowledge that those without such privileges had it worse; they were more vulnerable and more poorly treated, in ways that are systemic, predictable, historical, and unjust. Living in prison made the effects of belonging to a hierarchical social system that values some lives more highly than others experiential for justice action prisoners, it was not just something they knew intellectually to be true. Eyes were opened, fields of vision broadened, understandings strengthened; the prison standpoint enables more lucid and accurate vision.

NAVIGATING THE PRISON STANDPOINT

When they are released from prison, many justice action prisoners—and especially the women—go on to include prison reform or abolition in their activist work. By doing so, they can become powerful advocates for education, consciousness-raising, and institutional change. For example, the audiences who hear them speak expect to learn about disarmament and foreign policy, but they are also often told stories about prison. As former wards of the state, but also as people who are unashamed of their reasons for being incarcerated, justice action prisoners fill a special role from which to share about the U.S. justice system.

However, it is also important to note that it is—once again—their privilege that enables justice action prisoners' experiences to be so clearly heard by others. They are generally perceived to be "good" people, despite their criminal pasts.[54] They are trusted authorities, they are invited into classrooms and asked to speak on the radio. "Prisoners of conscience" thus occupy unique ground, from which they can (still again) be a "voice" for the voiceless: they can speak about the U.S. justice system as valid, authentic, and believable speakers—on subjects such as mass incarceration, the punitive nature of imprisonment, and the racism and classism inherent in these systems. Their presumed lack of belonging within this space bestows them with motivations that are not seen as self-serving; they are not perceived as whining about unfair conditions, but as truthfully reporting back about systems they have experienced to be real. In short, because of their constellations of privilege—social and personal—they can be widely, and accurately, *heard.*

Justice action prisoners may be valorized as truthful and righteous, and their stories also reach audiences who might otherwise be resistant to the information they have to share. Ordinary prisoners, on the other hand, most often cannot do the same for themselves. Discredited as guilty, as bad, as self-ish—the "most hated" population is largely unable to speak for themselves, and there are longstanding power dynamics that assure the perpetuation of these distinctions.

Justice action prisoners thus act from an exceptional place: considered "good people," they are also former prisoners. It is thus important that they speak. At the same time, justice action prisoners are always—as Fr. Bill explained—"visitors" in someone else's house. Learning about the prison through the stories of a justice action prisoner is a correct, truthful way to learn about the justice system and the ways that it impacts those who live within it. But learning from them can be a little bit like going to a travelogue, or to a lecture about "elsewhere" given by an anthropologist who has lived in that place but is not "from" there. Well-intentioned and informed as they may be, justice action prisoners are always also outsiders. By no means is this meant to diminish their experiences. They are convicted prisoners, guilty of the crimes that have been levied against them. Sometimes, they serve hard time. They are simply different, shaped by privileges that most prisoners can-not access.

Relying on this privilege is a form of power. It is a way to open hearts and make people think about the U.S. justice system. But it is worth consider-ing whether or not the "goodness" that prison witness relies upon can also consolidate the existing binary system: good and bad prisoners, the righteous versus the guilty, the deserving versus the undeserving. The translation of knowledge through the filter of one's identity—to reach people who may oth-erwise be resistant to or protected from such understandings—is a novel and important use of privilege. It is a truly unusual place from which to inform and transform. However, it must not be used to reinforce the hierarchical prison system, but to upend it. For those working so hard to rid the world of injustice, the double-edges of activating privilege are ever sharp.

CONCLUSION

The prison standpoint is a political achievement; it is a novel way of seeing and understanding the world, and it is a result of intentional effort. It is distinct for where it is achieved (the prison) and by whom (people of privilege), but it is not automatic. One must think about what has happened, in relation to one's previous knowledge, to gain better understandings with which to make sense of one's experiences, the social context, and what it all means. In the case of justice action prisoners, the biographical consequences of incarceration lend themselves to the production of knowledge of two basic types. One is systemic, and concerns the justice system itself; the ways that prison relies upon and reinforces oppressive racial and economic structures as it also dehumanizes and harms those it contains. The other is more personal, and is about knowing oneself as a human being within the prison, as well as in a greater context as a person of faith and privilege.

What happens to justice action prisoners when they are in prison—and the new ways of seeing that are enabled through it—are not necessarily "new." However, the prison standpoint is valuable not only for what its reveals, but how—and by whom. The perspective that is gained is bodily: it is felt, experienced, and witnessed. Prison provides the space for justice action prisoners' intellectual understandings, their well-informed political analyses, and their deeply held beliefs to be tested, and felt by them as real. Oppression, dehumanization, and privilege are not conceptual ideas, they *happen* to people. This changes what people know, but also how, in ways that are significant: justice action prisoners become unshakable in their beliefs. More convinced than ever that they are right in their understandings of selfish imperialism and violent geopolitics—and more committed than ever to a variety of justice-oriented causes.

The prison standpoint is significant for who gains its lines of sight: people of privilege, who are often those guarded against such understandings, and for what they can do with their embodied knowledge. The ground that justice action prisoners occupy, as speakers of and for the prison, is special: valorized as "good people," their personal stories may be distinctively heard. At the root, then, the prison standpoint can be another form of privilege-power; a way to speak-for, made possible because of one's belongings within various categories of status and power.

In different ways and to varying degrees—but without fail, prison transforms people, seemingly permanently. For some—and mostly the women as discussed in Chapter 5, they can never go back to their lives as they were, for the "burden of knowing" rests too heavily on them. For others, incarceration works more narrowly, as reinforcement of their disarmament goals: when one intimately knows a system to be broken and hurtful, the only route forward is continued resistance. For almost everyone, what is learned in the journey through the justice system results in a new way of understanding and making sense of the world, the achievement of a "prison standpoint."

NOTES

1. Rumpf, interview.

2. Larissa MacFarquhar has written a beautiful book about such extreme altruists, a personality type she came to understand with help from interviews with multiple members of the Berrigan family. See her acknowledgements in *Strangers Drowning: Impossible Idealism, Drastic Choices, and the Overpowering Urge to Help.* (New York: Penguin Press, 2016).

3. Doug McAdam. "The Biographical Consequences of Activism." *American Sociological Review* (1989): 744–760; and "Recruitment to High-Risk Activism: The Case of Freedom Summer." *The American Journal of Sociology* 92, no. 1 (1986): 64–90. See also Patrick Coy. *Protecting Human Rights: The Dynamics of International Nonviolent Accompaniment by Peace Brigades International in Sri Lanka.* (Dissertation. Syracuse University, 1997); Sara Koopman. "Making Space for Peace: International Protective Accompaniment in Colombia." *Geographies of Peace* (2014): 109–130; Sharon Nepstad and Christian Smith. "Rethinking Recruitment to High-Risk/Cost Activism: the Case of Nicaragua Exchange." *Mobilization: An International Quarterly* 4, no. 1 (1999): 25–40.

4. Standpoint is an idea from feminist philosophy positing that one's "location" within a matrix of identity categories (one's "place on the map" across lines of race, class, gender and so on) provides one's range of vision for making sense of the world.

5. Kathy Kelly, interview.

6. Sr. Flanigan, interview.

7. Sandra Harding, ed. *The Feminist Standpoint Theory Reader: Intellectual and Political Controversies* (Routledge, 2004). See also Nancy Hartsock. "The Feminist Standpoint: Developing the Ground for a Specifically Feminist Historical Materialism." In *The Feminist Standpoint Theory Reader: Intellectual and Political Controversies,* edited by Sandra Harding (New York: Routledge, 2004), 35–55; Patricia Hill Collins, *Black Feminist Thought: Knowledge, Consciousness, and the Politics of Empowerment* (New York: Routledge, 2020); Adrienne Rich, "Notes Towards a Politics of Location." In *Blood, Bread, and Poetry: Selected Prose* (London: Virago Press, 1984), 210–231; Alessandra Tanesini *An Introduction to Feminist Epistemologies* (Malden, MA: Blackwell Publishers, 1999).

8. W.E.B. DuBois. *The Souls of Black Folk* (Oxford: Oxford University Press, 1903). Indeed, the dominant have little incentive to see differently, and may actually have a "positive interest" in seeing the world "wrongly" according to Charles Mills, "White Ignorance," *Race and Epistemologies of Ignorance*, ed. Nancy Tauna and Shannon Sullivan (New York: SUNY Press, 2007), 26–31.

9. Harding, *The Feminist Standpoint Theory Reader*, 2004.

10. Serraglio, interview.

11. Kenneth Hayes, interview by author, Washington, DC, April 14th, 2012.

12. Fr. Frankel-Streit, interview.

13. Houston, interview. Illustrating this idea, Dr. Bill explained that he was in prison in September of 2001, and with his fellow inmates watched the two planes crash into the Twin Towers in New York City. He said that, though the range of reactions the attacks produced was the same as among those on the "outside," the distribution was different in the prison. He "had the impression that a far larger proportion of the prisoners could see why someone might want to do something like that . . . could see why they might hate the U.S. government" than could those on the outside.

14. Doty, interview.

15. Michel Foucault, *Discipline and Punish: The Birth of the Prison* (New York City: Vintage Books, 1979); Loic Wacquant, "Deadly Symbiosis when Ghetto and Prison Meet and Mesh," *Punishment & Society* 3, no. 1 (2001): 95–133; Wacquant, *Punishing the* Poor, 2009.

16. Michelle Alexander, *The New Jim Crow: Mass Incarceration in the Age of Colorblindness*, 10th anniversary ed. (New York: The New Press, 2020) and *Are Prisons Obsolete?* (New York: Seven Stories Press, 2011); Angela Davis, *Abolition Democracy: Beyond Empire, Prisons, and Torture* (Seven Stories Press 2011); Critical Resistance and Incite! "Statement on Gender Violence and the Prison-Industrial Complex." *Social Justice,* 30 (2003): 141–151; Michel Dylan Rodriguez, *Forced Passages: Imprisoned Radical Intellectuals and the US Prison Regime* (Minneapolis: University of Minnesota Press, 2006); Jael Silliman, Anannya Bhattacharjee, and Angela Yvonne Davis, eds., *Policing the National Body: Sex, Race, and Criminalization* (South End Press, 2002); Julia Sudbury, ed., *Global Lockdown: Race, Gender, and the Prison-Industrial Complex* (New York: Routledge, 2005).

17. Wacquant, *Punishing the Poor*, 2009.

18. Jackie Wang, *Carceral Capitalism*, Semiotexte, Intervention. vol. 21 (Boston: MIT Press, 2018).

19. For example, prisons provide a stable workforce for low-skilled workers in America's hinterlands, while prisoners themselves are a source of revenue. Prisons also provide a massive pool of cheap labor for private corporations and federal agencies—there are over 2.3 million people in America's prisons today, most of whom earn far less than $1.00 per hour working for companies such as Victoria's Secret and AT+T. See Lynne Haney, "Working through Mass Incarceration: Gender and the Politics of Prison Labor from East to West," *Signs* 36, no. 1 (2010): 73–97.

20. Ruth Wilson Gilmore, *Golden Gulag: Prisons, Surplus, Crisis, and Opposition in Globalizing California* (University of California Press, 2007).

21. Fr. Frankel-Streit, interview.

22. Kathy Kelly, interview. "Nothing but a minute" is a reference to justice action prisoners' relatively short sentences.

23. Sr. Pagosa, interview.

24. Fr. Vitale, interview.

25. Kramer, interview.

26. Crane, interview.
27. Heid, interview.
28. Kramer and Crane interviews.
29. Crowley, interview.
30. All of this section comes from my interview with Clare Grady.
31. See Philip Zimbardo, *The Lucifer Effect: Understanding How Good People Turn Evil* (New York: Random House, 2007).
32. Ellen Grady, interview.
33. Clare Grady, interview.
34. Johan Galtung, "Cultural Violence," *Journal of Peace Research* 27, no. 3 (1990): 291–305.
35. Berrigan, interview.
36. Tom, interview.
37. Personal letter, citing *In the First Circle.*
38. Kennon, interview.
39. Serraglio, interview.
40. Houston, interview.
41. Rumpf, interview.
42. Tom, interview.
43. Serraglio, interview.
44. Rumpf, interview.
45. Johanna B. Folk, Jeffrey Stuewig, Debra Mashek, June P. Tangney, and Jessica Grossmann. "Behind Bars but Connected to Family: Evidence for the Benefits of Family Contact During Incarceration." *Journal of Family Psychology* 33, no. 4 (2019): 453; "Lowering Recidivism through Family Communication," *Prison Legal News*, uploaded by Alex Friedmann, 04/15/2014, https://www.prisonlegalnews.org/news/2014/apr/15/lowering-recidivism-through-family-communication/.
46. Clare Grady, interview.
47. Clare Grady, interview.
48. Oldfield, interview.
49. Hayes, interview.
50. Heid, interview.
51. Heid, interview.
52. Desautels, interview.
53. Terrell, interview.
54. With thanks to Angela Davis for this insight.

Chapter 7

Journey through Prison Witness

The Significance of Privilege and Gender

I crossed the line at Fort Benning because I had the privilege to protest without being disappeared, kidnapped, tortured, and killed. I have a responsibility because of what my country is doing, and the freedom to do it because I don't face the same obstacles and risks that other people might.—Deligio (interview)

From the decision to act through release from prison, the journeys of justice action prisoners are fundamentally shaped by their identities as privileged American activists. Being accountable to their privilege is a common motivation for participation in nonviolent action, but the impacts of privilege reach far beyond reasons for engagement. Indeed, membership in various categories of identity—from white skin to professional status, personal resilience to a faith life that gives one courage and moral clarity—fuels the strategy of prison witness itself. Privilege also affects how it feels to act, how one's actions are received by others, how one experiences prison, and how one thinks about and learns from one's involvement overall. Indeed, the significance of privilege is omnipresent in the experiences of justice action prisoners, and developing a more lucid understanding of its role in systemic violence and its resistance is an area that this research is able to contribute towards.

Justice action prisoners are most often motivated to act in resistance by a sense of responsibility or obligation, realizing that their status as a Christian person, a U.S. citizen, or a "beneficiary of empire" demands that they protest militarized and imperial violence.[1] Acting in resistance is a way to bring word and deed into alignment, and justice action prisoners often decide to cross a line or hammer on a weapon to align what they *do* with their values.

Resistance is described as "doing the work I was put here to do," in Randy Serraglio's words; and it feels *good* to do it.[2] Clare Grady likened saying "yes" to prison witness to getting a chiropractic adjustment: "pscht!" she exclaimed, expressing a sense of relief that everything was now in its proper place, and working as it should.[3]

Privilege also gives strength to the strategy of prison witness itself. As a distinctive form of resistance, one that is high-risk and personalized, prison witness relies upon "privilege power," the power of one's mainstream status as a political force. Indeed, how the strategy of prison witness "works" depends on privilege. The "cognitive dissonance" that it inspires—the realization among the general public that there is a discrepancy between the crime committed and the punishment meted that deserves critical attention—crucially relies on an activist's identity as a "good person" (which is often linked with whiteness, professional status, and so on). Hence, the actor's "power," in terms of their own legitimacy but also their ability to spread their messages widely and deeply, is not solely connected to *what* they do, but also to "who they are" in terms of their subjective identities.

The power of one's privilege is also essential for the activation of "solidarity"—the troublesome but essential work of acting with and alongside those of more marginalized status, those who may not be able to "speak" (or be heard) themselves. For many justice action prisoners, solidarity is a crucial part of how they activate privilege "for good." For Brian DeRouen, enacting solidarity includes connecting his "whole suburban world" with uncomfortable truths (torture, prison, and so on), realities that are most often unknown among the people in his community—people who are similarly-privileged to Brian. However, Brian is a messenger they can hear. His task is thus one of translation, and his privileged identity is what makes the effort work. Relatedly, those who have been arrested at Fort Benning and chose to read the words of those affected by the school in their trial statements have used the opportunity as a chance for solidarity. They used their bodies, their identities, and their voices as vessels for translation—from Spanish to English, from marginalized to powerful, from south to north. The words they memorialized were not their own; their bodies are simply the medium for the message, not the message itself.

"Using privilege for good" must be handled carefully. Sr. Dorothy Pagosa warned that relying on privilege in attempts to "help" others can perpetuate inequalities between self and other. According to Sr. Ardeth Platte, the challenge is to create space for "those most affected to talk" and then to shut one's mouth and "listen to them," because, as Randy Serraglio pointed out, "that is what we're all about, right?" In other words, the challenge is to use one's privileges as Sr. Dorothy did when she worked with homeless veterans in Chicago, where she used her white privilege and sisterhood to "gain entrée" into spaces of power—but then stopped. Once "in," her job was to let the veterans talk, but not to speak for them. Sr. Kathleen Desautels described this as the work of "using" but not "abusing" privilege, knowing and honoring its capacities as well as its limits.[4] Using their own bodies as the platform for action, some of this book's participants articulated ways to undertake solidarity work that crosses lines of power ethically, skillfully, and accountably, and they deserve further attention.

Privilege also affects the experience of prison. Certainly, no one is immune from the potential violence stemming from the prison industrial complex, and this research shares stories illustrating some of the harms that the prison system may commit on its wards. However, *in general* those of compound privilege have an "easier" time in jail and prison than do people of marginalized or non-normative status. Connection to privilege is thus an important part of what makes the strategy of prison witness replicable, as well as relatively safe, for participants. In order to undertake an action that involves incarceration—and to do it again (or sincerely recommend it to others)—one should have an experience that is not marked by significant abuse. Further, the consequences of individuals and movements not facing the realities of unequal treatment for incarcerated activists are profound, ranging from the feeling of "resentment" toward the movements to which they belong to direct violence, but also to a reinforcement of the very types of systemic inequalities that justice action prisoners mean to uproot in the first place. Not all "people" have equal access to "power" at all times, and inequalities can (re)produce violence. Anyone connected to prison witness must fully understand these implications.

At the same time, something distinctive—and distinctively useful—can be learned from highly privileged people living in America's prisons. Justice action prisoners are often privileged by their subjective identities, but they are also buoyed by their characteristics and traits—in particular, by the fact that they are incarcerated by choice, as empowered citizens who feel proud of their illegal acts. As a result, justice action prisoners are in a special position to develop an analysis of the institution that is distinctive, and the analysis is valuable for this alone. The "prison standpoint" is a unique vantage point, from which a person of compound privilege may come to know themselves, the institution of the prison, and wider patterns of oppression and violence *differently*. As privileged political subjects, their perspectives may also be more readily "heard" by others—yet another form of privilege power.

The light that justice action prisoners can shine on the "injustice system" is an important part of their activist work. Justice action prisoners are frequently told that it is a "waste of time" to spend months or years in prison, when they could ostensibly be agitating more effectively from the outside. This attitude illuminates Kathleen Rumpf's observations that "prisoners are the most hated population" who are also the "disappeared in this country."[5] Hidden from view, prisoners can be neglected and abused. Justice action prisoners living among them, then, is a way to humanize the population for people living outside the prison walls, people who have not necessarily understood the actual mechanisms and costs of making the prison industrial complex work.

Further, at least for the justice action prisoners who are not severely abused during their tenures in prison, their incarcerations cannot be disregarded as a "waste of time." Their incarcerations have value for the impact of their witness on other prisoners as well as themselves, for what the public can learn through their stories, and also for the potential "efficacy" it can produce in terms of movement goals. In the work of social justice, expanding the area from which one can speak—increasing one's legitimacy and credibility—to greater and more diverse audiences, positively "works" to raise consciousness, increase awareness, and promote politicization. Raising consciousness is an essential part of the work of change, and to the extent that a prison stint can increase one's capacity for one's stories to be heard, the strategy must be understood as "effective."

The complexity of using of the master's tool of privilege in the aim of systemic change is nothing new, though it is ongoing. On the one hand, no matter what privileged white Western activists do "on behalf of" those most/made marginalized by practices of U.S. empire, they will be replicating and relying on longstanding legacies of inequality. It is difficult to move "forward" without some degree of assimilation of what came before; we are embedded in our unjust contexts. Justice action prisoners are among those who are willing to work with this imperfect reality as it is, making mistakes along the way—but never giving up, and continually engaging in struggles for change in earnest and full-bodied ways.

THE DIFFERENCE THAT GENDER MAKES

This research has contributed to the vast literature documenting the "difference" that gender—in a traditional binary sense—can make in shaping one's experience and knowledge, particularly gender as impacted by religious status. Both the "moment of action" and the experience of prison are crucially distinguished by gender, with women and men recalling different kinds of stories from one another, as well as articulating varying interpretations of what their experiences mean.

During interviews, the moment of action clearly emerged as one shaped by gender, a fact that is absent from nonviolence and social movement theorizing. In general, women experienced their participation as personally empowering, while men described the sense that they had engaged in a strategy that is powerful. This difference shows that—even among people who are otherwise similar—at the root, men ultimately feel "legitimate" as political actors, while women must often overcome barriers to their own participation. Belonging to radical communities and used to being "on the fringe," the sisters were the exception to this gendered story, showing that religious identity—and crucially, communities of belonging, may mitigate and inform one's experiences as a political subject and nonviolent resister.

Gender also impacts the experience of prison. In general, the men experienced prison as a solitary, sad, and deeply spiritual time, while the women lived in "communities" that they were actively a part of and worked to improve. The different ways of being in prison influenced how people left the institutions, with men more likely to return to lives as disarmament/foreign policy activists and women more likely to include a prison reform agenda in their activism—or to feel guilty for not doing so. Religious identity proved the exception in both cases, with priests more likely to keep up their activism when in prison, while nuns were more likely to return to their previous spheres of activism and without expressions of guilt. The specific limitations of this project's methodology (unstructured interviews with a younger woman) may have exaggerated the gendered variations relayed in various stories, with men proving themselves to be experts and women to be "companeras" during their interviews. That said, the reality and the consistency of *difference* holds true.

FINAL REFLECTIONS

The question I am most asked by others is one that this book does not actually answer, which is, "does prison witness work?" As briefly reviewed in Chapter 2, how to answer this question is not at all straightforward. If we are perfectly concrete and look only in terms of changing policy, we can say that in the cases of the Plowshares and SOA Watch movements, prison witness has not worked. After decades of resistance and over one hundred years spent in prison to protest it, the school is still open. Similarly, nuclear weapons have not been substantially threatened by Catholics with household hammers.

If we broaden our idea of impact even a tiny bit, however, the answer must be "of course prison witness works!" Some of this efficacy is only present in the unknowable histories of what has *not* happened across time: there is no way to know where we would be today without the centuries of resistance that have brought us here. With certainty, we can say that things would be worse for ordinary people. We know that there has been a constant pressure on those with power, by those with less power, to create ways of living that are more peaceful, just, and fair for everyone. We also know that only through coercion (including the most tender of nonviolent coercion) do those with power concede to the demands of those with less of it. Further, the history of nonviolent action demonstrates that change sometimes happens when least expected: unlikely people become allies, regimes "suddenly" topple—and almost always, these "sudden" changes are actually the result of years of collective organizing and resistance. In this, prison witness is very often a part. We also know that, collectively and over time, justice action prisoners have raised awareness, changed consciousness, organized people, made engaging in violent policies and practices of destruction less comfortable and sometimes even impossible for ruling authorities—and that participating in the activism itself has changed people.

Prison witness is also an important check on democratic governance, a parallel but essential contribution of this form of resistance. It is a fact that nuclear weapons, torture, and various kinds of warfare are illegal in the United States today. It is also true that citizens of this country have protected rights to protest, assemble, follow their religious beliefs, and be judged by a court of their peers. By providing compelling cases to judges and juries that center such issues as weapons, rights, and torture, justice action prisoners are providing legal pathways for regular citizens to reject nuclear weapons, drones, and schools of torture—as they simultaneously safeguard our bedrock democratic institutions and ideals.

When thinking about the contributions of justice action prisoners, we do well to remember that social change toward justice is rarely a quick or tangible achievement, but rather a long, hard, slog. Martin Luther King Jr. is famous for telling us that the universe "bends towards justice"—but we must add an essential corrective to this notion: the universe does not "bend," it must be "bent." Struggles for justice are active, they are intentional and ongoing, and they must be done by *people.* Justice action prisoners engage in a form of resistance that is universal and timeless, if relatively uncommon. It is complicated and challenging, but also powerful and important. In performing acts that are righteous, thoughtful, and really really hard—justice action prisoners are engaged in labor that benefits ordinary people, near and far. With all of their nonviolent might, they are bending. Bending. Bending this world toward justice.

NOTES

1. Kinane, interview.
2. Serraglio, interview.

3. Clare Grady, interview.
4. Interviews with Sr. Platte, Sr. Pagosa, Sr. Desautels, and Serraglio.
5. Rumpf, interview.

Appendix

List of Participants

Fr. Luis Barrios, *SOA Watch*. Washington, DC, April 14th, 2012

Jerome Berrigan, *Various anti-nuclear, anti war actions.* Syracuse, NY, April 13th, 2010

Susan Crane, *Plowshares.* Camden, NJ, September 5th, 2010

Ken Crowley, *SOA Watch*. Chicago, IL, March 7th, 2012

Tim DeChristopher, *Environmental action, "Bidder 70."* Nevada City, CA, January 2014

Elizabeth Deligio, *SOA Watch*. Chicago, IL, March 6th, 2012

Sr. Kathleen Desautels, *SOA Watch*. Chicago, IL, March 6th, 2012

Brian DeRouen, *SOA Watch*. Columbus, GA, November 18th, 2011

Meagan Doty, *SOA Watch*. Columbus, GA, November 19th, 2011

Sr. Mary Kay Flanigan, *SOA Watch*. Chicago, IL, March 8th, 2012

Alice Gerard, *SOA Watch*. Grand Island, NY, February 13th, 2012

Sr. Carol Gilbert, *Plowshares*. Baltimore, MD, April 13th, 2012

Jack Gilroy, *SOA Watch*. Interlaken, NY, February 8th, 2012

Clare Grady, *Plowshares*. Ithaca, NY, August 13th, 2010

Ellen Grady, *Plowshares*. Ithaca, NY, December 16th, 2011

Nancy Gwin, *SOA Watch*. 2010, Syracuse, NY, March 13th, 2013

Kenneth Hayes, *SOA Watch*. Washington, DC, April 14th, 2012

John Heid, *SOA Watch, Plowshares*. Tucson, AZ, May 15th, 2012

Martha Hennessey, *Plowshares*. Syracuse, NY, February 27th, 2012

William B. Houston Jr., *SOA Watch*. Yellow Springs OH, March 15th 2012.

Kathy Kelly, *Missouri Peace Planters, various anti-war actions.* Syracuse, NY, February 25th, 2012

Fr. Stephen Kelly, *Plowshares.* Oakland, CA, July 2012

Reverend Kenneth Kennon, *SOA Watch*. Tucson, AZ, May 13th, 2012

Ed Kinane, *SOA Watch*. Syracuse, NY, March 3rd, 2010

Rae Kramer, *SOA Watch*. Syracuse, NY, March 31, 2010

Thomas Mahedy, *SOA Watch*. Columbus, GA, November 18th, 2011

Elizabeth McAlister, *Plowshares*. Baltimore, MD, March 13th, 2012

Karl Meyer, *SOA Watch*. Telephone interview, March 27th, 2013
Julienne Oldfield, *SOA Watch*. Syracuse, NY, August 4th, 2010
Sr. Dorothy Pagosa, *SOA Watch*. Chicago, IL, March 7th, 2012
Michael P. Pasquale, *SOA Watch*. Syracuse, NY, March 27th, 2010
Sr. Ardethe Platte, *Plowshares*. Baltimore, MD, April 13th, 2012
Lois Putzier, *SOA Watch*. Tucson, AZ, May 13th, 2012
Sr. Megan Rice, *SOA Watch*. Solvey, NY, February 29th, 2012
Kathleen Rumpf, *SOA Watch*. Syracuse, NY, April 28th, 2010
Dr. Daniel Sage, *SOA Watch*. Syracuse, NY, April 8th, 2010
Doris Sage, *SOA Watch*. Syracuse, NY, April 8th, 2010
Randy Serraglio, *SOA Watch*. Tucson, AZ, May 13th, 2012
William Frankel-Streit, *Plowshares*. Camden, NJ, September 6th, 2010
Brian Terrell, *SOA Watch*. Columbus, GA, November 18th, 2011
Ann Tiffany, *SOA Watch*. Syracuse, NY, February 22nd, 2010
Derrlyn Tom, *SOA Watch*. Washington, DC, April 14th, 2012
Fr. Louis Vitale, *SOA Watch*. Oakland, CA, December 22nd, 2011

Bibliography

Ackerman, Peter, and Jack Duvall. "People Power Primed: Civilian Resistance and Democratization." *Harvard International Review,* (Summer 2005): 147–148.

Ackerman, Peter, and Christopher Kruegler. *Strategic Nonviolent Conflict: The Dynamics of People Power in the Twentieth Century.* Westport, CT: Praeger, 1994.

Adams, Katherine H., and Michael L. Keene. *Alice Paul and the American Suffrage Campaign.* Chicago: University of Illinois Press, 2010.

Alcoff, Linda Martin. "The Problem of Speaking for Others." In *Who Can Speak: Authority and Critical Identity*, edited by J. Roof and R. Wiegman, 97–119. Chicago: University of Illinois Press, 1995.

———. *Visible Identities: Race, Gender, and the Self.* New York: Oxford University Press, 2006.

———. "Epistemologies of Ignorance: Three Types." In *Race and Epistemologies of Ignorance*, edited by N. Tauna and S. Sullivan, 39–58. New York: SUNY Press, 2007.

———. "New Epistemologies: Post-Positivist Accounts of Identity." In *The Sage Handbook of Identities*, edited by Margaret Wetherell and Chandra Talpade Mohanty, 144–162. London: Sage Publications, 2010.

Alcoff, Linda Martin, Michael Hames-Garcia, and Satya Mohanty, eds. *Identity Politics Reconsidered.* New York: Palgrave Macmillan, 2006.

Alexander, Michelle. *The New Jim Crow: Mass Incarceration in the Age of Colorblindness*, 10th anniversary ed. New York: The New Press, 2020.

Alexander, M. Jacqui. *Pedagogies of Crossing: Meditations on Feminism, Sexual Politics, Memory, and the Sacred.* Durham: Duke University Press, 2005.

Amadeo, Kimberly. "US Military Budget, Its Components, Challenges, and Growth," *The Balance.* Updated 09/03/2020. https://www.thebalance.com/u-s-military-budget-components-challenges-growth-3306320#:~:text=Estimated%20U.S.%20military%20spending%20is,Defense%20alone2%EF%BB%BF%EF%BB%BF

Ancestral Pride. "Everyone Calls Themselves an Ally, until It Is Time to Do Some Real Ally Shit." *Warrior Publications.* January 29, 2014. https://warriorpublications.files.wordpress.com/2014/01/ancestral_pride_zine.pdf.

Arkin, William M., and Hans M. Kristensen. "US Deploys New Low-Yield Nuclear Submarine Warhead." Federation of American Scientists. January 29, 2020. https://fas.org/blogs/security/2020/01/w76-2deployed/.

Bailey, Alison. "Locating Traitorous Identities: Toward a View of Privilege-Cognizant White Character." *Hypatia* 13, no. 3 (1998): 27–47.

Barfield, Ellen. "Defending Resistance." *War Resisters League.* Spring 2011. http://www.warresisters.org/content/defending-resistance.

Bartkowski, Maciej J., ed. *Recovering Nonviolent History: Civil Resistance in Liberation Struggles.* Boulder: Lynne Rienner, 2013.

Beaumont, Judith. "Prison Witness: Exposing the Injustice." In *Swords into Plowshares: Nonviolent Direct Action for Disarmament,* edited by A. J. Laffin and A. Montgomery, 80–85. San Francisco: Harper and Row Publishers, 1987.

Berrigan, Daniel. *The Trial of the Catonsville Nine.* New York City: Fordham University Press, 2004.

———. *Essential Writings.* Maryknoll, NY: Orbis, 2009.

Berrigan, Philip, and Fred Wilcox. *Fighting the Lamb's War: Skirmishes with the American Empire.* Eugene, OR: Wipf and Stock Publishers, 1996.

Berrigan, Philip, and Elizabeth McAlister, *The Time's Discipline: The Beatitudes and Nuclear Resistance.* Eugene, OR: Wipf and Stock Publishers, 2010.

Beyerlein, Kraig, and Kelly Bergstrand. "Biographical Availability." In *The Wiley-Blackwell Encyclopedia of Social and Political Movements*, edited by David A. Snow, Donatella della Porta, Bert Klandermans, and Doug McAdam. Oxford: Blackwell Publishing, 2013.

Bhattacharjee, Anannya. "Private Fists and Public Force: Race, Gender, and Surveillance." In *Policing the National Body: Sex, Race, and Criminalization,* edited by J. Silliman, A. Bhattacharjee, and A. Y. Davis, 1–54. Boston: South End Press, 2002.

Biegelsen, Amy. "Divining Providence: Bill and Sue Frankel-Streit are Parents, Catholics, Felons and Anarchists. It's All pPrt of Their Mission to Serve God." *Style Weekly*, May 2010. http://www.styleweekly.com/richmond/divining providence/ Content? oid= 1369974.

Bigelow, Albert. *The Voyage of the Golden Rule: An Experiment with Truth.* Garden City, NY: Doubleday, 1959.

Boaz, Cynthia. "Must we Change our Jearts Before Throwing Off our Chains?" *Waging Nonviolence,* July 9, 2012. Accessed January 2021. http://wagingnonviolence.org/feature/must-we-change-our-hearts-before-throwing-off-our-chains/.

Bond, Doug. "Nonviolent Direct Action and the Diffusion of Power." In *Justice without Violence,* 59–79. Boulder: Lynne Rienner, 1994.

Bondurant, Joan V. *Conquest of Violence: The Gandhian Philosophy of Conflict.* Berkeley: University of California Press, 1965.

Boothe, Ivan, and Lee A. Smithey. "Privilege, Empowerment, and Nonviolent Intervention." *Peace & Change* 32, no. 1 (2007): 39–61.

Bosworth, Mary. "Gender, Race and Sexuality in Prison." In *Women in Prison: Gender and Social Control*, edited by Jim Thomas and Barbara Zaitzow, 137–154. Lynne Rienner Publishers, 2003.

Bosworth, Mary, and Emma Kaufman. "Gender and Punishment." In *The Sage Handbook of Punishment and Society,* edited by Jonathan Simon and Richard Sparks, 186–204. Fair Oaks: Sage Publications, 2012.

Bosworth, Mary, and Eamonn Carrabine. "Reassessing Resistance: Race, Gender, and Sexuality in Prison." *Punishment and Society* 3, no. 4 (2001): 501–515.

Boulding, Kenneth. *Three Faces of Power.* Newbury Park, CA: Sage Publications, 1989.

Bourgeois, Roy. *My Journey from Silence to Solidarity*. Yellow Springs, OH: fxBear, 2013.

———. "Excommunicated For 'Grave Scandal' of Ordaining Women." *Religion Dispatches.* 8/6/2013. http://www.religiondispatches.org/archive/sexandgender/7237/.

Brah, Avtar, and Ann Phoenix. "Ain't I a Woman? Revisiting Intersectionality." *Journal of International Women's Studies* 5, no. 3 (2004): 75–86.

Broad, William. "The Nun Who Broke into the Nuclear Sanctum." *New York Times.* August 11, 2012. https://www.nytimes.com/2012/08/11/science/behind-nuclear-breach-a-nuns-bold-fervor.html.

Brock, Peter. *Pacifism in the United States*. Princeton: Princeton University Press, 2015.

Bronson, Jennifer, and Ann Carson. "Prisoners in 2017." Bureau of Justice Statistics. Date published 04/22/2019. https://bjs.ojp.gov/library/publications/prisoners-2017.

Brink, Betty. "Hospital of Horrors: Time in Carswell's Prison Medical Facility Can Be a Death Sentence for Women Prisoners." *Fort Worth Weekly,* 10/19/2005. http://www.aclutx.org/2005/10/19/hospital-of-horrors-federal-medical-center-carswell-prison/.

Britton, Dana M. "Gendered Organizational Logic: Policy and Practice in Men's and Women's Prisons." *Gender & Society* 11, no. 6 (1997): 796–818.

Britton, Dana M. *At Work in the Iron Cage: The Prison as Gendered Organization*. New York City: NYU Press, 2003.

Brown, Gavin, and Jenny Pickerell. "Space for Emotion in the Spaces of Activism." *Emotion, Space, and Society* 2 (2009): 24–35.

Burdick, John. *Blessed Anastácia: Women, Race and Popular Christianity in Brazil*. London: Routledge, 2013.

Bureau of Prisons. "Our Locations." Accessed July 1, 2021. https://www.bop.gov/locations/list.jsp

———. "Total Federal Inmates." Last updated: October 1, 2021. https://www.bop.gov/about/statistics/population_statistics.jsp.

Butler, Judith. *Gender Trouble: Feminism and the Subversion of Identity*. London: Routledge, 2011.

Busch, Akiko. "The Invisibility of Older Women." *The Atlantic*. 02/27/2019. Accessed January 2021. https://www.theatlantic.com/entertainment/archive/2019/02/akiko-busch-mrs-dalloway-shows-aging-has-benefits/583480/.

Calhoun, Craig. "Putting Emotions in Their Place." In *Passionate Politics,* edited by J. Goodwin, et al., 45–57. Chicago, IL: University of Chicago Press, 2001.

Carastathis, Anna. "Identity Categories as Potential Coalitions." *Signs: Journal of Women in Culture and Society* 38, no. 4 (2013).

Carty, Linda, and Chandra Talpade Mohanty, eds. *Feminist Freedom Warriors: Genealogies, Justice, Politics, and Hope.* Chicago: Haymarket Books, 2018.

Chenoweth, Erica. *Civil Resistance: What Everyone Needs to Know.* London: Oxford University Press, 2021.

Chenoweth, Erica, and Maria Stephan. *Why Civil Resistance Works: The Strategic Logic of Nonviolent Conflict.* New York: Columbia University Press, 2011.

_____. "How the World Is Proving Martin Luther King Right about Nonviolence." *Washington Post.* January 19, 2016.

Cho, Sumi, Kimberly Williams Crenshaw, and Leslie McCall. "Toward of Field of Intersectionality Studies: Theory Applications and Praxis." *Signs,* 38, no. 4 (2013): 785–810.

Choo, Hae Yeon, and Myra Marx Ferree. "Practicing Intersectionality in Sociological Research: A Critical Analysis of Inclusions, Interactions, and Institutions in the Study of Inequalities." *Sociological Theory* 28 (2010): 129–149.

Clark, Howard, ed. *People Power: Unarmed Resistance and Global Solidarity.* London: Pluto Press, 2009.

Cole, Elizabeth R. "Coalitions as a Model for Intersectionality: From Practice to Theory." *Sex Roles* 59, no. 5–6 (2008): 443–453.

Cole, Elizabeth, and Zakiya Luna. "Making Coalitions Work: Solidarity across Difference within US Feminism." *Feminist Studies* 36, no. 1 (2010): 71–99.

Cook, Alice, and Gwyn Kirk. *Greenham Women Everywhere: Dreams, Ideas, and Actions from the Women's Peace Movement.* London: South End Press, 1983.

Coser, Walter H. "The United States: Reconsidering the Struggle for Independence, 1765–1775." In *Recovering Nonviolent History: Civil Resistance in Liberation Struggles,* edited by Maciej Bartkowski, 299–317. Boulder: Lynne Rienner, 2013.

Coy, Patrick G. *Protecting Human Rights: The Dynamics of International Nonviolent Accompaniment by Peace Brigades International in Sri Lanka.* Dissertation. Syracuse University, 1997.

————. "We Use It but We Try Not to Abuse It: Nonviolent Protective Accompaniment and the Use of Ethnicity and Privilege by Peace Brigades International." Paper presented at the Annual Meeting of the American Sociological Association, Washington, D.C. August 13, 2000.

————. "Shared Risks and Research Dilemmas on a Peace Brigades International Team in Sri Lanka." *Journal of Contemporary Ethnography* 30, no. 5 (2001): 575–606.

Crenshaw, Kimberly. "Mapping the Margins: Intersectionality, Identity Politics, and Violence Against Women of Color." *Stanford Law Review* 43, no. 6 (1991): 1241–1299.

Critical Resistance—Incite! "Statement on Gender Violence and the Prison-Industrial Complex." *Social Justice,* 30 (2003): 141–151.

Cusimano, Theresa. "A letter from Theresa Cusimano, recently released SOA Watch prisoner of conscience." *Nuclear Resister.* July 20, 2012. https://www.nukeresister. org/2012/07/20/a-letter-from-theresa-cusimano-soa-watch-prisoner-of-conscience/.

Dart, Ron. "The Christian Prophetic Tradition." *Clarion: Journal of Spirituality and Justice.* June 8, 2006. https://www.clarion-journal.com/clarion_journal_of_ spirit/2006/06/the_christian_p.html.

Davis, Angela. *Abolition Democracy: Beyond Empire, Prisons, and Torture.* Seven Stories Press, 2005.

———. *Are Prisons Obsolete?* New York City: Seven Stories Press, 2011.

Davis, Kathy. "Intersectionality as Buzzword: A Sociology of Science Perspectives on What Makes a Feminist Theory Successful." *Feminist Theory* 9 (2008): 67–85.

Davis, Lynn E., Stacie L. Pettyjohn, Melanie W. Sisson, and Michael J. McNerney. "U.S. Overseas Military Presence: What Are the Strategic Choices?" *Project Air Force.* RAND Corporation, 2012. http://www.rand.org/news/press/2012/09/12. html.

Day, Dorothy. *All the Way to Heaven: the Selected Letters of Dorothy Day.* New York: Image, 2012.

Delmas, Candice. *A Duty to Resist: When Disobedience Should Be Uncivil.* Oxford University Press, 2018.

DeVault, Marjorie. *Liberating Method: Feminism and Social Research.* Philadelphia: Temple University Press, 1999.

De Volo, Lorraine B. "Drafting Motherhood: Maternal Imagery and Organizations in the United States and Nicaragua." In *The Women and War Reader,* edited by Ann Lorentzen and Jennifer Turpin, 240–254. New York: NYU Press, 1998.

Dear, John. "A Peace Movement Victory in Court." *National Catholic Reporter.* Sept. 21, 2010. https://www.ncronline.org/blogs/road-peace/peace-movement-victory-court.

———. "An Interview with Phil Berrigan." Accessed January 2021. http://www. jonahhouse.org/archive/interviewJohnPhil.htm.

Debs, Eugene V. "Statement to the Court, September 18, 1918." E.V. Debs Internet Archive. Accessed June 20, 2021. https://www.marxists.org/archive/debs/ works/1918/court.htm

Del Vasto, Joseph. *Warriors of Peace: Writings on the Technique of Nonviolence.* New York: Alfred Knopf, 1974.

Disarm Now Plowshares, 2009. http://disarmnowplowshares.wordpress.com.

Droogendyk, Lisa, Stephen C. Wright, Micah Lubensky, and Winnifred R. Louis. "Acting in Solidarity: Cross-Group Contact between Disadvantaged Group Members and Advantaged Group Allies." *Journal of Social Issues* 72, no. 2 (2016): 315–334.

DuBois, William Edward B. *The Souls of Black Folk.* Oxford: Oxford University Press, 1903.

Dudouet, Veronique. "Nonviolent Resistance and Conflict Transformation in Power Asymmetries." Berghof Research Center for Constructive Conflict Management, 2008. www.berghof-handbook.net.

Dunier, Mitchell. *Sidewalk.* New York: Macmillan Press, 1999.

DuVall, Jack. "Civil Resistance and the Language of Power." International Center for Nonviolent Conflict. November 19, 2010. https://www.nonviolent-conflict.org/resource/civil-resistance-and-the-language-of-power/.

———. "Dream Things True: Nonviolent Movements as Applied Consciousness." *Cosmos and History: The Journal of Natural and Social Philosophy* 10, no. 1 (2014): 106–117, 109.

Ellis, Alan. "Federal Prison Designation Update, 2021." Accessed June 24, 2021. https://alanellis.com/prison-designation-transfers-disciplinary-matters-medical-and-other-problems/

Euripides. *Hecuba.* In *The Actor's Book of Classical Monologues,* ed. Stefan Rudnicki, adapted by John Barton and Kenneth Cavander, translated by Kenneth Cavander. New York: Penguin Books, 1988.

Evans, Marcel. "Nicaragua: Ortega announces withdrawal from US Army School of the Americas." *Costa Rica Star.* 9/12/2012. http://news.co.cr/nicaragua-ortega-announces-withdrawal-from-us-army-school-of-the-americas/14348/.

Fosl, Catherine. *Subversive Southerner: Anne Braden and the Struggle for Racial Justice in the Cold War South.* Lexington: University Press of Kentucky, 2006.

Friedman, Alex. "Lowering Recidivism through Family Communication." *Prison Legal News.* 04/15/2014. https://www.prisonlegalnews.org/news/2014/apr/15/lowering-recidivism-through-family-communication/.

Freeberg, Ernest. *Democracy's Prisoner: Eugene V. Debs, the Great War, and the Right to Dissent.* Boston: Harvard University Press, 2008.

Folk, Johanna B., Jeffrey Stuewig, Debra Mashek, June P. Tangney, and Jessica Grossmann. "Behind Bars but Connected to Family: Evidence for the Benefits of Family Contact During Incarceration." *Journal of Family Psychology* 33, no. 4 (2019): 453.

Gallo-Cruz, Selina. *Political Invisibility and Mobilization: Women Against State Violence in Argentina, Yugoslavia, and Liberia.* New York: Routledge, 2020.

———. "Negotiating the Lines of Contention: Counterframing and Boundary Work in the School of the Americas Debate 1." In *Sociological Forum*, vol. 27, no. 1, pp. 21–45. Oxford, UK: Blackwell Publishing Ltd, 2012.

Galtung, Johan. "Cultural Violence." *Journal of Peace Research* 27, no. 3 (1990): 291–305.

Garza, Alicia. "Ally or Co-Conspirator?: What it Means to Act #InSolidarity." *Move to End Violence.* 9/26/16. https://movetoendviolence.org/blog/ally-co-conspirator-means-act-insolidarity/

Gilmore, Ruth Wilson. *Golden Gulag: Prisons, Surplus, Crisis, and Opposition in Globalizing California.* Berkeley: University of California Press, 2007.

Gill, Leslie. *The School of the Americas: Military Training and Political Violence in the Americas.* Duke University Press, 2004.

Gilligan, Carol. *In a Different Voice: Psychological Theory and Women's Development.* Cambridge, MA: Harvard University Press, 1993.

Goodwin, Jeff, James Jasper, and Francesca Polletta, eds. *Passionate Politics: Emotions and Social Movements.* Chicago: University of Chicago Press, 2001.

Grewal, Inderpal, and Caren Kaplan. "Introduction: Transnational Feminist Practices and Questions of Postmodernity." In *Scattered Hegemonies: Postmodernity and Transnational Feminist Practices,* edited by Grewal and Kaplan, 2–33. Minneapolis: University of Minnesota Press, 1997.

Gramsci, Antonio. *Selections from the Prison Notebooks of Antonio Gramsci: Edited and Translated by Quintin Hoare and Geoffrey Nowell Smith*, edited by G. Nowell-Smith, & Q. Hoare. New York City: International Publishers, 1971.

Gusterson, Hugh. "Empire of Bases." *The Bulletin of Atomic Scientists.* 03/10/2009. http://thebulletin.org/empire-bases.

Hames-Garcia, Michael. *Identity Complex: Making the Case for Multiplicity.* Minneapolis: University of Minnesota Press, 2011.

Haney, Lynne A. "Working through Mass Incarceration: Gender and the Politics of Prison Labor from East to West." *Signs* 36, no. 1 (2010): 73–97.

———. "Motherhood as Punishment: The Case of Parenting in Prison." *Signs* 39, no. 1 (2013): 105–130.

Harding, Sandra. "Introduction." In *The Feminist Standpoint Theory Reader: Intellectual and Political Controversies,* edited by S. Harding, 1–16. London: Routledge, 2004.

Hartsock, Nancy. "The Feminist Standpoint: Developing the Ground for a Specifically Feminist Historical Materialism." In *The Feminist Standpoint Theory Reader: Intellectual and Political Controversies,* edited by S. Harding, 35–55. New York: Routledge, 2004.

Hedin, Benjamin. *In Search of the Movement: The Struggle for Civil Rights Then and Now*. San Francisco, CA: City Lights Books, 2015.

Hill, Dana. *Opening Our Eyes: How Activist Women in Ecuador Learn Critical Political and Self-aware Consciousness.* Syracuse University Press, 2014.

Hill Collins, Patricia. *Black Feminist Thought: Knowledge, Consciousness, and the Politics of Empowerment*. New York: Routledge, 2000.

Holmes, Robert L. *On War and Morality*. Princeton: Princeton University Press, 1989.

Hunt, Mary, and Diann Neu, eds., *New Feminist Christianity: Many Voices, Many Views.* Nashville: Skylight Paths Publishing, 2010.

Hussain, Murtaza. "It's Time for America to Reckon with the Staggering Death Toll of the Post-9/11 Wars." *The Intercept.* 11/19/2018, 8 p.m. https://theintercept.com/2018/11/19/civilian-casualties-us-war-on-terror/.

Isherwood, Lisa. "The Embodiment of Feminist Liberation Theology: The Spiraling of Incarnation." *Feminist Theology* 12, no. 2 (2004): 140–156.

Jagger, Alison. "Introduction." In *Just Methods: An Interdisciplinary Feminist Reader,* edited by A. M. Jagger, 1–14. Boulder, CO: Paradigm Publishers, 2008.

Johnson, Paula. "Women and Power: Toward a theory of effectiveness." *Journal of Social Issues 32* (1976): 99–110.

Johnson-Reagan, Bernice. "Coalition Politics: Turning the Century." In *Home Girls: A Black feminist anthology,* edited by Beverly Smith, 343–358. New Brunswick, NJ: Rutgers University Press, 1983.

Jonah House. 2021. http://www.jonahhouse.org.

Juris, Jeffrey. "Performing Politics: Image, Embodiment, and Affective Solidarity during Anti-Corporate Globalization Protests." *Ethnography* 9, no. 1 (2008): 61–97.

Karatnycky, Adrian, and Peter Ackerman. *How Freedom Is Won: From Civic Resistance to Durable Democracy*. New York: Freedom House, 2005.

Kearney, Mathew. *The Social Order of Collective Action: The Wisconsin Uprising of 2011*. Lanham, MD: Lexington Books, 2018.

Kelly, Kathy. *Other Lands have Dreams: From Baghdad to Pekin Prison*. Petrolia, CA: CounterPunch and AK Press, 2005.

Kennon, Kenneth. *Prisoner of Conscience: A Memoir*. Indiana: Xlibris, 2002.

Kerman, Piper. *Orange is the New Black: My Year in a Women's Prison*. New York: Random House LLC, 2011.

Kinane, Ed. "Think Global, Act Local: Grassroots Opposition to Weaponized Drones." Presented at Historians Against War conference on "The New Faces of War." Towson University, Towson, Maryland, April 2013.

Kinane, Ed, et al. "Two Dozen Get Prison Time for Crossing S.O.A. Line." *The Nuclear Resister*. 07/01/2001. http://www.nukeresister.org/static/nr124/nr1242dozen.html.

King, Martin Luther, Jr. "Letter from Birmingham Jail." In *Liberating faith: Religious Voices for Justice, Peace, & Ecological Wisdom*, Roger Gottlieb, 177–187. Lanham, MD: Rowman & Littlefield, 2003.

Kings Bay Plowshares 7, https://kingsbayplowshares7.org/

Kirk, Gwyn. *Our Greenham Common: Feminism and Nonviolence*. New York: Routledge, 2018.

Kohn, Stephen Martin. *Jailed for Peace*. New York: Praeger Publishers, 1987.

Koopman, Sara. "Field Note: Columbus, Georgia, USA." *Women's Studies Quarterly*, (2006): 90–93.

———. "Imperialism Within: Can the Master's Tools Bring Down Empire?" *ACME: An International E-Journal for Critical Geographies* 7, no. 2 (2008a): 283–307.

———. "Cutting through topologies: Crossing lines at the School of the Americas." *Antipode* 40, no. 5 (2008b): 825–847.

———. "Making space for peace: International protective accompaniment in Colombia." *Geographies of peace* (2014): 109–130.

Kraemer, Kelly Rae. "Solidarity in Action: Exploring the Work of Allies in Social Movements." *Peace & Change* 32, no. 1 (2007): 20–38.

Kristensen, Hans, and Robert Norris. "Global Nuclear Weapons Inventories, 1945–2013." *Bulletin of the Atomic Scientists* 69, no. 5 (2013): 75–81.

Laffin, Arthur. "A History of the Plowshares Movement—A Talk by Art Laffin. *Nuclear Resister.* October 22, 2019. https://www.nukeresister.org/2019/11/02/a-history-of-the-plowshares-movement-a-talk-by-art-laffin-october-22-2019/.

Laffin, Arthur, and Anne Montgomery, eds. *Swords into Plowshares: Nonviolent Direct Action for Disarmament, Peace and Social Justice*. San Francisco: Harper and Row Publishers, 1987.

Lakey, George. "'Suffragette' Raises Question of Property Destruction's Effectiveness." Waging Nonviolence. 2015. https://wagingnonviolence.org/2015/11/suffragette-raises-question-property-destruction-effectiveness/.

Lang, Berel. "Civil Disobedience and Nonviolence: A Distinction with a Difference," *Ethics*, vol. 80, no. 2 (January 1970): 156.

Lempe-Santangelo, Gretchen. "The Radical Conscientious Objectors of World War II." *Radical History Review* 45 (1989): 5–29.

Lorde, Audre. "The Master's Tools Will Never Dismantle the Master's House." In *Feminist Postcolonial Theory: A Reader,* edited by R. Lewis and S. Mills, 23–28. London: Routledge, 2003.

Lovell, James. *Crimes of Dissent: Civil Disobedience, Criminal Justice, and the Politics of Conscience.* New York: NYU Press, 2009.

Luna, Zakiya. "Who Speaks for Whom? (Mis)representation and Authenticity in Social Movements." *Mobilization: An International Quarterly* 22, no. 4 (2017): 435–450.

Lynd, Staughton, and Alice Lynd, eds. *Nonviolence in America: A Documentary History.* New York: Orbis Books, 1995.

Lyshaug, Brenda. "Solidarity without 'Sisterhood'? Feminism and the Ethics of Coalition Building." *Politics & Gender* 2, no. 1 (2006): 77–100.

MacFarquhar, Larissa. *Strangers Drowning: Impossible Idealism, Drastic Choices, and the Overpowering Urge to Help.* New York: Penguin Press, 2016.

MacFarquhar, Neil. "Why Charges against Protesters are being Dismissed by the Thousands." *The New York Times.* 11/09/2020. https://www.nytimes.com/2020/11/19/us/protests-lawsuits-arrests.html.

Mansbridge, Jane. "Complicating Oppositional Consciousness." In *Oppositional Consciousness: The Subjective Roots of Protest,* edited by J. Mansbridge and A. Morris, 238–264. Chicago: University of Chicago Press, 2001.

Mansbridge, Jane, and Aldon Morris, eds. *Oppositional Consciousness: The Subjective Roots of Social Protest.* Chicago: University of Chicago Press, 2001.

Marantz, Andrew. "How to Stop a Power Grab." *The New Yorker,* 11/16/2020. https://www.newyorker.com/magazine/2020/11/23/how-to-stop-a-power-grab.

Martin, Brian. "How Nonviolence Is Misrepresented." *Gandhi Marg* 30, no. 2 (2008): 235–257.

McAdam, David. *Freedom Summer.* Oxford: Oxford University Press, 1988.

———. "Recruitment to High-Risk Activism: The Case of Freedom Summer." *American Journal of Sociology* 92, no. 1 (1986): 64–90.

———. "The Biographical Consequences of Activism." *American Sociological Review* (1989): 744–760.

McCall, Leslie. "The Complexity of Intersectionality." *Signs: Journal of Women in Culture and Society* 30, no. 3 (2005): 1771–1800.

McElwee, Joshua. "Berrigan's Message to Peacemakers: Persevere." *National Catholic Reporter,* 12/08/2010. https://www.ncronline.org/news/people/berrigans-message-peacemakers-persevere.

Merriman, Hardy. "Theory and Dynamics of Nonviolent Action." In *Civilian Jihad,* 17–29. New York: Palgrave Macmillan, 2009.

Merton, Thomas. *A Thomas Merton Reader.* New York: Image, 1974.

Mills, Charles. "White Ignorance." In *Race and Epistemologies of Ignorance,* edited by N. Tauna and S. Sullivan, 13–38. New York: SUNY Press, 2007.

Minh-ha, Trinh T. *Women, Native, Other: Writing Postcoloniality and Feminism.* Bloomington: Indiana University Press, 1989.

Mohanty, Chandra Talpade. "Under Western Eyes: Feminist Scholarship and Colonial Discourses." *Feminist Review* 30 (1988): 61–88.

———. "Introduction: Cartographies of Struggle: Third World Women and the Politics of Feminism." In *Third World Women and the Politics of Feminism,* edited by C. T. Mohanty, A. Russo, and L. Torres, 1–51. Indiana: Indiana University Press, 1991.

———. *Feminism without Borders: Decolonizing Theory, Practicing Solidarity.* Durham: Duke University Press, 2003.

———. "Social Justice and the Politics of Identity." In *The Sage Handbook of Identities,* edited by M. Wetherall and C. T. Mohanty, 529–540. London: Sage Publications, 2010.

Mohanty, Satya P. "The Epistemic Status of Cultural Identity: On *Beloved* and the Postcolonial Condition." *Cultural Critique* 24 (1993): 41–80.

Mollin, Marian. *Radical Pacifism in Modern America: Egalitarianism and Protest.* University of Pennsylvania Press, 2013.

———. "Women's Struggles within the American Radical Pacifist Movement." *History Compass* 7, no. 3 (2009): 1064–1090.

———. "The Limits of Egalitarianism: Radical Pacifism, Civil Rights, and the Journey of Reconciliation." *Radical History Review* 88, no. 1 (2004): 112–138.

Montgomery, Ann. "Divine Obedience." In *Swords into Plowshares: Nonviolent Direct Action for Disarmament,* edited by A. J. Laffin and A. Montgomery, 25–31. San Francisco: Harper and Row Publishers, 1987.

———. "Spiritual Power Behind Bars." In *Swords into Plowshares: Nonviolent Direct Action for Disarmament,* edited by A. J. Laffin and A. Montgomery, 73–75. San Francisco: Harper and Row Publishers, 1987.

Mountz, Alison, and Jennifer Hyndman. "Feminist Approaches to the Global Intimate." *Women's Studies Quarterly* 34, no. 1/2 (2006): 446–463.

Moya, Paula. "What's Identity Got to Do with It? Mobilizing Identities in the Multicultural Classroom." In *Identity Politics Reconsidered,* edited by L. M. Alcoff, M. Hames-Garcia, and S. P. Mohanty, 96–117. New York: Palgrave Macmillan, 2006.

Moya, Paula, and Michael Hames-Garcia, eds. *Reclaiming Identity: Realist Theory and the Predicament of Postmodernism.* Berkeley: University of California Press, 2000.

Muste, A. J. "The Pacifist Way of Life." *Fellowship* 7, no. 12 (1941): 198.

Myers, Ched. "By What Authority? The Bible and Civil Disobedience." In *The Rise of* Christian Conscience, 243. San Francisco: Harper & Row, 1987.

———. *Who Will Roll Away the Stone? Discipleship Queries for First World Christians.* Maryknoll, NY: Orbis Books, 1994.

Myers, Daniel. "Ally Identity: The Politically Gay." In *Identity Work in Social Movements*, edited by Jo Reger, Daniel Myers, and Rachel Einwohner, vol. 30, 167–87. University of Minnesota Press, 2008.

Naess, Arne. *Gandhi and Group Conflict: An exploration of Satyagraha. Theoretical Background*. Oslo, Norway: Universitetsforlaget, 1974.

Nagler, Michael. *Is There No Other Way? The Search for a Nonviolent Future*. Berkeley: Berkeley Hills Press, 2001.

Nepstad, Sharon Erickson. *Catholic Social Activism*. NYU Press, 2019.

———. *Nonviolent Struggle: Theories, Strategies, and Dynamics*. Oxford: Oxford University Press, 2015.

———. "School of the Americas Watch." *Peace Review* 12, no. 1 (2000): 67–72.

———. *Religion and War Resistance in the Plowshares Movement*. Cambridge: Cambridge University Press, 2008.

———. "Oppositional Consciousness among the Privileged: Remaking Religion in the Central America Solidarity Movement." *Critical Sociology* 33, no. 4 (2007): 661–688.

———. *Convictions of the Soul: Religion, Culture, and Agency in The Central America Solidarity Movement*. New York: Oxford University Press, 2004a.

———. "Persistent Resistance: Commitment and Community in the Plowshares Movement." *Social Problems* 51, no. 1 (2004b): 43–60.

Nepstad, Sharon, and Christian Smith. "Rethinking Recruitment to High-Risk/Cost Activism: The Case of Nicaragua Exchange." *Mobilization: An International Quarterly* 4, no. 1 (1999): 25–40.

The Nuclear Resister. "Colville Sentenced, Kelly Released." April 21, 2021. http://www.nukeresister.org/wp-content/uploads/2021/05/NR197web.pdf.

O'Neill, Patrick. "Peace Activist Peter DeMott Dead After Fall." *Common Dreams,* 2/21/2009. http://www.commondreams.org/headline/2009/02/21-5.

Paechter, Carrie. "Masculinities and Femininities as Communities of Practice." *Women's Studies International Forum* 26, no. 1 (2003): 69–77.

Parkins, Wendy. "Protesting like a Girl: Embodiment, Dissent and Feminist Agency." *Feminist Theory* 1, no. 1 (2000): 59–78.

Peace Brigades International. "Making Space for Peace." 2014. http://www.peace-brigades.org.

Peaceful Uprising. "Tim's Story." 2013. http://www.peacefuluprising.org/tim-dechristopher/timsstory.

Phelps, Shirelle, and Jeffrey Lehman. "Necessity." *West's Encyclopedia of American Law* 7, no. 2. Detroit: Gale, 2005.

Phillips, Holiday. "Performative Allyship is Deadly (Here's What to Do Instead)," *Forge*, 05/10/2020. https://forge.medium.com/performative-allyship-is-deadly-c900645d9f1f.

Phoenix, Ann, and Pamela Pattynama. "Intersectionality." *European Journal of Women's Studies*, 13, no. 3 (2006): 187–192.

Polner, Murray. *Disarmed and Dangerous: The Radical Life and Times of Daniel and Philip Berrigan, Brothers in Religious Faith and Civil Disobedience*. New York: Routledge, 2018.

Popiel, John. "Prison Cannot Crush Their Spirit: The Ideological Impact of Incarceration on Emma Goldman, Alexander Berkman, and Eugene V. Debs." PhD dissertation, the University of Houston Clear-Lake, 2020.

Prison Policy Initiative. "Section III: The Prison Economy." Accessed 12/12/2020. https://www.prisonpolicy.org/prisonindex/prisonlabor.html.

Public Affairs, UC Berkeley. "Words of freedom: video made from Mario Savio's 1964 'Machine Speech.'" September 30, 2014. https://news.berkeley.edu/2014/09/30/words-of-freedom-video-made-from-mario-savios-1964-machine-speech/.

Rabuy, Bernadette, and Daniel Kopf. "Prisons of Poverty: Uncovering the pre-incarceration incomes of the imprisoned." Prison Policy Initiative, 07/09/2015. https://www.prisonpolicy.org/reports/income.html.

Raven, Bertram. "The Bases of Power: Origins and Recent Developments," *Journal of Social Issues* 49, no. 4 (1993): 227–251.

――――. "A power/interaction model of interpersonal influence: French and Raven thirty years later." *Journal of Social Behavior & Personality* 7, no. 2 (1992): 217.

Reif, Kingston. "Would the United States Ever Actually Use Nuclear Weapons?" *Atomic Bulletin,* 2013. http://thebulletin.org/would-united-states-ever-actually-use-nuclear-weapons.

Reinherz, Shulamit, and Lynne Davidman. "Conclusions." In *Feminist Methodologies in Social Research.* New York, Oxford University Press, 1992.

Rich, Adrienne. "Notes Towards a Politics of Location." In *Blood, Bread, and Poetry: Selected Prose,* 210–231. London: Virago Press, 1984.

Riegle, Rosalie G. *Doing Time for Peace: Resistance, Family, and Community.* Nashville: Vanderbilt University Press, 2012a.

―――. *Crossing the Line: Nonviolent Resisters Speak Out for Peace.* Eugene, OR: Cascade Books, 2012b.

Rivers, Larry E. *Rebels and Runaways: Slave Resistance in Nineteenth-Century Florida.* Chicago, University of Illinois Press, 2012.

Roberts, J. W. "Factories with Fences: The History of Federal Prison Industries." UNICOR. Accessed 12/15/2020. https://www.unicor.gov/publications/corporate/FactoriesWithFences_FY19.pdf.

Rodriguez, Dylan. *Forced Passages: Imprisoned Radical Intellectuals and the US Prison Regime.* Minneapolis: University of Minnesota Press, 2006.

Roth, Guenther. "Socio-Historical Model and Developmental Theory: Charismatic Community, Charisma of Reason and the Counterculture." *American Sociological Review* (1975): 148–157.

Rubin, Joel. "What Nuclear Weapons Cost Us—It's the Right Time for a Debate." Ploughshares, 12/20/2011. http://www.ploughshares.org/what-nuclear-weapons-cost-us.

Ruddick, Sara. *Maternal Thinking: Toward a Politics of Peace, with a New Preface.* Boston: Beacon Press, 1995.

Russo, Chandra. *Solidarity in Practice: Moral Protest and the US Security State.* Cambridge: Cambridge University Press, 2018.

―――. "Allies Forging Collective Identity: Embodiment and Emotions on the Migrant Trail." *Mobilization: An International Quarterly* 19, no. 1 (2014): 67–82.

Rutgers University. "Children and families of the incarcerated fact sheet." *National Resource Center on Children and Families of the Incarcerated,* 2014. https://nrccfi.camden.rutgers.edu/files/nrccfi-fact-sheet-2014.pdf.

Sawyer, Wendy, and Peter Wagner. "Mass Incarceration: The Whole Pie." *The Prison Policy Initiative*, 03/24/2020. Accessed 12/11/2020. https://www.prisonpolicy.org/reports/pie2020.html.

Scarry, Elaine. *Thermonuclear Monarchy: Choosing Between Democracy and Doom.* New York: W.W. Norton & Company, 2014.

Schock, Kurt. "Nonviolent Action and Its Misconceptions: Insights for Social Scientists." *PS: Political Science and Politics* 36 (2003): 705–712.

———. *Unarmed Insurrections: People Power Movements in Nondemocracies.* Minneapolis: University of Minnesota Press, 2005.

School of the Americas Watch. Retrieved at http://soaw.org

Seelye, Katherine. "Dianna Ortiz, American Nun Tortured in Guatemala, Dies at 62." *The New York Times,* Feb 20, 2021. https://www.nytimes.com/2021/02/20/us/dianna-ortiz-dead.html.

Sentencing Project. "Fact Sheet: Incarcerated Women and Girls." 2013. http://www.sentencingproject.org/doc/publications/cc_Incarcerated_Women_FactsheetSep24sp.pdf.

Sharp, Gene. *The Politics of Nonviolent Action, 3 vols.* Boston: Porter Sargent, 1973.

Sider, Ronald. *Nonviolent Action: What Christian Ethics Demands but Most Christians Have Never Really Tried.* Ada, MI: Brazos Press, 2015.

Silliman, Jael, Anannya Bhattacharjee, and Angela Y. Davis, eds. *Policing the National Body: Sex, Race, and Criminalization.* Boston: South End Press, 2002.

Snow, David, and David McAdam. "Identity Work Processes in the Context of Social Movements: Clarifying the Identity/Movement Nexus." In *Self, Identity, and Social Movements,* edited by S. Stryker, et al., 41–67. Minneapolis: University of Minnesota Press, 2000.

Sorensen, Majken J., and Brian Martin. "The Dilemma Action: Analysis of an Activist Technique." *Peace & Change* 39, no. 1 (2014): 73–100.

Stephan, Maria, and Erica Chenoweth. "Why Civil Resistance Works: The Strategic Logic of Nonviolent Conflict." *International Security* 33, no. 1 (2008): 7–44.

Sudbury, Julia. "A World without Prisons: Resisting Militarism, Globalized Punishment, and Empire." *Social Justice* 31, no. 1–2, (2004): 9–30.

———. *Global Lockdown: Race, Gender, and the Prison Industrial Complex.* New York: Routledge, 2005.

———. "Maroon abolitionists: Black Gender-Oppressed Activists in the Anti-Prison Movement in the US and Canada." *Meridians: Feminism, Race, Transnationalism* 9, no. 1 (2008): 1–29.

Tanesini, Alessandra. *An Introduction to Feminist Epistemologies.* Malden, MA: Blackwell Publishers, 1999.

Terrell, Brian. "The Pro Se Defense in the Catholic Worker Tradition." *Voices for Creative Nonviolence,* 2011. http://vcnv.org/categories/writings-by-brian-terrell.

———. "From FPC Yankton." The Nuclear Resister, 2/15/2013. file:///Users/anyastanger/Desktop/POC%20docs/Articles/~%20from%20FPC%20Yankton,%20by%20Brian%20Terrell%20«%20The%20Nuclear%20Resister.webarchive.

———. "A Judge's 'Doubtful Proposition' on Nuclear Weapons." *Consortium News*, 11/18/2019. https://consortiumnews.com/2019/11/18/a-judges-doubtful-proposition-on-nuclear-weapons/.

The Atlantic. "Mass Incarceration, Visualized." 09/11/2015. Accessed 12/11/2020. https://www.theatlantic.com/video/index/404890/prison-inherited-trait/.

Thoreau, Henry David. "Civil Disobedience." In *The Power of Nonviolence: Writings by Advocates of Peace*, introduction by Howard Zinn, edited by Beacon Press, 15–36. Boston: Beacon Press, 2002.

Thurber, Ann, et al., "Staying Off the Megaphone and in the Movement: Cultivating Solidarity and Contesting Authority Among White Anti-Racist Activists." *Understanding and Dismantling Privilege* 5, no. 2 (2015): 1–20.

Tickner, Jean A. *Gender in International Relations: Feminist Perspectives on Achieving Global Security*. Columbia University Press, 1992.

Tobey, Kristen. "Beyond Religious Freedom: Religious Activity in the Civil Disobedience Trials of Plowshares Antinuclear Activists." *The Journal of Religion* 96, no. 2 (2016): 234–251.

———. *Plowshares: Protest, Performance, and Religious Identity in the Nuclear Age*. University Park: Pennsylvania State University Press, 2016.

———. *Performing Marginality: Identity and Efficacy in the Plowshares Nuclear Disarmament Movement*. Dissertation, University of Chicago, 2010.

Tracy, James. *Direct Action: Radical Pacifism from the Union Eight to the Chicago Seven*. Chicago, IL: University of Chicago Press, 1996.

Transform Now Plowshares. "Legal Arguments." Accessed January 21, 2021. http://transformnowplowshares.wordpress.com/legal-arguments.

Wacquant, Loïc. "Deadly symbiosis when ghetto and prison meet and mesh." *Punishment & Society* 3, no. 1 (2001): 95–133.

———. *Punishing the Poor: The Neoliberal Government of Social Insecurity*. Durham, NC: Duke University Press, 2009.

Wang, Jackie. *Carceral Capitalism, vol. 21*. Boston: MIT Press, 2018.

War Resisters League. "The Parameters of Nonviolent Action: What Makes an Action Nonviolent" essays. Accessed January 2021. https://www.warresisters.org/nva/nva-july-august-2001/parameters-nonviolent-action-what-makes-action-nonviolent.

Warner, Elizabeth. "The Gold Standard of Nuclear Spending." *Ploughshares*, 7/10/13. http://www.ploughshares.org/blog/2013-07-10/gold-standard-nuclear-spending.

Wink, Walter, ed. *Peace is the Way: Writings on Nonviolence from the Fellowship of Reconciliation*. Maryknoll, NY: Orbis Books, 2000.

Wittner, Lawrence S. *Rebels Against War: The American Peace Movement, 1933–1983*. Philadelphia: Temple University Press, 1984.

Witness for Peace. 2014. http://www.witnessforpeace.org.

Vanzetti, Bartolomeo. "The Last Speech of Bartolomeo Vanzetti." Workers' Liberty, submitted by Martin, June 22, 2010. https://www.workersliberty.org/story/2010/06/22/last-speech-bartolomeo-vanzetti.

Varon, Jeremy. *Bringing the War Home: The Weather Underground, the Red Army Faction, and Revolutionary Violence in the Sixties and Seventies*. Berkeley: University of California Press, 2004.

Vinthagen, Stellan. *A Theory of Nonviolent Action: How Civil Resistance Works*. London: Zed Books Ltd, 2015.

Yoder, John Howard. *Nevertheless: The Varieties and Shortcomings of Religious Pacifism*. Herald Press, 1992.

YouTube. "Kings Bay Plowshares 7 Guilty Verdict 10-24-2019." October 25, 2019. https://www.youtube.com/watch?v=MONkguTdryA&feature=youtu.be.

Yuval-Davis, Nira. "Intersectionality and Feminist Politics." *European Journal of Women's Studies* 13 (2006): 193.

Zak, Dan. "The Prophets of Oak Ridge." *The Washington Post,* 4/30/2013. http://www.washingtonpost.com/sf/wp-style/2013/09/13/the-prophets-of-oak-ridge/.

Zakiya, Luna. "Who Speaks for Whom? (Mis) Representation and Authenticity in Social Movements." *Mobilization: An International Quarterly* 22, no. 4 (2017): 435–450.

Zimbardo, Philip. *The Lucifer Effect: Understanding How Good People Turn Evil*. New York: Random House, 2007.

Zinn Education Project. "Nov. 15, 1917: Suffragists Beaten and Tortured in the 'Night of Terror.'" Accessed June 1, 2021. https://www.zinnedproject.org/news/tdih/suffragists-beaten-and-tortured/.

———. "June 15, 1955: Protest of Nuclear Attack Drills." Accessed January 2021. https://www.zinnedproject.org/news/tdih/nuclear-attack-drill-protest.

Zinn, Howard. *The Zinn Reader: Writings on Disobedience and Democracy*. New York: Seven Stories, 1997.

———. *A People's History of the United States: 1492–present*. New York City: Routledge, 2015.

———. *The Power of Nonviolence: Writings by Advocates of Peace*. Boston: Beacon Press, 2002.

Zunes, Stephen. "Weapons of Mass Democracy: Nonviolent Resistance is the Most Powerful Tactic Against Oppressive Regimes." *Yes Magazine,* 2009. http://www.yesmagazine.org/issues/learn-as-you-go/weapons-of-mass-democracy.

Zunes, Stephen, Lester Kurtz, and Sara Asher, eds. *Nonviolent Social Movements: A Geographical Perspective*. London: Blackwell Publishing, 1999.

Index

About the Author

Anya Stanger earned her PhD in Social Science from Syracuse University in 2015. She currently teaches women's and gender studies and sociology at Sierra College and conflict studies at Syracuse University.

www.ingramcontent.com/pod-product-compliance
Lightning Source LLC
Chambersburg PA
CBHW022311280326
41932CB00010B/1064